Those who hoped the collapse of financial markets would usher in the end of neo-liberalism and rehabilitate support for traditional social democratic policies have been disappointed. It is not only the irrationality of markets that is the focus of public discontent, but also the inefficiency of states and the inability of elected governments to humanise and control global market capitalism.

Despite recent successes, social democratic parties in the EU have become locked in a cycle of electoral underperformance. The crisis remedies of the right appear more simple and direct in their diagnosis, casting the state as restrictive, wasteful and inefficient. Abstract theoretical debates on the left about a 'paradigm shift' in western capitalism in the aftermath of the crisis have had little traction.

So, in the aftermath of the 2008 crash prompted by the failure of the US financial services conglomerate Lehman Brothers, this book addresses a deceptively simple question: what is to be done? It makes the case for a new, post-crisis settlement harnessing the dynamic traditions of social liberalism and social democracy as the foundation for progressive reforms geared towards alleviating crisis aftershocks and addressing the deep-seated structural challenges afflicting western capitalist democracies.

In the series:

After the Third Way: The Future of Social Democracy in Europe
Edited by Olaf Cramme and Patrick Diamond
ISBN: 978 1 84885 992 0 (HB); 978 1 84885 993 7 (PB)

Europe's Immigration Challenge: Reconciling Work, Welfare and Mobility
Edited by Elena Jurado and Grete Brochmann
ISBN: 978 1 78076 225 8 (HB); 978 1 78076 226 5 (PB)

Left Without a Future? Social Justice in Anxious Times
Anthony Painter
ISBN: 978 1 78076 660 7 (HB); 978 1 78076 661 4 (PB)

Progressive Politics after the Crash: Governing from the Left
Edited by Olaf Cramme, Patrick Diamond and Michael McTernan
ISBN: 978 1 78076 763 5 (HB); 978 1 78076 764 2 (PB)

Governing Britain: Power, Politics and the Prime Minister
Patrick Diamond
ISBN: 978 1 78076 581 5 (HB); 978 1 78076 582 2 (PB)

The Europe Dilemma: Britain and the Challenges of EU Integration
Roger Liddle
ISBN: 978 1 78076 222 7 (HB); 978 1 78076 223 4 (PB)

Edited by Olaf Cramme, Patrick Diamond
and Michael McTernan

progressive politics after the crash

Governing from the Left

I.B. TAURIS

LONDON · NEW YORK

Published in 2013 by I.B.Tauris & Co. Ltd
6 Salem Road, London W2 4BU
175 Fifth Avenue, New York NY 10010
www.ibtauris.com

Distributed in the United States and Canada Exclusively by Palgrave Macmillan
175 Fifth Avenue, New York NY 10010

ISBN: 978 1 78076 763 5 (HB)
ISBN: 978 1 78076 764 2 (PB)

A full CIP record for this book is available from the British Library
A full CIP record is available from the Library of Congress

Library of Congress Catalog Card Number: available

Printed and bound in Great Britain by T.J. International, Padstow, Cornwall

About Policy Network

Policy Network is a leading thinktank and international political network based in London. It promotes strategic thinking on progressive solutions to the challenges of the twenty-first century and the future of social democracy, impacting upon policy debates in the UK, the rest of Europe and the wider world.

Through a distinctly collaborative and cross-national approach to research, events and publications, the thinktank has acquired a reputation as a highly valued platform for perceptive and challenging political analysis, debate and exchange. Building from our origins in the late 1990s, the network has become an unrivalled international point-of-contact between political thinkers and opinion formers, serving as a bridge between the worlds of politics, academia, public policy-making, business, civil society and the media.

www.policy-network.net

About the Foundation for European Progressive Studies (FEPS)

FEPS is the first progressive political foundation established at the European level. Created in 2007 and co-financed by the European Parliament, it aims at establishing an intellectual crossroad between social democracy and the European project. It puts fresh thinking at the core of its action and serves as an instrument for pan-European intellectual and political reflection.

Acting as a platform for ideas, FEPS relies first and foremost on a network of members composed of more than 40 national political foundations and thinktanks from all over the EU. The Foundation also closely collaborates with a number of international correspondents and partners in the world that share the ambition to foster research, promote debate and spread progressive thinking.

www.feps-europe.eu

'Instead of making sweeping generalisations and putting together unrealisable manifestos, the cast of contributors deliberately concentrate on providing cutting-edge, evidence-based analysis and workable solutions – on hard choices rather than hot air. Social democrats everywhere can draw both ammunition and even a measure of confidence from every single page. Highly recommended.'

Tim Bale, Chair in Politics, Queen Mary, University of London

'*Progressive Politics after the Crash* is a major contribution to ongoing debates about the future of the left. The onset of the "great recession" in 2008 seemed, for a moment, to promise a revival in the fortunes of the centre-left, but it has not yet happened. The argument made here is that the fortunes of parties of the centre-left will not improve until parties and thinkers on the left develop a model of governance premised on a deeper understanding of the nature of contemporary global capitalism, and of the constraints it places on the state and state finances and on traditional, social-democratic policies for growth and redistribution. Progressive politics on this reading requires not so much a new rhetoric or vision but rather novel approaches to creating a fair society – "social investment", for example, and measures aimed at "predistribution" – as well as persistent efforts to create or recreate the institutional basis for centre-left politics. These finely crafted chapters will be essential reading for anyone who cares about the future of progressive politics.'

James Cronin, Professor of History, Boston College and affiliate of the Center for European Studies, Harvard University

'The Great Financial Crisis has raised major policy challenges for all advanced democracies. Yet, very few policy thinktanks have addressed these questions comprehensively and even fewer take the perspective of the centre-left. *Progressive Politics after the Crash* is a concise and highly readable collection of chapters that includes some of the world's most stimulating and reflective academics. It is a very valuable contribution to a new centre-left agenda of establishing a political economy in the western world based on the reconciliation of economic development, equal access to assets and human capital, and redistribution.'

Anke Hassel, Professor of Public Policy, Hertie School of Governance

'If it is to win the battle of ideas, the centre-left urgently needs a new reform agenda. The essays in this book, drawing on the twin traditions of social liberalism and social democracy, begin to show the way forward.'

Andrés Velasco, Edward Larocque Tinker Visiting Professor at the Columbia School of International and Public Affairs, and former finance minister of Chile

Contents

Acknowledgements

This volume originates in the collaboration between Policy Network and the Foundation for European Progressive Studies (FEPS). As international progressive thinktanks based in London and Brussels, we have drawn together our respective political networks to engage centre-left parties, academics, policy experts and thinkers on the challenges of governing from the left in a post-crisis world. *Progressive Politics after the Crash* draws on the rich vein of policy ideas and political frameworks presented and debated at numerous conferences, seminars and meetings across Europe and North America.

In particular, a concerted effort has been made to strengthen the dialogue between the American political tradition of progressivism and liberalism, and European social democracy. Pressures on living standards, hardening of attitudes towards redistribution and a more challenging global economic environment all strengthen the case for more sustained transatlantic dialogue between progressives. We would like to convey our thanks to Nuffield College, University of Oxford, and the Institute for Global Law and Policy (IGLP), Harvard University, for the partnership that facilitated and informed a two-day conference in Oxford in July 2012. The conference provided the genesis for this volume, and we are extremely grateful and indebted to the presenters and discussants at that transatlantic gathering.

Thanks are also due to the Wiardi Beckman Stichting, the Dutch social democratic thinktank, and the other European and American thinktanks and universities that have contributed to our debates.

We are grateful to Seamus Nevin, Renaud Thillaye and Claudia Chwalisz in the Policy Network team for their support in the editorial process. Roger Liddle, Policy Network's chair, was a constant source of inspiration in giving counsel and guidance. Finally, we would like to thank Alfred Gusenbauer, Ania Skrzypek and Ernst Stetter of FEPS for the rewarding and productive partnership.

Olaf Cramme, Patrick Diamond and Michael McTernan

Contributors

A.B. Atkinson is Honorary Fellow at Nuffield College, University of Oxford, and Centennial Professor at the London School of Economics. He primarily writes on income distributions. He is the author of *The Changing Distribution of Earnings in OECD Countries* (2008) and *Empirical Studies of Earnings Mobility* (2001), as well as many other books.

Sheri Berman is a Professor of Politics at Barnard College, Columbia University. Her research interests include European history and politics, political development, social theory and the history of the left. She is the author of *The Social Democratic Moment* (1998) and *The Primacy of Politics* (2006).

Wendy Carlin is Professor of Economics at University College London and Research Fellow at the Centre for Economic Policy Research (CEPR). Her research focuses on macroeconomics, institutions and economic performance, and the economics of transition. Her latest book is *Macroeconomics and the Financial System* (with David Soskice, forthcoming 2014*)*.

Olaf Cramme is Director of Policy Network and a visiting fellow at the London School of Economics' European Institute. He is also Co-founder of *Das Progressive Zentrum*, a Berlin-based thinktank. Olaf publishes widely on the future of the EU and European social democracy. He is co-editor (with Patrick Diamond) of *Social Justice in the Global Age* (2009) and *After the Third Way* (2012).

Colin Crouch is Professor Emeritus of the University of Warwick and External Scientific Member of the Max Planck Institute. He is Vice-president for Social Sciences of the British Academy. His research focuses on comparative European sociology, industrial relations and economic sociology. His most recent books include *The Strange Non-death of Neoliberalism* (2011) and *Making Capitalism Fit for Society* (2013).

Patrick Diamond is Senior Research Fellow at Policy Network. He is a lecturer in Public Policy at Queen Mary, University of London, and Gwilym Gibbon Fellow at Nuffield College, Oxford. He is the former head of policy planning in 10 Downing Street. His recent books include *After the Third Way* (co-edited, 2012) and *Governing Britain* (forthcoming 2013).

Jeffry A. Frieden is Professor of Government at Harvard University. He specialises in the politics of international monetary and financial relations. His recent publications include *Lost Decades: The Making of America's Debt Crisis and the Long Recovery* (co-edited, 2011) and *Global Capitalism: Its Fall and Rise in the Twentieth Century* (2006), as well as many other publications.

Andrew Gamble is Professor of Politics and a fellow of Queens' College at the University of Cambridge. He is a fellow of the British Academy and the UK Academy of Social Sciences. His main research interests lie in political economy, political theory and political history. In 2005 he received the Isaiah Berlin Prize from the Political Studies Association for lifetime contribution to political studies. His most recent book is *The Spectre at the Feast* (2009).

Alfred Gusenbauer is Chair of the Foundation for European Progressive Studies (FEPS) 'Next Left' programme. He is the former federal chancellor of Austria and the former leader of SPÖ. He is also the first Leitner Global Fellow at the Columbia University School of International and Public Affairs and is a guest lecturer at the IGLP of Harvard Law School. He is also Senator of the European Academy of Science and a president of Renner Institut.

Jacob S. Hacker is Director of the Institution for Social and Policy Studies and Stanley B. Resor Professor of Political Science at Yale

University. He is also Vice-president of the National Academy of Social Insurance. He writes primarily on the politics of US health and social policy and is the author, most recently, of *Winner-Take-All Politics* (with Paul Pierson, 2011) and *The Great Risk Shift* (2008).

Peter A. Hall is Krupp Foundation Professor of European Studies at the Minda de Gunzburg Center for European Studies at Harvard University as well as Co-director of the programme on Successful Societies for the Canadian Institute for Advanced Research. His most recent books are *Social Resilience in the Neoliberal Era* (co-edited, 2013) and *The Politics of Representation in the Global Age* (co-edited, forthcoming 2014).

Anton Hemerijck is Dean of the Faculty of the Social Sciences and Professor of Institutional Policy Analysis at the VU University Amsterdam. He writes primarily on comparative social policy and institutional policy analysis. As an academic expert, he has advised the European Commission and several EU presidencies on social policy developments. His most recent book is *Changing Welfare States* (2013).

Jane Jenson is Professor of Political Science at the Université de Montréal, where she holds the research chair in Citizenship and Governance. Her current research focuses on analysis of changes to social policy paradigms in the direction of the social investment perspective in the EU and Latin America. She publishes widely in scholarly journals in English and French and is a former editor of *Lien social et Politiques*.

Lane Kenworthy is Professor of Sociology and Political Science at the University of Arizona. He studies the causes and consequences of living standards, poverty, inequality, mobility, employment, economic growth and social policy. His books include *Social Democratic America* (forthcoming 2014), *Progress for the Poor* (2011), *Jobs with Equality* (2008) and *Egalitarian Capitalism* (2004).

Onawa Promise Lacewell is a post-doctoral researcher in the Democracy and Democratization programme at the Social Science Research Centre Berlin (WZB). She works on the research project 'The political sociology of cosmopolitanism and communitarianism', which focuses on emerging political cleavages in Europe.

Will Marshall is President and Founder of the Progressive Policy Institute (PPI), a centre for political innovation in Washington DC. He is also a co-founder of the Democratic Leadership Council, serving as its first policy director, and currently serves on the board of directors for the National Endowment for Democracy. He is editor or co-editor of many books, including *Memos to the New President* (2009).

Wolfgang Merkel is Director of the Democracy and Democratization programme at the Social Science Research Centre Berlin (WZB) and Professor of Political Science at the Humboldt University Berlin. He is a member of the Berlin-Brandenburg Academy of Sciences and Humanities. His most recent publications include *The Future of Representative Democracy* (co-edited, 2009) and *Social Democracy in Power* (2008).

Michael McTernan is Deputy Director of Policy Network. His research focuses on elections, government and party politics, looking at how centre-left parties are affected by the emergence of new distributional conflicts, the rise of populism and the decline of political trust. He is Editor of the Policy Network Observatory and the monthly *State of the Left* report.

David Miliband is a former UK foreign secretary and former Labour MP. He served as an MP for 12 years and on the frontbenches for 11 of those. Prior to election he worked as Head of Policy for former UK prime minister Tony Blair, and was head of the prime minister's policy unit between 1997 and 2001. In April 2013 David stood down as an MP and will start his new role as President and CEO of the International Rescue Committee in New York in September 2013.

Pippa Norris is Laureate Fellow and Professor of Government and International Relations at the University of Sydney and the McGuire Lecturer in Comparative Politics at the John F. Kennedy School of Government, Harvard University. Her honours include receiving the 2011 Johan Skytte Prize in Political Science. Her most recent research is the Electoral Integrity Project, generating a planned trilogy of books.

Bruno Palier is CNRS Research Director at Sciences Po, Centre d'études européennes. His primary research focus is on welfare reforms in Europe. He is a former scientific co-ordinator of the European Network of Excellence RECWOWE. His recent publications include *The Age of Dualization* (co-edited, 2012) and *Towards a Social Investment Welfare State?* (co-edited, 2012).

Ania Skrzypek is Senior Research Fellow at the Foundation for European Progressive Studies (FEPS). She co-ordinates the 'Next Left' programme and specialises in the political history of the European Union, with a focus on the development of pan-European party political systems. She previously worked as a researcher in the Institute of Political Sciences at the University of Warsaw.

Ernst Stetter has been Secretary General of the Foundation for European Progressive Studies (FEPS) since its creation in 2008. He is an economist and political scientist who comments regularly on EU affairs. He formerly worked for the Friedrich Ebert Stiftung (FES) holding various positions, including Head of the Central Europe Unit, Head of Africa Department, Director of the Paris office and Director of the EU office in Brussels.

Loukas Tsoukalis is Professor of European Integration at the University of Athens, President of the Hellenic Foundation for European and Foreign Policy (ELIAMEP), and Visiting Professor at the College of Europe in Bruges. He is also a former special adviser to the president of the European Commission. His publications include *The New European Economy* (1997) and *The Delphic Oracle on Europe?* (co-edited, 2011).

Preface

Ernst Stetter

Progressives everywhere believed that the 2008 crash would mark a historical turning point. The magnitude of the economic and financial crisis was supposed to expose the destructive nature of financial capitalism. The overpowering strength of mainstreaming, neo-liberal philosophy would be undermined. A new space was open that would enable centre-left parties to break free from their political and intellectual captivity, otherwise known as 'TINA' (there is no alternative). And, despite the harshness of the crisis itself, there was a sense of anticipation that, after hard times, a new, more inclusive economic settlement would emerge. People widely thought that it would be impossible to return to 'business as usual'.

These great expectations were not to be met, however. The crisis evolved and encompassed further spheres, which quickly inflicted electoral pain on progressive parties. Attempts to propose alternatives were met with disbelief, as a consequence of popular distrust, disillusionment and the political right's success at framing the financial collapse as a crisis of debt induced by 'reckless' government spending. This situation instilled little confidence among electorates that a way out was in sight or that the centre-left had a credible exit strategy. In turn, the core principles of democracy, both as an ideal and as a process, came under pressure. And, even if this gloomy picture has been lightened from time to time by positive electoral results, those results did not form a trend that could be seen as either stable or consistent. Progressives continue to search for answers to their historical mission of finding a compromise between the current capitalism settlement, democracy and social stability.

This book provides academic testimony to these explorations. The distinguished authors try to look beyond the usual, extensively developed analyses of the current crisis. Instead, they put forward a set of policy and political frameworks that can inform and shape progressive politics after the crash. This innovative approach points to the importance of liberating political and academic debates from the confinement of short-term crisis deliberations, and looking forward to the long-term politics of growth, reform and social stability.

The volume is divided into two sections. The first looks at the fabric of the post-crisis environment and contemporary politics. The focus is on understanding the political conflicts that cut across western capitalist democracies and, in turn, on thinking about the distinctive values and traditions of progressive politics that can be drawn upon to reinstate democracy as both an ideal and a process, through which individuals and societies can pave a path towards their desired, prosperous future.

The second section moves on to consider the pillars of a new agenda and narrative to underpin sustainable growth and progressive economic reform. In each contribution the authors consider the challenges of consolidating an agenda that promotes innovation and new drivers of growth, finds space for human capital investment to raise productive potential and tackles widespread societal inequalities. These crossings are matched with an ambition to formulate a new progressive narrative that will be powerful enough to appeal to broad constituencies and restore a sense of solidarity, responsibility and reciprocity capable of reuniting progressive majorities in a struggle for a better future for all, particularly with reference to social investment and youth opportunity.

The papers gathered in this book represent outcomes of research and debates that the FEPS has intensively held over a number of years, together with its respective members and especially in co-operation with Policy Network. These exchanges gathered leading scholars and analysts to explore the future of progressive politics on both sides of the Atlantic, and as such have already resulted in a number of intellectually inspiring and politically bold proposals. In this context I would especially like to thank Alfred Gusenbauer, chair of the FEPS Next Left research programme, for his exceptional contribution in framing this project. I would also like to express my sincere gratitude to Roger Liddle, chair of Policy Network, and Olaf Cramme, director of Policy Network, for their outstanding co-operation.

Foreword
Progressive Politics after the Crash

David Miliband

This volume of essays addresses a pressing need in modern politics: for the centre-left to engage in a serious way in the battle of ideas about the future of policy and politics in western industrialised democracies. Away from the tactical battles that dominate day-to-day politics, and separate from the topical but essentially short-term debate about the need for Keynesian counter-cyclical fiscal policy at a time of balance-sheet recession, the authors gathered here focus on some of the big structural questions that face social democrats in the second decade of the twenty-first century.

These kinds of contributions are badly needed. It is not just that a lot of centre-left parties are finding it hard to win elections. It is also that those that do get elected quickly find that, while the nostrums of what Tony Judt called 'defensive social democracy' can strike a chord when a party is in opposition, they are insufficient for government. The welfare state needs defence in the face of unfair attacks. But it also needs reform. Inequality is undoubtedly a modern menace exacerbated by austerity, but macroeconomic policy and even full employment will not tackle its roots. Those at the bottom need a voice, but the middle class is also feeling squeezed. The public sector and its services have been a civilising force in western societies, but they need to operate very differently to meet the twin challenges of changing public expectations and needs and limited public funds.

Francis Fukuyama has written:

> It has been several decades since anyone on the left has been able to articulate, first, a coherent analysis of what happens to the structure of advanced societies as they undergo economic change and, second, a realistic agenda that has any hope of protecting middle class society.[1]

I think this is more unfair when it comes to analysis than in the case of prescription. But we who are on the centre-left should take this challenge seriously. There is not an 'off-the-shelf' model of social democracy, though there are powerful examples of what can make a positive difference (as well as what doesn't).

There are many ways of describing the changing context for what the US columnist David Brooks[2] has called the debate about 'how to rejuvenate mature industrialised societies'. To my eye, there are four key global changes underway that explain why this feels like a decade of disorder.

There is the shift in economic power from west to east (and to some extent from north to south), as outsourcing and what Al Gore calls 'robo-sourcing' (i.e. technological change) alter the economic prospects of millions of people. Around 50 million people a year are joining the global middle class in Asia, while norms of employment are being overturned. This has massive domestic consequences in industrialised societies, but is also creating a new power structure in the international system.

There is the resource crunch, which predated the credit crunch and is exemplified by a mismatch in the supply and demand for resources that is driving up their price. Shale gas discoveries in the US are important but they do not invalidate this issue. The oil price remains high, and non-oil commodities have risen fast enough in the last decade to eradicate the price cuts of the previous hundred years. As the urban middle-class global population is continuing to grow, it is hard to see this trend going into reverse.

There is the radical extension of the open society to the nooks and crannies of economic and social life, public and personal. This is fuelling democratic revolutions in the undemocratic world and frustration with democracy as traditionally practised in the established democracies. Across the public–private divide, the bar for the legitimate exercise of authority is being raised.

And there is the pressing nature of interdependence, local and international, that demands new forms of co-operation at precisely the time when people want more power for themselves. The Lehman moment showed that the pre-existing definition of which institutions posed systemic risk was not properly thought through. But, as I write, European politicians are saying that Cyprus is 'unique' and even hermetically sealed. Surely we have learned that in a hyper-connected world the ring-fencing of problems is easier said than done.

It is the interaction of these global changes that has reframed the political equation in western democracies. It is not just that needs are rising but also that tax revenues are declining. The welfare state is costing more, but investment in supporting wealth creation is an increasingly urgent claim on public funds. Wages are being squeezed, and immigration is causing resentment. There is a crisis of employment and opportunity among young people, but they don't vote in heavy numbers, so politics is skewed towards the old. The shift to low carbon is a necessity, but there is a collective-action problem when global negotiations are stuck. Societies have become more diverse in cultural as well as racial terms, and this has opened up a new and challenging axis of division in politics, which makes the construction of coherent electoral and governing coalitions more difficult. The putative conflict between cosmopolitans and communitarians has been a real one, in the Netherlands and elsewhere.

In the 1990s it seemed that economics and politics were both pushing in the same direction. Globalisation was driving down inflation; education and training were offering opportunities for social mobility; social justice seemed like the counterpart of economic efficiency. The heart of the conundrum facing centre-left parties today is that economics and politics are systematically pulling in opposite directions. The economics calls for more sharing of sovereignty, but the politics is more nationalist or localist. The economics calls for more migration, the politics for less. The economics says switch welfare spending from the old to the young, but the politics of that are horrible. And so on.

Meanwhile, politics itself is increasingly seen as broken – and not just seen as broken but actually broken. This is not just about corruption scandals. It is also about political systems that for too many people have lost their capacity to engage and include. Party systems are controlled by small groups (President Hollande's exemplary election by open primary excepted). Money creates a sense of popular disempowerment. Parliaments are gridlocked and enfeebled. For parties of the left, who take pride in the power of politics to check the abuse of power in markets, these are not peripheral concerns.

The essays in this book try to address these questions. The starting point is not that the centre-left is wrong to continue to see the importance of Keynesian insights, or wrong to see an important role for government in economy and society, or wrong to defend the poorest, who rely on the welfare state. It is that these articles of faith are insufficient for navigating the rapids of government.

I was once told by a Swedish friend of mine – a successful politician in his own right – that good politics starts with empathy, then proceeds to analysis, then sets out values and establishes the vision, before getting to the nitty-gritty of policy solutions. A lot of politics focuses on the last point, but maybe that is why it fails to connect to a lot of the public. If this is right, it seems to me that three sets of issues, interlocking in nature, will be defining for the future of the centre-left.

The first is how we respond to the public desire for more protection from risks beyond their control – without falling into the trap of big-state solutions that can neither be afforded nor delivered. These can be global risks of an economic, environmental or security-related nature. They can be personal risks, such as unemployment, dementia or crime. In each case the traditional mechanisms for collective insurance against risk through the state are under pressure.

The second is how we meet people's expectations for more power and control over their own lives – at a time when interdependence and inequality are making this seem like a pipe dream. The sense of disempowerment can be economic, in workplaces that lack the collective power of trade unions but where employee satisfaction and opportunity are limited. It can be social, in communities where crime or neglect sap individual and collective strength. Or it can be in public services, where budgets or decisions are out of the reach of the people who use the services.

In truth the Third Way discussions of the 1990s were too weak in addressing issues of economic power, in the workplace and elsewhere. There seemed to be sufficient common ground to facilitate win–win solutions. But the stagnation of wages, among other matters, has shown that this perception was optimistic at best. Economic empowerment needs a harder edge.

The third is how to foster a sense of belonging when people are more mobile and identities more complex. This is partly, but not only, about immigration. It is also about the loneliness of too many elderly people and the lack of security of people of all ages.

Each of these areas of study captures social democratic concerns with equity and mutuality. But they look at them in different ways, through the lens of the way people lead their lives rather than the overall structure of society. What is more, they challenge the still-dominant paradigm of Anglo-Saxon politics – for or against state or market, for or against public or private sector. They speak much more clearly to the continental European notion of a social market economy, in which public values and mores define market rules and norms, and in which the state is respectful of private enterprise and personal liberty. Where Labour had ended up in Britain by 2010 – too hands on with the state and too hands off with the market – shows the perils of not getting this clear.

People sometimes ask – or lament – why the financial crisis of 2008 has not led to an upsurge of support for the centre-left. One answer is that in many countries parties of the centre-left were in government, and so got the blame, but this is insufficient. In truth there was a major market failure, and in particular a failure of under-regulated markets. But there was state responsibility too. And, as Stan Greenberg has written: 'a crisis of government legitimacy is a crisis of liberalism'.[3] That is why reforming the state as well as reforming the market is a necessity not a luxury.

The essays in this book offer some quite stark messages. I would highlight six.

The first is that, while fiscal stimulus may be a short-term remedy for low demand, fiscal prudence is a medium-term necessity. Keynesianism is after all a hard task master.

The second is that the politics of production require social democrats to address the structural challenges to western economies as engines of wealth creation. Sometimes this is reduced to a debate about the importance of 'manufacturing', but that is not enough, as the border between manufacturing and services becomes blurred, and as services take up a much larger share of the economy and require higher degrees of skill.

The third is that the tendency of markets towards inequality and instability needs to be countered by action upstream in order to curb abuse of power, and to empower citizens and employees with rights, information and control. 'Predistribution' does not fit on an electoral pledge card, but the idea is right and so is the challenge of developing new ways, either through individual rights or collective organisation, to tilt the balance of power towards ordinary people.

The fourth is that the state needs to do more with less, and that requires big reform. Reform is one of those words that can lose meaning through excessive and loose use. But for social democrats the specifics of decentralisation of power, transfer of budgets to people, integration of back offices, flexibility for the front line and challenge from private- and voluntary-sector providers should all be geared towards the goal of a public sphere that can serve its founding purpose: representing the public and its interest against threats of injustice and insecurity.

The fifth is that fighting globalisation is futile and damaging, but that the processes of global integration nevertheless need to be managed by regional co-operation in the absence of stronger global governance. It is striking that, despite the travails of the European Union, around the world there is a tendency towards regional association – in the Pacific Alliance in South America (20 per cent greater GDP than Brazil), for example. This is the way for medium-sized states to have influence.

The sixth message is that the challenge for parties and politics is as big as the challenge to policy. Assembling a winning coalition is one thing; holding it is harder. That makes the achievement of the Obama campaign quite remarkable. He was helped by his opponent, but he made his own luck through a drive street by street and voter by voter to maintain his winning coalition. Presidential elections are different from parliamentary systems, but there is read-across nonetheless.

Across the countries covered in this volume, left-of-centre politicians in national and local government are protecting their citizens from global storms, giving them more power over public services and economic destiny, and building communities worthy of the name. They are the best advertisement for our politics. But the threads and lessons need to be drawn together. And for that we need more books like this one.

March 2013

Notes

1. Francis Fukuyama, 'The future of history: Can liberal democracy survive the decline of the middle class?', *Foreign Affairs*, January/February (2012). Available at www.foreignaffairs.com/articles/136782/francis-fukuyama/the-future-of-history (accessed 4 July 2013).
2. David Brooks, 'The collective turn', *New York Times* (21 January 2013). Available at www.nytimes.com/2013/01/22/opinion/brooks-the-collective-turn.html?_r=0 (accessed 10 July 2013).
3. Stanley Greenberg, 'Why voters tune out Democrats', *New York Times* (30 July 2011). Available at www.nytimes.com/2011/07/31/opinion/sunday/tuning-out-the-democrats.html?pagewanted=all&_r=0 (accessed 4 July 2013).

Introduction
Governing from the Left

Olaf Cramme, Patrick Diamond and Michael McTernan

In today's world, social democratic parties and governments are operating on uncertain and volatile terrain. Not only has the west experienced among the most serious financial crises in history – symbolised by the bankruptcy of the US financial services conglomerate Lehman Brothers in 2008 – but capitalism itself is undergoing profound change through the process of technological innovation and the demise of Fordist mass production. The advanced economies are on the brink of a 'third' disruptive industrial revolution that is destabilising and undermining long-established institutions. Moreover, fiscal pressures unleashed by the crisis are placing unprecedented strain on public finances, welfare and the future of the state; crisis aftershocks are accentuating the impact of long-term structural trends, ranging from the ageing society to declining fertility rates; and the international context has been further reshaped by the rising industrial powers and the decline of the west.

As the world has changed, the agenda of centre-left parties has too often been trapped in the doctrines and strategies of the past. When the Bretton Woods system collapsed in the 1970s following the OPEC (Organization of the Petroleum Exporting Countries) oil-price shocks and the spillover effects of conflict in the Middle East and Vietnam, the left looked increasingly helpless in the face of 'stagflation'. An outdated conception of markets and social justice granted political initiative and momentum to the right. This time has been little different – at least in Europe. As Andrew Gamble observes,[1] the financial crisis largely benefited the right rather than the left. What began as a crisis of market fundamentalism has quickly evolved into a crisis of debt and government deficits.

So, five years after the crash, the authors in this collection address a deceptively simple question: what is to be done? The arguments developed in this book are based on one central proposition: if the left is to fulfil its vision of a social democratic society reconciling economic efficiency, social justice and ecological sustainability, it must develop a new governing strategy and structural reform agenda that addresses the socio-economic challenges and political aftershocks that define the post-crisis environment. The simplistic debate over fiscal austerity versus Keynesian stimulus should be abandoned. Those who argue that premature fiscal consolidation damages growth, employment and living standards have been proved correct. On the other hand, failure to deal with the long-term debt overhang bequeathed by the crisis weakens credibility with the international markets, and threatens long-term competitiveness. What the advanced economies of Europe need is neither masochistic austerity nor Keynesian pump-priming, but rather long-term structural reforms that raise productive potential, tackle new forms of inequality, and reinvent a sustainable growth model for our societies.

This, in turn, necessitates recasting the role of the state. The crisis has served to remind policy-makers of the fundamental importance of public institutions in upholding the regulatory and legal framework required for a flourishing market economy. But too often the remedies of the right have appeared more prescient and politically salient, with the state always cast as restrictive, wasteful and excessive. The political question, therefore, is whether the centre-left can respond with a coherent governing programme that rebuilds confidence in the active state not only in ensuring crisis-management intervention, but in leading the process of stabilisation, innovation and long-term rebalancing of our economies. The focus of the state will continue to evolve from the traditional welfare role towards an agent of industrial modernisation and economic reform.

The Post-Crisis Environment

In the face of this challenge, centre-left parties must re-evaluate their governing purpose and political identity. European social democracy has to identify new policy instruments and strategies that determinedly address the post-crisis environment.

Debt Overhang and Low Growth

The most immediate concern is rising public debt and the increase in the public-sector deficit. This has been most severe in countries such as Ireland and Spain, where sovereign debt has been contaminated by financial-sector debt. In other countries, such as the UK, huge levels of private debt overhang the economy and severely constrain growth. Many western economies now face the prospect of an 'L-shaped' recovery and a Japanese-style decade of stagnation, which will further undermine growth and any sustainable recovery in the public finances.

Fragile Tax Systems

The pressure on the public finances resulting from bail-outs and low growth has been exacerbated by declining tax revenues and the fragility of the tax system in many countries. Lack of attention to the resilience of the tax base, complacency about personal and corporate tax evasion, and inattention to the overall tax take have compromised the public finances of EU member states.

Vulnerable Welfare States

The fiscal aftershock is all the more acute because the crisis is accentuating the impact of long-term trends: an ageing society, soaring health costs and rising demands for public and social-care services.[2] The International Monetary Fund (IMF) has warned that the impact of demography on public spending far outweighs the financial crisis: in Europe, the cost of pensions will rise from 10.2 per cent of GDP to 12.6 per cent by 2060, and health-care will increase from 6.7 to 8.2 per cent.[3] The unemployment rate (a 'lagging indicator' of declining growth) has also markedly increased since the crisis, further weakening the fiscal viability of welfare systems.

Growing Societal Inequalities

The austerity burden and the process of fiscal consolidation exacerbate income and intergenerational inequality. In the wake of the crisis, Gini coefficients are moving in the wrong direction. Younger cohorts are most adversely affected, manifested in rising youth unemployment, as older people stay active in the workforce for longer. The squeeze on state spending reduces investment in education and human capital; measures to support children and low-income families are readily sacrificed. On the other hand, the crisis threatens pension incomes in countries with high levels of private-sector provision and a rapidly ageing population: pension fund assets are being eroded by falling equity markets.

Fresh thinking and radical reform are required to address these long-term challenges. The authors in this book present a range of bold and forward-looking ideas from 'predistribution' and the new politics of production to social investment and measures to remedy declining living standards. Reforms to address socio-economic challenges such as worklessness and lack of skills require upfront investment and ruthless prioritisation of policies. Nonetheless, securing the mandate to tackle structural challenges means addressing the fiery political aftershocks of the crisis.

Hardening of Attitudes Towards Redistribution

Governing parties are operating in what Peter Hall terms an economically insecure climate of *sauve-qui-peut* politics – where voters are more concerned with preserving what they have and thus resist the redistribution of resources to the needy.[4] Public-opinion surveys demonstrate that citizens are aggrieved by the lack of reciprocity in the welfare state. This is borne out in hardening attitudes towards immigration, welfare and social security.

'Conservative Biases' in Welfare

The crisis has reinforced support for traditional welfare entitlements such as higher pensions and public expenditure on health care. The entrenched public commitment to those elements of the welfare state is a worthy endorsement of postwar centre-left achievement. However, it is becoming more difficult to redirect spending to address new social risks that traditional social protection is poorly equipped to handle. This includes measures to remedy structural changes in labour markets and demography, alongside gender equality and family instability.

Populism and New Political Conflict Lines

The system of representative democracy is under stress in many countries. This is manifested in the rise of populist parties (which are mobilising along new cultural cleavages in relation to identity) and new conflicts about the distribution of resources. At the European level, a new division has emerged between north and south over the symmetry of crisis adjustment, the pace of structural reform, and the burden of debt. Lines of accountability in the EU are becoming increasingly contested.

The 'Collective Action' Problem

The centre-left does not possess the organising capacity of the postwar era. Political parties, civil-society groups and trade unions are increasingly hollowed out. New spaces have emerged in the form of social movements and new media, but these remain largely untapped by mainstream parties. The consequence is that parties are no longer able to carry the coalition of interest groups that is required to implement contentious structural reforms, a situation exacerbated by the rise of anti-politics. Progressive politics no longer has a self-identified historical agent such as the organised working class.

The Right's Formidable Sweep of Ideas

Against this backdrop, abstract theoretical debates on the left about a 'paradigm shift' in western capitalism in the aftermath of the crisis have had little impact. Despite recent successes in France and the Netherlands, social democratic parties in the EU are locked in a cycle of electoral underperformance. This apparent weakness is fundamentally a consequence of the refusal to adapt to today's needs and challenges. Those who hoped the collapse of financial markets would rehabilitate support for traditional socialist programmes have been disappointed. It is not only the irrationality of markets that is the focus of public discontent, but also the inefficiency of states and the inability of elected governments to humanise and control global market capitalism.[5]

In contrast, the right has appeared to offer distinctive, clear-cut remedies: in relation to deteriorating public finances, the response was to cut public expenditure to rebalance the economy and reduce the level of public-sector debt – a proxy for rolling back the frontiers of the state. This led to a wave of austerity across the EU, alongside a sharp contraction of aggregate demand. The right's analysis is that failure to reduce government debt and an increase in the structural deficit would provoke a meltdown in confidence among international investors, leading to the withdrawal of credit and economic Armageddon. The economics may be wholly deficient, but the political message is devastatingly straightforward.

Moreover, parties of the right have a clear-cut solution to restoring stable economic growth. In order to galvanise growth in the wake of the crisis, an accumulation strategy is promulgated requiring market liberalisation and further deregulation of labour and capital markets. The crisis is the symptom of state-driven pathologies in the macroeconomy: over-regulation inhibits the free movement of market forces and prevents developed economies from competing with countries that have a lower cost base. The solution for restoring accumulation is to get government out of the way, which entails less state intervention and greater freedom for market forces.

The final argument invoked by the right to consolidate their advantage in a climate of economic insecurity emphasises the hardening of public attitudes towards welfare and redistribution. Cutting costs helps to reduce the size of the state and public-sector borrowing while addressing the resentment created by the 'undeserving poor'. This argument coalesces with the rise of *sauve-qui-peut* politics in the US and Europe.

In short, the right seeks a mandate to sweep away stagnation and sclerosis by curtailing the forces of 'big government', enabling markets to thrive while restoring the dynamism of the global economy. Against this formidable armoury of New Right rhetoric and policy remedies, the left appears cautious and defensive. Its programmes lack the simplicity and cutting edge of the ideological right. The strategy of Keynesian demand management requires increased public borrowing despite rising debt and structural deficits. This goes against the grain of how households perceive economic management: fundamentally, why is more borrowing a better long-term answer to public and private indebtedness?

The politics of debt are crucial in Europe and the US: the crisis was fuelled by the accumulation of public- and private-sector debt, leading to unsustainable asset bubbles and imbalances in the world's developed economies.[6] Where centre-left parties are complacent about the need to reduce public and private debt, they neglect the importance of economic rebalancing. This reinforces the perception of centre-left parties as not trustworthy in relation to the economy, and as failing to grip the debt problem that leads inevitably to higher spending and taxes.

Merely urging a faster rate of growth, the default impulse of 'Left Keynesianism', does not amount to a viable economic management strategy in the wake of the crisis. The assumption that growth is anaemic since public expenditure is being cut overstates the multiplier effect popularised by Keynes. This recalls the theory of the Phillips Curve advocated by Keynesians in the 1960s[7] and the presumption that there is a trade-off between unemployment and inflation. The notion of a trade-off between unemployment and inflation was undermined by the breakdown of the international economic system in the 1970s and the onset of crippling 'stagflation'.

The premature contraction of fiscal policy is an inadequate, at best partial, explanation for economic stagnation. While in the UK judgement about the pace of fiscal consolidation may have been flawed, and while in the eurozone the policies of the European Commission may ignore the spillover effects on demand of simultaneous fiscal tightening, this is not an ordinary cyclical recession. We have experienced an unprecedented breakdown and paralysis in the financial sector, and many countries, including the UK, have experienced a dramatic loss of liquidity. The capacity of the economy to recover has been severely undermined: the financial sector's role in directing money from savers to investors broke down in the aftermath of the crisis, to the extent that it will take years for the conventional business model to be restored, as Cambridge University's Helen Thompson has argued.[8] Where debt in the financial-services sector remains abnormally high, there is no alternative to a long and arduous process of deleveraging before business lending returns to normal.

In other words, the impact of the crisis and the manner of the recovery will be slow and laborious, leaving in their wake a debt overhang and a significant adjustment burden. Classical Keynesian remedies fail to address the underlying structural weaknesses of advanced economies such as the United Kingdom: a low rate of investment in plant and capital; a weak culture of innovation and information and communications technology absorption; too few workers with technological and intermediate skills; an unsustainable current-account deficit; and an inadequate export base. There can be no return to the pre-crisis growth paradigm in the industrialised west.

A Post-Crisis Centre-Left Agenda

Centre-left parties will not recover politically and electorally by accommodating themselves to the orthodoxies of the right. They need to reaffirm and embed the values of social democracy, and emphasise how the left's ideological vision can be advanced in tough times. This means drawing on a rich social democratic tradition based on mutually reinforcing ideals:

- first, *economic efficiency* through an acceptance of markets alongside acknowledgement of the disruptive and polarising effects of capitalism – in other words, decoupling markets from the forces of rapacious financial capital;
- second, a belief that *social justice* equalises access to opportunities while securing a fair distribution of the outcomes and rewards earned through the market;
- finally, *ecological sustainability and solidarity* that accept the limits to personal consumption and the importance of sustainable production, while cultivating a sense of community and local identity.

Applying these values entails a centre-left accumulation strategy after the crisis built on public investment in infrastructure, human capital and productive assets, with state-led modernisation through industrial strategy, planning and co-ordination across the public and private sectors. The recession has meant that both current and capital expenditure are under pressure. Governments of the left have too often chosen to prioritise current spending over long-term investment in protecting the value of existing welfare benefits, even where these are poorly directed. Growth-enhancing expenditure on human capital, physical infrastructure and social investment is at risk of being too readily sacrificed, diminishing future growth capacity and global competitiveness. The consumption bias is all too pervasive, especially in the UK and the US, resulting in escalating public-sector deficits and a mountain of speculative debt in private households, fuelled by asset bubbles.

But while the financial crisis has underlined the importance of a credible, centre-left economic strategy, there are social institutions and bonds that exist beyond capitalist markets that are fundamental to citizens' well-being: identity, social capital and cohesion, and the ties and traditions of community civility and neighbourliness. A period of economic crisis ought to emphasise the importance of cultivating institutions and resources that give meaning and security to people's lives outside competitive markets and economic exchange.

The contention of this volume is that social democracy has to be animated by a coherent governing strategy that ensures our societies and institutions are more resilient and better able to withstand domestic and external shocks. Moreover, structural reforms are required that boost economic growth, living standards and jobs while expanding life-chances and opportunities for all 'from the cradle to the grave'. For policy-makers on the left, this means challenging some long-cherished nostrums and governing practices. Key examples follow below.

Living Standards, not Per Capita GDP

The purpose of economic management is to ensure stability and growth and to prioritise investment in the productive sectors of the economy. The conditions in which we are living are similar to those described by Keynes in the 1930s. This is an era of 'radical uncertainty'. As such, there is a premium on sound financial management, including transparent instruments such as independently monitored budgetary, fiscal and monetary rules. However, GDP growth alone is a weak proxy for economic and social development in the advanced countries. Measures should focus on improving household disposable incomes, especially for those in the lower and median range of the income distribution.[9]

Moreover, it is evident that GDP can rise and fall without any discernible impact on household incomes. It is essential to measure *median*, rather than mean, income growth, monitoring whether its fruits are being fairly shared across society. The societal objective of economic growth in GDP per se is crude and myopic. Alternative measures are required, as captured in the deliberations of the Stiglitz Commission.[10] Growth is important, but its primary function is to ensure effective adaptation to long-term challenges such as climate change, while using new technologies to solve major human problems from disease to deprivation in the developing world.

The New Age of Distributional Conflict

The distributional cleavages affecting western societies can no longer be addressed simply through income redistribution. There is always scope for progressive taxation to smooth excessive income differentials, to prevent the excessive accumulation of capital in a few hands, and to create a fairer distribution of wealth. For example, significant revenues can be raised from higher taxation of wealth and property, and lifetime gifts as well as inheritances. The risk, however, is that the reduction of inequality per se may distract from wider goals such as early intervention to reduce life-course disadvantage, while making labour markets fairer.[11] Indeed, generational inequalities have proved increasingly significant. These are characterised as a conflict between relatively affluent 'baby boomers' of pensionable age and younger families with children suffering from austerity policies. The issue of equity between the generations is of serious concern. The OECD has averred that 'the risk of poverty for older people has fallen, while poverty among young adults and families has risen'.[12] As Bruno Palier notes: 'We still have old-age biased welfare states.'[13] While public expenditure on pensions rose from 6.6 per cent of GDP to 8.3 per cent between 1980 and 2007, spending on vocational education and training has fallen in most countries.[14] Moreover, cost containment in public expenditures such as health, social care and pensions will be needed to protect resources for future investment in growth-enhancing public goods.

There is a case for an intergenerational pact that balances benefit entitlements for the current population of pensionable age with the needs of younger cohorts, for example: the removal of tax privileges for the affluent elderly would create a surplus to invest in the human capital capabilities of the young. Enhanced growth is necessary to underpin future pensions and social-care systems; everyone gains rather than there being a zero-sum trade-off imposed. Indeed, the cleavages within generational cohorts are often as great as the differences between cohorts. Approaches are still required to tackle pensioner poverty and to support the elderly population with the most acute needs.

Another dimension of inequality is equity between men and women. In many European countries, there are persistent inequalities in gender pay, in the division of labour in the household and caring responsibilities, and through labour-market segmentation.[15] Service-intensive welfare states with high-quality, affordable child-care help to raise the female employment rate while improving outcomes for children.[16] This enhances long-term competitiveness and equity. Gender equality has to be a key pillar of social investment strategies.

The issue of how to contain costs in state-funded services such as health and social care remains controversial. However, the process is certain to require a mixed economy of managed competition in public provision: only through contestability between providers is it possible to contain rising costs while enhancing quality.[17] Social democrats must not confuse their legitimate criticism of financial capitalism with the need for 'quasi-market' mechanisms to distribute goods and services in a free society operating within a public interest framework. Moreover, forging a culture of public-sector innovation will be crucial in ensuring value for money and optimal outcomes in a period of austerity. This requires incentives that encourage providers in the public sector to innovate, experiment, raise productivity and improve outcomes.

Reclaiming Supply-Side Reform: Towards Predistribution

Public policy should no longer be concerned merely with addressing post hoc inequalities, as the literature on 'predistribution' has emphasised.[18] The postwar legacy of welfare state redistribution has been only a modest impact on inequality in many developed states, including Britain and America, where poverty has remained intractable. Moreover, as markets become more globalised, they produce ever more extreme outcomes: governments have to run faster to achieve objectives that merely check the rise of income inequality, just as austerity reduces the scope for government-led redistribution.

Governments have to alter the underlying pattern of market rewards, addressing supply-side factors such as infrastructure and human capital while increasing the demand for high-skilled labour through new strategies of production. All countries need to move up the economic value chain; the propensity of manufacturers to relocate to the west given rising costs in Asia presents major opportunities. Globalisation processes can be rebalanced in favour of domestic production if public investments are targeted judiciously. The rebirth of western manufacturing should not obscure the ongoing importance of the new economy: specifically, innovation and 'data-driven growth', including the internet, social media, telecommunications and 'big data' to harness global flows of information and knowledge.[19] Moreover, it is likely that in the present international context developed economies will continue to derive comparative advantage from financial services and banking, even in the wake of the post-2008 financial crisis.

Tackling inequality also means addressing unequal outcomes in the labour market. The individualisation of pay bargaining since the 1970s has further eroded the labour-market position of low-skilled workers. The restoration of collective bargaining through the institutions of social partnership ought to be a reform priority in casualised, low-wage sectors. Moreover, the capacity of workers to upgrade their skills, another factor in the persistence of inequality, varies enormously across Europe. The EU employment rate for those with 'high' skills is 83.9 per cent, compared to 48.1 per cent for those with 'low' skills.[20] Non-professional workers are far less likely to access education and training than the highly skilled, according to Figures I.1 and I.2.

Closing the skills gap between 'professional' and 'non-professional' employees entails social investment in human capital and lifetime learning as the route to high-value competitiveness. The private sector must contribute; for example, through the introduction of a Europe-wide skills levy. The progressive taxation of capital transfers and inheritance is both more *efficient* (in helping to create a sustainable tax base less reliant on taxing incomes) and more *egalitarian* (in ensuring that wealth

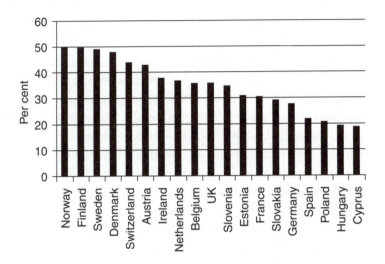

FIGURE I.1   Percentage of respondents who have upgraded their skills in the past 12 months, 2012.
Source: European Social Survey 2012.

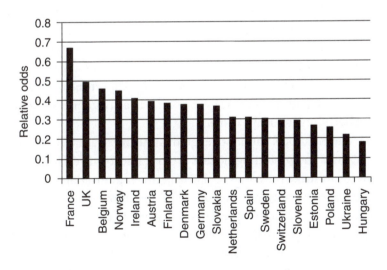

FIGURE I.2   Relative odds of non-professional workers receiving training in the past 12 months, 2012.
Source: European Social Survey 2012.

is fairly shared). The taxation system needs to focus on unearned wealth rather than earned income, rebalancing the distribution of rewards in favour of labour rather than capital.

The social policy expert Jane Jenson argues that social democratic governments have attempted the impossible task of squaring a circle: promising to improve social policy while keeping taxes low.[21] The inference has been that it is possible to combine US tax rates with public services of Nordic quality. This leads to a strategy of 'residualisation' in which citizens pay tax but services and benefits are increasingly targeted for reduction. Families are forced to seek provision through private markets, undermining the universal and solidaristic principles of the welfare state. Instead, paying taxes should be seen as the mechanism by which citizens share risk and ensure access to high-quality services that would never be provided through the market.

Public Policy and Risk: Reinventing Governance

Public policy has traditionally focused on protecting individuals and institutions from 'risks' that they cannot bare alone. Since the end of World War II, this has been an important prerogative of welfare states in most European countries. The latest European Social Survey data demonstrate that European citizens believe that governments have wide-ranging responsibilities in ensuring a minimum level of welfare for their citizens. Nonetheless, while citizens generally support the maintenance of the welfare state, they are sceptical of its capacity to provide security and opportunity in today's climate.

In western Europe, nation states gradually evolved as mechanisms for sharing risks and protecting citizens 'from cradle to grave'. However, the left needs to strike the correct balance between innovation and regulation: an excessive accumulation of rules imposes mounting compliance costs on business and entrepreneurs. The key is to pursue strategies that are genuinely 'risk-based': overseeing financial markets is an imperative given their impact on the real economy. An effective approach to regulation means reinventing government as an enabler rather than a barrier to change.

Moreover, strategies for tackling exclusion have to recognise that they should not simply protect individuals from risk and that, by taking chances, individuals can avoid permanent entrapment in poverty. The structure and organisation of the welfare state should acknowledge this in programmes ranging from urban regeneration to 'welfare to work', as full employment remains a fundamental social democratic goal. Tackling unemployment is essential, not least because a high rate of worklessness perpetuates resentment against the welfare state; moreover, long-term unemployment undermines basic human 'capabilities'. The contributory principle has a role in maintaining support for social security. But it is not a panacea: there are a range of strategies to entrench support for the welfare state. These include ensuring that those who 'pay in' to the system receive comprehensive benefits; that entitlements are conditional so that there is an obligation to work for those who can; and that there is a role for 'relational welfare', where individuals are rewarded for under-taking useful work in the community, including volunteering and caring for others. Across public policy, there is space between the market and the state: the realm of community, belonging, neighbourliness, reciprocity and solidarity should be actively cultivated by social democrats.

The Limits of Nation-State Social Democracy: Multilevel Governance

The 'permissive consensus' which carried European integration over many decades has run its course. The institutions of the EU are struggling to respond to citizens' demands for more transparency and accountability. Moreover, the EU is far larger than was envisaged by its 'founding fathers', with 28 member states and more new members in prospect. The project of the past decade, focused on monetary integration and the single currency, has come under strain following the eurozone crisis. Reforms to create a more accountable EU – for example, through direct election of the European Commission president – are necessary and urgent. But a more profound rethinking of the international dimension is needed that addresses the imperative of 'multilevel' governance through the appropriate distribution of local, regional, national, European and global power.

On the one hand, this entails transnational systems of governance to compliment the nation state in providing a sustainable supply of public goods and social welfare, as reflected in the importance of the European social model. On the other hand, systems of multilevel governance need to genuinely engage citizens in the policy-making process. At whatever level the process of governing occurs, decision making requires messy compromises and trade-offs between competing interests. The danger is that politics is forever doomed to disappoint, leading to growing cynicism, disillusionment and mistrust. It is vital that democracies actively involve citizens in the challenge of governing, championing new forms of participation in the democratic process. Politics is the only credible counterweight to the dominance of financial markets and unaccountable corporate power.

Conclusion: Progressive Politics after the Crash

A window of opportunity has been created for fundamental reform where institutions are recast to deal with pressing domestic and global problems which are increasing in their urgency. The state is more necessary than ever in advanced economies as an agent of structural reform and economic rebalancing. The challenge, however, is to embed an enduring consensus about the role of government so that public institutions are not swept away by the periodic resurgence of market liberalism.

For the left, the stakes are huge. The twentieth-century social democratic state was predominantly a *welfare* state. The political mobilisation of the postwar settlement as a distinctive, left-of-centre project was influenced by several phenomena: the transition to universal suffrage and a newly empowered electorate; rising longevity and the importance of protection in old age through viable public pension systems; and faster economic growth, which created a surplus of investment in social protection.

A defence of the traditional welfare state has been hardwired into European social democratic parties. Despite the narrative of ideological 'renewal' in the 1990s, there has been a reluctance to examine how the state itself should be modernised and reinvented: how the capacities and powers of government might be enhanced in the light of structural pressures, including globalisation and the internationalisation of capital, labour and product markets.

This book makes the case for a new, *post-crisis settlement* harnessing the dynamic traditions of progressive social liberalism and social democracy as the bedrock for structural reforms geared towards alleviating crisis aftershocks and addressing the profound structural challenges afflicting western capitalist democracies. The task is to show that, even in tough times, economic efficiency, social justice and ecological sustainability go hand in hand.

Notes

1. Andrew Gamble, *The Spectre at the Feast: Capitalist Crisis and the Politics of Recession* (Basingstoke: Palgrave Macmillan, 2009).
2. A. Sapir, 'The crisis of global governance', in A. Hemerijck, B. Knapen and E. van Doorne (eds), *Aftershocks: Economic Crisis and Institutional Choice* (Amsterdam: Amsterdam University Press, 2011), pp. 177–84.
3. See Howard Glennerster, 'Financing the welfare state: a new partnership model', in S. Griffiths, H. Kippin and G. Stoker (eds), *The Public Services: A New Reform Agenda* (London: Bloomsbury, 2013).
4. See Chapter 1 in this volume.
5. See Gamble, *The Spectre at the Feast*.
6. See Gamble, *The Spectre at the Feast*. C. Hay and D. Wincott, *The Political Economy of Welfare Capitalism* (Basingstoke: Palgrave Macmillan, 2012). M. Wolf, *Fixing Global Finance* (New Haven, CT: Yale University Press, 2009). Robert Hunter Wade, 'Globalization, growth, poverty, inequality, resentment and imperialism', in John Ravenhill (ed.), *Global Political Economy* (Oxford: Oxford University Press, 2011), pp. 373–409.
7. Helen Thompson, 'No way back: the legacy of a financial sector debt crisis' (Policy Network, 2012). Available at www.policy-network. net/pno_detail.aspx?ID=4233&title=No-way-back-the-legacy-of-a-financial-sector-debt-crisis (accessed 1 May 2013).
8. See Thompson, 'No way back'.
9. See Chapter 15 in this volume.

10. Ibid.

11. See Chapter 11 in this volume.

12. OECD, *Growing Unequal? Income Distribution and Poverty in OECD Countries* (2008), p. 3. Available at www.oecd.org/els/soc/growing unequalincomedistributionandpovertyinoecdcountries.htm (accessed 1 May 2013).

13. See Chapter 13 in this volume, p. 184.

14. OECD, *Growing Unequal?*

15. See Chapter 13 in this volume.

16. See Gøsta Esping-Andersen, *The Incomplete Revolution: Adapting to Women's New Roles* (Cambridge: Polity Press, 2008).

17. See Glennerster, 'Financing the welfare state'.

18. See Chapter 8 in this volume.

19. See Chapter 9 in this volume.

20. See Chapter 13 in this volume.

21. See Chapter 12 in this volume.

CHAPTER 1

The Limits of Technocratic Social Democracy

Renewal in the Post-Crisis Landscape

Peter A. Hall[1]

What are the prospects for progressive politics on the two sides of the Atlantic? I approach this question through reflection on the accomplishments and evolving dilemmas of social democracy since the middle of the twentieth century. While my emphasis is on European social democracy, many of the observations apply, *mutatis mutandis*, to the progressive side of American Democratic politics. This is a tale of three crises. In its modern form, social democracy was created in response to the bitter class conflict of the 1930s, which culminated in world war and a yearning for something new. Social democracy was then transformed – and some would say lost its way – in response to the economic crises of the late 1970s. Today, the issue is: what will it forge out of the global economic crisis that began in 2008?

There is no need to rehearse the history of postwar social democracy told so well elsewhere.[2] At the core of its trajectory were two issues: what policies could progressive parties implement and how were electoral coalitions assembled for them? Each side of this double movement was dependent on the other. In many respects, the 30 years that followed World War II were golden years for social democracy as well as the western economies. An industrial working class, drawn away from the radical right by its association with a devastating war, gave solid support to parties of the political left. The class-based grievances those parties aimed to rectify were still very real: it is sometimes forgotten that a significant proportion of British dwellings lacked indoor plumbing as late as 1958.

Social democratic parties were weaned from their initial inclination to nationalise the commanding heights of the economy by the

Keynesian promise that full employment could be secured through macroeconomic management. In conferences from Blackpool in the UK to Bad Godesberg in Germany, they devoted themselves to building full-employment welfare states founded on social and educational policies that T.H. Marshall could legitimately describe as 'class abatement'.[3] Many of those policies were also vehicles for cross-class coalitions that sustained social democracy, as growing employment in services and the public sector transformed the occupational structure.[4]

By the 1960s, social democratic parties were exploiting a modernisation paradigm, popular in the public sphere as well as in social science and notable for its faith in the capacities of states to improve society. The election of Harold Wilson in 1964 on a promise to transform Britain in the white hot heat of the scientific revolution was the high-water mark of a modernist vision that saw democratic states as vehicles for harnessing scientific knowledge to a popular will, whose vanguard social democracy could legitimately claim to represent.[5]

Although this vision was fraying around the edges by the 1970s, in the face of student revolts and a New Left more *autogestionnaire* than statist, it was dealt a mortal blow by the failure of governments to restore economic growth after the stagflation that followed the oil-price shocks of 1973–4. Virtually every government in office during this period was defeated at the next election; but social democracy suffered the most, because the apparent failure of Keynesian policies, often tied to state-led income policies, inspired a deep disillusionment with state intervention, tantamount in some countries to a crisis of legitimacy for the state.[6] Seeking a solution to persistently high rates of unemployment, as well as ways to absolve governments of responsibility for it, political elites on both the left and right turned towards market-oriented approaches to economic management. With the elections of Margaret Thatcher in 1979 and Ronald Reagan in 1980, an emphasis on the efficiency of markets became the hallmark of a neo-liberal era that was to last for 30 years.[7]

The Legacy of Neo-Liberalism

Despite some landmark events, including the election of the first socialist governments in Fifth Republic France and postwar Spain, the neo-liberal era has been a troublesome one for social democracy and progressive democrats. To some extent, social democracy was the victim of its own success. With the establishment of generous social programmes, the most appealing item in its platform was firmly in place by the early 1980s, when declining rates of growth diminished the scope for further expansion.[8] The question 'what's next?' has never been fully answered. Three decades of prosperity augmented by this social safety net reduced the incidence of abject deprivation, which had lent an edge to postwar politics, and blurred the boundaries of social class that were central to the appeal of many social democratic parties.[9]

By the early 1980s, the traditional class cleavage was also cross-cut by a values-cleavage that ranged the younger generations of many western societies committed to post-materialist values against others (often older or less educated) inclined to defend traditional values.[10] Progressive parties rose to this challenge by embracing post-materialist positions and recruiting more white-collar workers and professionals, rendering class dealignment more or less complete. However, these moves left blue-collar workers with traditional values without a natural home, creating an electoral opening for radical right parties in Europe and groups such as the 'moral majority' in the US. From the early 1980s, for instance, the National Front has commanded a fairly consistent 15–18 per cent of the vote in France, and sometimes a plurality of the votes from the manual working class.

More ominously, the traditional patterns organising political thinking have become disorganised. For instance, in France, the country that invented the left–right spectrum, barely more than half the voters are now willing or able to place themselves on that spectrum. To some extent, this reflects the policy choices made by social democratic governments in recent decades. Their platforms moved in neo-liberal directions and, even when their rhetoric remained leftist, their policies often were not (see Figure 1.1). In Europe, much of the impetus came from the Single European Act of 1986, which turned the European Commission into an agent for market liberalisation; and, even as they inveighed against globalisation, many social democratic governments implemented its European equivalent.[11] It is not surprising that voters were confused.

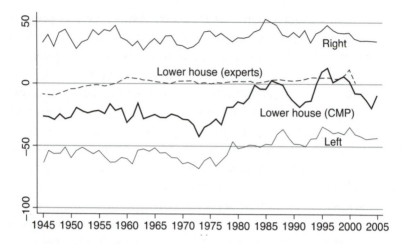

FIGURE 1.1   Movement of party platforms in 18 OECD countries between 1945 and 2005. Higher values on the y-axis indicate more neo-liberal positions on eight economic items in party platforms. The 'lower house (CMP)' line represents averages value for economic ideology weighted by share of seats. The dotted line is left–right orientation of legislature by share of seats.
Source: Courtesy of Torben Iversen, 'Class politics is dead! Long live class politics! A political economy perspective on the new partisan politics', *APSA-CP Newsletter* 17/20 (2006), pp. 1–6.

In this context, with no lodestone other than a concern to ensure the least affluent were not further disadvantaged, social democratic parties made heroic attempts to distinguish themselves from their conservative counterparts. In some cases, these efforts were largely rhetorical. Declaring himself in favour of a 'market economy' without a 'market society', Tony Blair tried to define and defend a Third Way in the UK.[12] Social policy was relabelled 'social investment' and the kinds of sums once spent on industrial policy were devoted to more or less active manpower policy in many parts of the continent.[13] Ironically, social policies once designed to reduce the dependence of workers on markets were reoriented to ensure that workers entered labour markets and had the skills to do so.[14] However, the era also saw some distinctively social democratic accomplishments, especially with regard to the distribution of income. The French socialists, for example, made taxation more progressive in order to expand social spending; and, even though high incomes rose dramatically, the British Labour Party kept the gap between low and median incomes narrow, while parties in Spain and Portugal built modern welfare states.

Fear of Falling

A decade after the turn of the millennium, however, the distinctiveness of what social democracy offers and who supports it is less clear than it has been at many previous moments in history. American progressives and European social democrats are seen as competent managers of liberal capitalism, more humane than their opponents, but not animated by especially powerful visions. Paradoxically, to the extent that the position of progressive parties remains distinctive, as in the US, it is largely because their opponents have moved a long way to the right, taking the political spectrum as a whole with them (see Figure 1.2).

Thus, the question is: can European social democrats and American progressives fashion an effective response to the current economic crisis and build from it a durable electoral coalition? The challenges are daunting. In principle, recession should increase support for the social

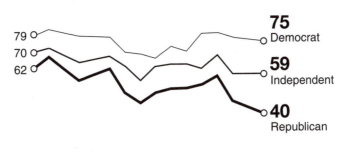

FIGURE 1.2 Change in views about the responsibility of government in the US between 1987 and 2012, in response to the statement: 'It is the responsibility of the government to take care of people who can't take care of themselves.' As explained alongside the original figure: 'Republicans have become less supportive of the social safety net while Democratic views have shown little change.'
Source: Pew Research Center, *Trends in American Values 1987–2012* (Washington: Pew Research Center, 2012).

protection offered by parties of the political left, and such trends are visible in European opinion. However, this is no ordinary recession. Several features make it unusually difficult to resolve.

First, this recession is rooted not in the business cycle, but in a debt crisis that was the culmination of several decades of lax regulation that saw vast increases in public- and private-sector debt, accompanied by disproportionate expansion in the financial sectors of some countries.[15] Therefore, the problem has become one of securing growth amid deleveraging, in terms that will promote a return to fiscal balance over the medium term. Although growth is by far the best solution to this problem, some (on both the left and right) argue that it demands a politics of austerity.[16]

Second, where banking systems are overextended or levels of public debt are high, governments face pressure from international financial markets for contractionary policies that are difficult to resist. While the image of the Cabinet waiting in the garden of 10 Downing Street to hear whether J.P. Morgan could secure a loan for Britain in 1931 reminds us that this phenomenon is not new, the demands of international finance limit the room for manoeuvre available to many contemporary governments.[17]

Third, in the eurozone, the problem is complicated by rules that prohibit the European Central Bank (ECB) from purchasing government debt, cumbersome decision-making processes that require transnational consensus and the challenges of securing agreement to transfer resources across national borders. The response to the euro crisis resembles the desperate, and politically disastrous, efforts to maintain the gold standard of the 1920s.[18] It borders on a transnational Ponzi scheme in which the European Union (EU) lends funds to national governments that are then sequestered to pay the interest on previous loans from the EU, while those governments borrow to bail out banks that are in turn lending to them with the encouragement of the ECB.

Social democratic parties can be forgiven for not having a distinctive solution to these problems. Moreover, high levels of unemployment, sluggish growth and threats of further recession are making the politics they face more challenging. Economic insecurity has given rise to a *sauve-qui-peut* politics in which people are worried about holding onto

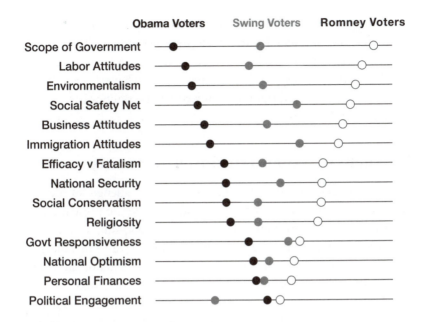

FIGURE 1.3 Attitudes of swing voters relative to those of Obama and Romney supporters, 2012. The original figure explanation reads: 'Each line shows the position of swing voters relative to the positions of Obama and Romney supporters on each of 14 values indices based on related survey questions. On most issues, opinions of swing voters fall squarely between those of Obama and Romney supporters. On others they tilt closer to Obama voters or Romney voters.'
Source: Pew Research Center, *Trends in American Values 1987–2012* (Washington: Pew Research Center, 2012).

what they have and more resistant to measures that might redistribute resources to others.[19] There is evidence for this in American public opinion, where swing voters, including many on modest incomes who are natural Democrats, were drawn to the Republican Party in 2012's presidential campaign, not by the religious or moral concerns usually cited but by the strong stance that party took against redistribution (see Figure 1.3). In much the same way, economic hard times tend to increase hostility to immigrants.[20] These developments pose special dilemmas for social democratic parties because they evoke a 'fear of falling' that the radical right can exploit to attract working-class voters.[21]

Some of the effects can be observed in the bitter polarisation of political debate in the US, where a battle rages between Republicans committed to reducing social spending and Democrats trying to preserve the social safety net. In continental Europe, electoral systems built on proportional representation sustained generous welfare states in good times, but, during the politics of bad times, these systems have given legislative footholds to the radical right. In many countries, politics has not been so ugly since the 1930s.

The Limits of Technocratic Social Democracy

In this context, social democrats face the challenge of devising programmes that will promote sustainable economic growth and an imagery of social justice appropriate for the twenty-first century. This is easier said than done and these programmes have to be tailored to the circumstances of each country. But some elements of the current conjuncture offer opportunities for social democracy. Unlike the recession of the 1970s, the current crisis cannot be blamed on the failure of state intervention. Instead, it has dealt a severe blow to the overweening faith in markets that was a fixture of the neo-liberal era. Survey evidence suggests that many people blame the crisis on the banks at least as much as they do on governments, and support for 'free markets' is waning in many countries (see Table 1.1). This crisis is also associated with rising

TABLE 1.1   Support for Free Markets, 2007–12.

| | *Percentage completely or mostly agree* | | | | |
	2007	*2010*	*2012*	*2007–12 change*	*2010–12 change*
Britain	72	64	61	−11	−3
Czech Republic	59	—	50	_9	—
France	56	67	58	+2	−9
Germany	65	73	69	+4	−4
Greece	—	—	44	—	—
Italy	73	—	50	−23	—
Poland	68	68	53	−15	−15
Spain	67	62	47	−20	−15
US	70	68	67	−3	−1

Source: Pew Research Center, *European Unity on the Rocks* (Washington: Pew Research Center, 2012).

levels of income inequality: many people resent the high rates of pay in the financial sector and more than a few wonder why the banks were bailed out when individuals were not.

In other words, the faith in free markets that was a dominant element of the neo-liberal creed has been shaken, and there is a new willingness to believe that governmental initiatives can make important contributions to economic growth. Social democrats should respond to this, especially in the Anglo-American democracies, by making a new commitment to public investment, understood to mean investment in human as well as material infrastructure. In countries like the US, the need to replace ageing physical infrastructure is manifest, and this kind of commitment evokes a distinctively social democratic confidence in the ability of states to advance social welfare. Although some might claim that the demands of austerity stand in the way of such policies, the best way to reduce debt is to inspire growth. Where real interest rates are at unprecedented lows, borrowing to make public investments offering higher returns than the cost of the loans makes eminent sense.[22]

However, social democrats need more than good sense. They can speak effectively to those disillusioned with neo-liberal policies and the politics of self-interest only by articulating a moral vision of a better society focused not only on what states can do for societies, but also on how better societies can be built. The technocratic social democracy of previous decades, marked by claims to operate market economies as efficiently as the right, has reached its limits. In this context, one of the central pillars of the social democratic vision should be its commitment to fairness – understood as equal treatment, fair dealing, respect and equal opportunity (long a core social democratic value). In the wake of a new gilded age, this could again be the keystone of progressive platforms. Many people are animated today by a diffuse sense of unfairness, born of promises not kept and expectations unfulfilled. In the developed democracies, markets have not delivered to ordinary citizens many returns.

What matters most in substantive terms is equality in life-chances, the central element of a fair society, now threatened by a market culture gone wild. Despite the rhetoric linking markets to meritocracy, the income inequality generated by unfettered competition has eroded equality

Intergenerational earnings elasticity

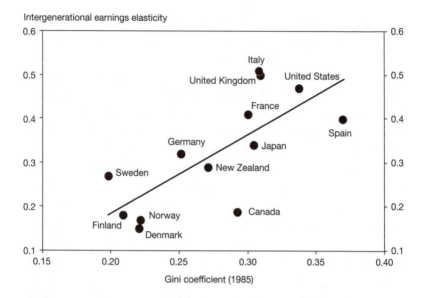

FIGURE 1.4   The relationship between income inequality and social mobility.
Source: Economic Report of the President 2012 (Washington DC: GPO 2012), Fig.
6.7.

of opportunity. Recent studies show that intergenerational mobility
varies inversely with the level of income inequality across nations, and
in many societies social mobility is stagnant or declining (see Figure
1.4).[23] In short, highly unequal incomes do not simply confer privilege;
they perpetuate it, as children without access to good housing, effective
schools, solid career tracks or parents with time off work and dedicated
to them are unable to find footholds to a secure life. In this context,
the incomes of the very rich may not matter much to the facts on the
ground for most people, but they symbolise a fundamental unfairness
about which social democrats should be thinking and talking.

That conversation may not always be comfortable, however, because
this is not simply a matter of redistribution as usual. The challenge is
to rethink what people owe one another, with a view to refashioning
the social contract for a new century. Some long-standing policies may
have to be reconsidered. Western welfare states, for instance, are typically more generous towards the elderly than the young. Unemployed
youth in Europe might well have the impression that welfare states

are a preserve for the old, and the American Tea Party movement is partly an effort by the elderly to defend their Medicare benefits at the cost of providing health insurance to the young.[24] Thus, complex issues of intergenerational redistribution are involved in rewriting the social contract, especially in economies facing high levels of debt and slow rates of growth.

In much the same way, Europeans have to decide what they owe to citizens of other member states. In the context of the Euro crisis, does social solidarity stop at national borders? And, after decades in which racial inequality, which is still serious, was the primary focus of attention, Americans are now discovering gaps in educational achievement across social classes that loom even larger than those across races.[25] Social democracy has to construct a new understanding of social justice for an era profoundly different from the prosperous age following World War II, when its modern principles were forged. The challenge is to confront rather than avoid these dilemmas.

Active Government and Social Imagination

In the Anglo-American democracies, a case will also have to be made for the effectiveness of active government. One of the principal impediments to the social democratic project is the prevalent view, pounded into people by three decades of neo-liberalism, that government is part of the problem rather than the solution. In contemporary economic doctrine, governments appear primarily as sources of inefficiency in the economy. While that is a minority view in parts of Europe, elsewhere it is an ideological totem that will not disappear overnight. The argument for effective government will have to be made, in new and inventive ways, by intellectuals and politicians.

Here, the concept of a government that is investing in its people, with a view to making a better future for all of them, has real promise. Although too often used to dress up policies designed to force people into dead-end jobs, the idea of social investment still has power. It deserves to be rescued and applied in programmes that confer new skills and seed new enterprises.[26] Public facilities (such as libraries, neighbourhood sports halls, extramural learning programmes and health clinics) have pay-offs that extend into the community well beyond their immediate users. It is time to give new meaning to the notion of public services.

Moreover, if the objective is a fairer society, governments can do more than redistribute, and social democrats offer more on this front than their opponents. After three decades in which market principles have penetrated ever more spheres of social life, people yearn for more decent social relations, which vacuous aspirations for a 'Big Society' are unlikely to supply. The social capital embodied in Britain's robust voluntary sector, for instance, was long dependent on how governments funded social services.[27] Ordinary people draw social resources, crucial to their health and well-being, from social connections in the local community, and studies suggest that these can be augmented or eroded by public policy.[28] Thus, governments attentive to the conservation of social, as well as natural, resources can make it easier for people to help themselves. As Jacob Hacker observes in this volume and elsewhere, the burden on governments to redistribute can also be reduced by regulations that ensure the distribution of market resources is more equitable.[29] By mandating private pensions that are more generous, higher minimum wages and better working conditions, governments can create fairer societies where new norms of social justice take hold.

To sustain such endeavours, however, social democratic parties need social allies. One of the most striking developments during the neo-liberal era has been the collapse of trade unions. Their membership is now half of what it was across the OECD three decades ago. As a result, people who once earned a decent wage no longer do so and many countries have seen their most prominent tribunes for social justice enfeebled.[30] It is time for progressive governments to acknowledge that trade unions are not only important political allies, but also bulwarks for fairness in the allocation of resources that progressive societies cannot do without.

Ultimately, the construction of such a society is not simply a matter of allocating resources, but one of constructing a moral vision of what people in a common community of fate owe one another. The effects of the current crisis have exposed many of the neo-Victorian myths in the social vision of neo-liberalism. And, if one legacy is still a residual cynicism about what governments can do and how people should behave, another is a void in the social imagination that deserves to be filled by something more than simple-minded nationalism. That is a task for which social democracy is in many ways fitted. As a General Secretary of the British Labour Party famously said, that party has long owed more to Methodism than to Marxism. If it is to appeal to a new electorate, its leaders will have to explain why social democracy is important in human and moral terms. Compassion can be as powerful a force in politics as cynicism, and people will respond to calls to create a better society. In this respect, the fate of social democracy lies in its own hands. The failure of market-oriented policies provides a new opening, but to step through it political progressives will have to shake off the shibboleths of their own past and evoke the passions to improve the world that can inspire new generations.

Notes

1. I am grateful to Michael McTernan and Rosemary C.R. Taylor for comments on an earlier draft.
2. Donald Sassoon, *100 Years of Socialism: The West European Left in the Twentieth Century* (London: I.B.Tauris, 1996); Gerassimos Moschonas, *In the Name of Social Democracy* (London: Verso, 2002); Sheri Berman, *The Primacy of Politics: Social Democracy and the Making of Europe's Twentieth Century* (New York: Cambridge University Press, 2006).
3. T.H. Marshall, *Citizenship and Social Class and Other Essays* (Cambridge: Cambridge University Press, 1950); Anthony Crosland, *The Future of Socialism* (London: Jonathan Cape, 1956).
4. Andrew Martin, 'The dynamics of change in a Keynesian political economy: the Swedish case and its implications', in C. Crouch (ed.), *State and Economy in Contemporary Capitalism* (London: Croom Helm, 1979); John Goldthorpe, *Social Mobility and Class Structure in Modern Britain* (Oxford: Clarendon Press, 1987).
5. Samuel H. Beer, *Patterns of Government* (New York: Random House, 1974).
6. Michel Crozier, Samuel P. Huntington and Joji Watanuki, *The Crisis of Democracies* (New York: New York University Press, 1974).

7. David Harvey, *A Brief History of Neoliberalism* (Oxford: Oxford University Press, 2005); Colin Crouch, *The Strange Non-Death of Neo-Liberalism* (Cambridge: Polity Press, 2011).
8. Evelyn Huber Stephens and John Stephens, *Development and Crisis in the Welfare State* (Chicago: University of Chicago Press, 2001).
9. Peter A. Hall, 'The political origins of our economic discontents: contemporary adjustment problems in historical perspective', in M. Kahler and D. Lake (eds), *Politics in the New Hard Times* (Ithaca: Cornell University Press, 2013).
10. Ronald Inglehart, *Culture Shift in Advanced Industrial Society* (Princeton: Princeton University Press, 1990); Herbert Kitschelt and Philipp Rehm, 'Economic redistribution and socio-political governance: when and where do second dimension voter alignments matter?' Paper presented to the Conference of Europeanists, Montreal (April 2010).
11. Peter A. Hall, 'The politics of social change in France', in P.D. Culpepper, P.A. Hall and B. Palier (eds), *Changing France: The Politics that Markets Make* (Houndsmills: Palgrave Macmillan, 2006), pp. 1–26.
12. Cf. Anthony Giddens, *The Third Way and Its Critics* (Cambridge: Polity Press, 2000).
13. Jane Jenson and Denis Saint-Martin, 'New routes to social cohesion? Citizenship and the social investment state', *Canadian Journal of Sociology* 28/1 (2003), pp. 77–99.
14. Gøsta Esping-Andersen, *Politics Against Markets: The Social Democratic Road to Power* (Princeton: Princeton University Press, 1988).
15. Menzie D. Chinn and Jeffry A. Frieden, *Lost Decades: The Making of America's Debt Crisis and the Long Recovery* (New York: Norton, 2011).
16. Wolfgang Streeck, 'The crises of democratic capitalism', *New Left Review* 71 (2011), pp. 5–29.
17. Cf. Ralph Miliband, *Parliamentary Socialism: A Study in the Politics of Labour*, 2nd edn (London: Merlin Press, 1972), p. 138 *et passim*.
18. Cf. Karl Polanyi, *The Great Transformation: Political and Economic Origins of Our Time* (Boston: Beacon Press, 1944).

19. James Alt, *The Politics of Economic Decline* (New York: Cambridge University Press, 1979); Amos Tversky and Daniel Kahneman, 'Loss aversion in riskless choice: a reference-dependent model', *Quarterly Journal of Economics* 106/4 (1991), pp. 1039–61.

20. Lucy Barnes and Peter A. Hall, 'Neo-liberalism and social resilience in the developed democracies', in P.A. Hall and M. Lamont (eds), *Social Resilience in the Neo-Liberal Era* (New York: Cambridge University Press, 2013).

21. Barbara Ehrenreich, *Fear of Falling: The Inner Life of the Middle Class* (New York: Pantheon Books, 1989).

22. Lawrence B. Summers, 'Look beyond interest rates to get out of the gloom', *Financial Times* (3 June 2012). Available at www.ft.com/cms/s/2/7ad17ac2-ab42-11e1-b675-00144feabdc0.html#axzz2S2nBE5la (accessed 1 May 2013).

23. Alan Krueger, 'The rise and consequences of inequality in the United States'. Paper presented to Center for American Progress, Washington DC (12 January 2012). Available at www.whitehouse.gov/blog/2012/01/12/chairman-alan-krueger-discusses-rise-and-consequences-inequality-center-american-pro (accessed 21 May 2013).

24. Theda Skopcol and Vanessa Williamson, *The Tea Party and the Remaking of American Conservatism* (New York: Oxford University Press, 2012).

25. Sean F. Reardon, 'The widening educational achievement gap between the rich and the poor: new evidence and explanations', in R. Murnane and G. Duncan (eds), *Whither Inequality? Rising Inequality and Uncertain Life Chances of Low-Income Children* (New York: Russell Sage, 2011).

26. Nathalie Morel, Bruno Palier and Joakim Palme (eds), *Towards a Social Investment Welfare State?* (London: Policy Press, 2011).

27. Peter A. Hall, 'Social capital in Britain', *British Journal of Political Science* 29 (1999), pp. 473–517.

28. Peter A. Hall and Rosemary C.R. Taylor, 'Health, social relations and public policy', in P.A. Hall and M. Lamont (eds), *Successful Societies: How Institutions and Cultural Affect Health* (New York: Cambridge University Press, 2009).

29. See Chapter 8 in this volume and Jacob S. Hacker, 'The foundations of middle-class democracy', in *Priorities for a New Political Economy: Memos to the Left* (London: Policy Network, 2011).

30. See Barnes and Hall, 'Neo-liberalism and social resilience'.

CHAPTER 2

Coming to Terms with Capitalism
Austerity Politics and the Public Household

Andrew Gamble

I n his famous essay on 'The Ends of History' reflecting on the eclipse of socialism at the end of the twentieth century, Perry Anderson set out four possible futures for the movement which for much of the twentieth century had seemed to supporters and opponents alike to be in the ascendancy.[1] The first possibility was *oblivion*: that the various socialist and social democratic parties and movements of the twentieth century might disappear without trace, and if remembered at all would come to be regarded as historical curiosities, political experiments that belonged to the process of transition to the modern world but that left no lasting legacy. The second possibility was *transvaluation*: that, after a period of demoralisation and defeat (which might last decades or even centuries), some of the ideas and objectives might be resurrected in a new form and new context, and influence later movements for social change and social justice. The third possibility was *mutation*: that there would be no sharp break in continuity. Instead, the parties and movements of the left and centre-left might successfully adjust and evolve in the face of new circumstances, while retaining a recognisable identity and connection with the traditions of the past. The final possibility was *redemption*: that at the nadir of its fortunes socialism might be reborn. Liberalism had recovered from decline and defeat between 1914 and 1945 to re-emerge triumphant again, and become the dominant doctrine and common sense of the postwar world.

Anderson, writing at the beginning of the 1990s, speculated that some new world crisis might make socialism once again relevant and necessary, although he conceded that, as with the earlier rebirth of liberalism after 1945, this would have to be a socialism purged of its flaws and past mistakes and reinvigorated by its inclusion of other traditions.

All four possibilities are still in play, but, in the midst of a new world crisis, there are as yet few signs of a rebirth of socialism or of the parties and movements of the left and centre-left. Instead, the left hovers uneasily between mutation and transvaluation, occasionally flirting with oblivion. It still has much to say about social justice, human rights and public services, but it no longer has much to say about capitalism. In the past a particular analysis of capitalism and how it might be reformed or replaced was what defined the left. Unless the left can recapture a sense of how it wants to reform capitalism, rather than simply relying on capitalism to provide the state with resources to redistribute, it is hard to see it regaining a meaningful role. When Francis Fukuyama presented his reworking of the end of history, the crux of his argument was that capitalism and democracy reigned supreme because all the alternatives to them, including all versions of socialism, had been tried and found wanting.[2] History had ended because there was no fundamental principle that any longer divided left and right in the various senses that had persisted since the French Revolution. The terms were redundant because no one contested any longer on grounds of principle the existence of either democracy or of capitalism.

Fukuyama may have recanted some of his views, but his basic argument still dominates debate on the future of the left. Is it any longer possible to imagine a different way of organising the economy? This question is hard enough, but there are two further questions, about class and about the state, that the left must answer in thinking about whether or not there is a future for socialism or for social democracy.

Statecraft and the Interest Groups

The reason why the left has become disorientated is that many of the frameworks through which it once viewed the world and imagined the future no longer seem to represent reality accurately. It is now sometimes forgotten how central class was to political thinking on the left. It generated powerful sets of assumptions, one of the most deep-rooted of which was 'the forward march of Labour', the idea that the combination of collective organisation of the industrial working class in trade unions and mass political parties in the new era of universal suffrage would prove unstoppable. Whatever setbacks were encountered, these would prove temporary, and the eventual triumph of the organised Labour movement would be assured. Its industrial and political strength would prevail, since it represented the great majority of workers and voters. Eric Hobsbawm suggested in the 1980s that these comforting beliefs were no longer valid, if they had ever been. The forward march of Labour had halted both industrially and electorally.[3] There was no guarantee that capitalism was producing its own gravediggers, or even its own reformers, in the shape of a powerful organised interest of labour, and others demonstrated that parties of the left could not succeed by relying on the votes of the working class alone.

Following the restructuring of national economies in the 1980s, those parts of the working class most associated with centre-left political parties have declined, often precipitately. The distribution of occupations and sectors in the economy now looks very different. Some centre-left parties have become more dependent on the votes of public-sector workers, but this will not generate lasting electoral majorities. The problem for any kind of progressive politics is serious. If the old interest base of left politics based on class has disappeared or is at least seriously weakened, what can replace it? It is very hard to imagine a successful politics that does not rely on interests. Parties have to articulate and be identified with the interests of a sufficient bloc of voters to stand any chance in elections.

The second set of assumptions concerns the state. It became axiomatic on the left in the twentieth century that any meaningful socialist political economy meant the extension of the powers of the state over the market. The purpose of social democracy was conceived as taming the powers of the market, offering countervailing powers to the market and governing the market in the interests of the majority rather than of the capitalist oligarchy. One of the most influential analyses that underpinned this perspective came from Karl Polanyi. He argued that the liberal market economy did not emerge spontaneously but had been politically constructed in the nineteenth century and had now broken down, because it had systematically eroded and weakened the institutions and communities that were necessary to sustain it.[4]

The spontaneous reaction of society to the workings of market capitalism had created the collectivist movements of the twentieth century, all of which proposed a big extension of the state to exert control over the market and restore a sense of security and community to modern societies. Polanyi's 'double movement' was the movement first to market freedom and then to collective security. Only the second had democratic legitimacy. What we have seen, however, is a second double movement: the revival of market freedom and the erosion of many of the gains in the enlargement of public services and lessening of social inequality that were achieved after 1945. Optimists think that this second double movement has given us 30 years of liberalisation but will be followed by a reaction, a new counter-movement (the re-imposition of social control), only this time at the international as well as the national level.[5] Pessimists think that there will be no reaction, that the return to liberal political economy and the subordination of the state to the market are the synthesis of Polanyi's double movement and represent a terminus, not a new point of departure, or at least that the neo-liberal wave has not yet run its course. The present world crisis is the opportunity for the start of the second movement, the turn to the re-engagement of the state and the renewal of the fortunes of the left. The opportunity is undeniable, but so far there is little sign it is being seized.

These are two critical problems for the centre-left in thinking about the future, and whether neo-liberalism is the last word or whether we can imagine a paradigm shift that can take us beyond neo-liberalism. What is the next stage for the development of capitalism, and how might a distinctive centre-left perspective emerge that can both articulate the interests of the majority and provide a viable governing strategy? Many of the critiques of centre-left parties and governments in the past 20 years have argued that they did not try to reshape the assumptions on which public policy were based, but worked within these assumptions to pursue their particular objectives.[6] They accepted in particular the shape of the new international economy that had emerged from the travails of the 1970s and they did not seek to disturb it. States still had significant freedoms and autonomy within the new liberal international order; it was still an embedded liberalism in Ruggie's sense[7] that nation states with their own distinctive national agendas pursued those agendas within the framework of a liberal international order.

The Power of Transnational Markets

The problem for the centre-left (both now and in the past) in seeking to assert democratic political control over market forces is that markets have increasingly become transnational and would require transnational governance to control them. The international system of states, with its complex regional arrangements and deadlocked international negotiations, reacts more slowly than markets, and so is more frequently in the position of having to adjust to agendas set by market agents than it is able to set agendas proactively itself. The penalty for social democratic governments (or any other kind of government) in leaving the international market system and setting up a closed economy is usually judged both by elites and electorates to be too high. It has hardly ever happened in the past 60 years; the decision by Greece to seek to stay in the eurozone is the most recent example of a country under extreme pressure hesitating at the brink. But staying within the international market system does not enable these governments to change the shape of this system very much, because doing so needs alliances and the co-operation of the leading states, who often refuse to give it.

A viable centre-left politics needs a reformed international market system, particularly in areas such as finance, corporate governance, trade and the environment. There are many proposals for change, but gaining political agreement to move ahead on a reform agenda has been extremely slow. The default position is always the existing international market system, with the well-known flaws in its governance and in its policies that were so exposed by the 2008 crash. The international market system is a precious asset but it urgently needs modification. Ha-Joon Chang and Dani Rodrik have separately argued that unqualified free trade can damage economies and societies.[8] States require a certain level of economic security to develop, and should have the right to pursue their own industrial policy and not fall foul of international trade rules (a right that the US already asserts for itself).

The objective should not be to implement substantive policy at the global level. That would require the formation of a world government for which there is little support and no realistic prospect. The task is rather to reform the existing institutions of global governance so that the rules that they uphold and attempt to enforce provide more support for national governments pursuing centre-left programmes. This may look forlorn at times, and the difficulties may seem insuperable. This is one of those areas where, as Weber puts it, politics is 'slow, strong drilling through hard boards'.[9] But, without significant reform and movement in this area, it is hard to see a future for the centre-left.

National controls, protectionism and the building of bilateral arrangements between states with similar regimes and objectives is the main alternative, and, if the world crisis deepens, these measures may be forced on all states and lead to a negative and destructive downward spiral. But reforming the rules of the international market system would clearly be preferable, if it could be achieved, and would be both less costly and less likely to lead to conflicts between states. The risk, as the present situation in the European Union makes plain, is that electorates will grow impatient with elites that seem incapable of delivery and appear to be locked in interminable negotiations with other elites. The risk of a fracturing of the system through populist rebellion has been avoided so far, but it is likely to increase if substantial reforms to international institutions cannot be agreed quickly.

Framing the Centre-Left Political Economy

The second requirement for the centre-left is to find new ways to talk about the economic crisis and to engage in the politics of austerity. At present it is losing this argument. One of the reasons for this is that politicians of the centre-right have generally been more adept at employing a discourse about an international market system that must obey the impersonal rules of 'market forces' alongside a discourse about the public household. In this discourse the public household is often reduced by analogy to a private household (which must subordinate everything to balancing its income with its expenditure) or to a corporate household (which subordinates everything to the bottom line and the pursuit of efficiency).

What the centre-left needs is a new discourse about the public household that resurrects the importance of this concept for a distinctive centre-left political economy. The importance of the concept of a household, as Hayek noted, is that it is organised on very different principles from a market.[10] The conflicts between states and markets can be traced to this fact. But the distinction between states and markets needs to be broken down. Markets are multiple and highly varied, in part because of the way they are constituted by different kinds of households. There are not only public households (states) but also corporate households and private households, none of which are organised on market principles yet all of which are essential in order for markets to exist. It is this complexity of the political economy of capitalism that offers scope for a distinctive centre-left perspective. The idea of the public household involves not just the budget (which lays bare the skeleton of the state, as Goldscheid argued),[11] but also the institutions and processes that define the overarching rules for private and corporate households, and for the market order itself.

All citizens are members of the public household, and the way the public household is ordered is key to understanding the political economy.[12] Centre-right politicians have a conception of the public household too, but it tends to be a minimalist one. Centre-left conceptions should be maximalist, but they have in recent years often tended to be minimalist too. 'Maximalist' does not mean that everything should be included within the public household, as many early socialists advocated, but it does mean that the public household is the place where the common management of the nation's affairs should be debated and decided, and rules determined. The biggest leap of all that needs to be made is countering the assumption that the market order is a spontaneous creation that works best if it is left as unhindered in its operations as possible. Many of the most serious contributors to the liberal tradition of political economy, from Adam Smith to Keynes, have argued otherwise, and this idea used to be a staple of socialist political economy as well, from Marx to Tawney. Recapturing the confidence to affirm the importance of politics in determining the rules that shape the way markets are governed and companies are governed is an essential step to a new centre-left political economy. So too is the need to address questions of intergenerational justice, the organisational ecology of civil society and our environmental dilemmas. None of these questions can be left to markets alone.

Drilling through Hard Boards

There are many new ideas on the centre-left about economic policy. These include ideas around redistribution, intervening to shape the distribution of income and assets before tax as well as after it, as discussed by Wendy Carlin.[13] The campaign for a living wage is a major initiative here, as are some of the radical ideas around asset-based welfare. Along with efforts to raise investment in human capital to the levels already achieved in the Nordic economies, these ideas offer new policy instruments with which to start to counter the market trends that in the past 30 years have widened inequality. Another major area for reform is corporate governance, following the banking scandals and the renewed focus on how transfer pricing allows transnational companies to reduce the amount of tax they pay. Ideas around stakeholding briefly flourished in the 1990s and were then buried, but they need reviving. The centre-left has never taken reform of company law seriously enough, but it is one of the key building blocks in reshaping the relationship between the state and the market – a relationship that has become distorted.[14] None of this need mean a large increase in central control. Another area currently receiving attention is how to develop a more diverse organisational ecology, promoting co-operative, charitable and other forms of social and community enterprise.

It sometimes seems that it is harder to achieve change than it was in the past. Neo-liberalism is well entrenched, international agreement to reform the international market system and global governance remains elusive, the class base of social democracy has been seriously weakened, and the current politics of austerity is dominated by the tropes of fiscal conservatism. There have so far been few attempts to put together a new vision that is comprehensive. There is a yearning for a new Keynes to appear and chart the way ahead. But that is a false hope. Real change is more likely to come from the active involvement of a wide spectrum of individuals and groups in developing a serious programme of reform. What is required is a critique of neo-liberalism and its failings alongside recognition of its strengths and successes, a credible commitment and strategy to reform international rules and institutions, a strategy to build a new majority electoral coalition, and a new philosophy and political economy of the public household. If such a programme is to emerge, it will be through many small local initiatives: a patchwork of ideas about how existing institutions and policies can be reformed and new coalitions built to press for change. Mutation is probably no longer sufficient. If it is to influence the next phase of capitalist development, the centre-left will need some transvaluation and perhaps a dose of redemption too. Otherwise it really may be facing oblivion.

Notes

1. Perry Anderson, 'The ends of history', in *A Zone of Engagement* (London: Verso, 1992).
2. Francis Fukuyama, *The End of History and the Last Man* (London: Hamish Hamilton, 1992).
3. Eric Hobsbawm, *The Forward March of Labour Halted?* (edited by M. Jacques and F. Mulhern; London: NLB, 1981). See also Göran Therborn, 'Class in the twenty first century', *New Left Review* 78 (2012), pp. 5–29.
4. Karl Polanyi, *Origins of Our Time: The Great Transformation* (London: Gollancz, 1945).
5. Robert Cox, *Approaches to World Order* (Cambridge: Cambridge University Press, 1996).
6. Colin Hay, *The Political Economy of New Labour: Labouring Under False Pretensions* (Manchester: Manchester University Press, 1999).
7. John Ruggie, *Constructing the World Polity* (London: Routledge, 1998).
8. Ha-Joon Chang, *Kicking Away the Ladder: Economic Development in Historical Perspective* (London: Anthem, 2002); Dani Rodrik, *The Globalization Paradox: Democracy and the Future of the World Economy* (New York: Norton, 2011).
9. Max Weber, 'Politics as a vocation', in *Political Writings* (edited by Peter Lassmann and Ronald Speirs; Cambridge: Cambridge University Press, 1994), p. 369.
10. F.A. Hayek, *Law, Legislation and Liberty* (London: Routledge, 1982), vol. II, pp. 107–32.

11. See Joseph Schumpeter, 'The crisis of the tax state', in R. Swedberg (ed.), *The Economics and Sociology of Capitalism* (Princeton: Princeton University Press, 1990), p. 100. Rudolf Goldscheid was an Austrian socialist and pioneer of fiscal sociology, and was quoted by Schumpeter in this essay.
12. Daniel Bell, *The Cultural Contradictions of Capitalism* (New York: Basic Books, 1976).
13. See Chapter 10 in this volume.
14. John Parkinson, Andrew Gamble and Gavin Kelly (eds), *The Political Economy of the Company* (London: Hart, 2000).

CHAPTER 3

The Many Faces of Distributional Conflicts
Recovery and Fiscal Adjustment

Jeffry A. Frieden

The world is in the midst of the most serious economic crisis since the 1930s. The downturn has been longer and deeper than any recession in 75 years, and it has affected almost every developed, emerging and developing economy.

Even more troubling is the fact that recovery from this Great Recession has been limited and halting. Europe is now in its second recession in five years, with skyrocketing unemployment in some countries and generalised stagnation in the region as a whole. The US is doing better, but even there the improvement in economic conditions has been very weak.

This does not seem to be a typical cyclical recession – and it isn't. The world is suffering through a series of interrelated debt crises. And debt crises are different from cyclical recessions, for both economic and political reasons. We have already lost one decade to the current crisis, as the economic gains of 2001–7 have since been erased. If we are to avoid losing another decade, we need to understand how this crisis is different and what can be done to limit its negative effects. Indeed, as events of the past couple of years show, the danger is not just of losing another decade but of spending the remainder of this decade in a near-constant state of crisis and stagnation, with the threat of a truly global depression not so distant on the horizon.

The crisis is the result of a decade of debt-financed consumption. In some countries, this was led by the public sector, with large-scale deficits. In other countries, the borrowing was largely or entirely private, typically by or through the financial system. In virtually all cases, borrowing was not associated with increased investment, public or private, but rather with increased consumption. This expansion of consumption led to a boom – especially in asset and housing markets – and then a bubble, which eventually burst.

Such a debt crisis leaves a very difficult economic and political residue. On the economic front, it saddles society with a serious debt overhang that hampers recovery. Debtors, burdened with more debts than they can easily service, need to reduce consumption and increase savings in order to mobilise resources. Creditors, encumbered with trillions in debts they know to be bad or fear may be bad, have to struggle to adjust their balance sheets to compensate for expected losses. On both sides, then, growth is constrained by limited spending and limited lending. Indeed, in the major debtor nations in the US and Europe, adjustment has not proceeded at anything like the pace necessary to restore balance. It will undoubtedly be several years before we see American and European consumers spending in the usual ways, and before we see the American and European financial systems playing their appropriate role as intermediaries between savers and investors.

The Many Faces of Distributional Conflict

Politically, debt crises lead to conflict over the distribution of the adjustment burden. When, as in the current case, cross-border debts are at issue, there are two dimensions of conflict. First, creditor countries and debtor countries square off to see which will undertake the bulk of the costly adjustment: creditors demand debtor austerity to maintain debt service, while debtors demand debt restructuring to make the debt more manageable. Typically, some compromise is worked out – after all, both sides have an incentive to reach agreement – but the battle over the compromise can be hard fought and drawn out.

A second dimension of conflict erupts *within* countries, over who domestically will be asked to contribute to dealing with the debt overhang. In creditor countries, for example, the question might be whether it will be financial institutions or taxpayers. In debtor countries, the issue is the distributional incidence of the austerity measures necessary to maintain debt service: taxpayers or beneficiaries of government services, workers or managers, the private or the public sector. Debt crises are never resolved easily; they always lead to substantial international and domestic political tension. The current crisis and its aftermath have been no exception, and in some instances the tension has only begun to manifest itself.

The crisis and its aftermath present the countries of the west with serious economic and political problems – both short term and long term.[1] In the short run, the over-riding imperative is to rekindle economic growth. Ironically, given the debt-overhang problem, this almost certainly requires stimulative fiscal policy. One saving grace is that, at this point, many governments are able to borrow at such low interest rates that it is almost certainly the case that the social cost of public borrowing is far outweighed by the social benefits of the stimulus. So we should have no compunction about insisting that, so long as unemployment remains unacceptably high and recovery lags, governments should pursue aggressive monetary and fiscal policies to speed growth.

There is another aspect to recovery, related to the heavy debt burden that weighs on economies. Simple fiscal stimulus will help, but it will not do much to address the very substantial debts that are slowing economic activity. Recovery will be retarded so long as these trillions of dollars in bad and questionable debts continue to constrain both creditors and debtors. This calls for a substantial restructuring of existing debts, such as takes place in virtually every debt crisis. There is no doubt that, where debts cannot be serviced as contracted, it is in the interests of both creditors and debtors to find a resolution that allows a resumption of normal financial relations – after all, that is what bankruptcy proceedings are for.

In some instances, debts can be restructured by negotiation. The current round of sovereign debt crises in Europe may fall into this category: there are a few debtors and a (relatively) few creditors, so negotiation is an option. However, most of the troubled debts today are of households, not sovereigns, and it is not feasible to plan a negotiated restructuring of tens of millions of mortgages and other household obligations. This suggests the value of a traditional way of reducing the real burden of accumulated debts: inflation. Several years of modest inflation, in the 3–5 per cent range, would substantially reduce the extent to which debts foul the balance sheets of households in Europe and North America.

Debt restructuring is highly political, for whatever resolution is worked out – whether by explicit negotiation or by inflation – will harm some more than others. The crux of the problem is the asymmetry of the adjustment burden. Debtors have no choice but to adjust, inasmuch as they face grave difficulties with further borrowing; so, creditors can insist that debtors do most of the sacrificing. But this inflames debtors, and often ends up with an explicit refusal to service debts. More generally, the result typically throws debtors and creditors into a game of chicken, which can lead to a dramatic exacerbation of the political conflict. It can also cause grave delays in settling the issue, and delay only raises the cost of a debt crisis. Europe, of course, finds itself deeply embroiled in this characteristic, dangerous tug of war.

Growth and Debt Restructuring

Thus, the immediate need in both Europe and the US is for stimulative measures to rekindle economic growth, and systematic plans to restructure household and sovereign debts. Both sets of policies are highly controversial, involving as they do major conflicts of interests. But, without both, the current recession is certain to lead to another lost decade as economies continue to stagnate and debts continue to hang over national economies.

Growth in and of itself is not enough: even with a rapid return to the growth rates of the early 2000s, many industrial societies would still be hampered by outstanding debts. For some, accumulated public-sector debts will seriously restrict the ability of governments to address national problems. For others, the debt burden weighs most heavily on households, and growth will not sufficiently ease this burden to allow households to return to normal spending patterns. Even in creditor countries, financial institutions are unlikely simply to be able to 'grow out of' their problems without artificially restraining their lending in ways that themselves would limit economic activity. Governments will have to work both to rekindle growth and to reduce the debt overhang.

However, there are longer-term problems that western governments need to address. Most OECD countries will face serious fiscal choices over the next couple of decades. Government revenues will not keep up with the demands of retirement and health-care programmes in most of the developed world. This is part of a more general phenomenon that afflicts many rich economies: the political difficulty of getting populations to agree to pay for the social and other programmes they want. In its basic form, this is not a question of how much governments should spend on social insurance, the military or education, but simply of how they will pay for the things that voters want and are unwilling to see cut. For much of the past 20 years, governments have run deficits rather than fund their current expenditures, but deficit spending at these levels is unlikely to be feasible for the next 20 years. This is due both to the scale of the current financial crisis and to the inexorable increase in spending as populations age. Therefore, one long-term problem is the need to find a way to square governments' retirement and health-care commitments with their fiscal positions.

Fiscal pressures on governments are likely to become more binding; but future prosperity also depends upon expanding other important government programmes, and these in turn are sure to require more spending. Virtually all observers believe that the developed countries need substantial increases in the quality of their education systems and economic infrastructures. This is particularly pressing as the pace of international competition is quickening, inevitably, as the easy exports and easy consumption of the past decade fade into a distant memory. Economic growth will require substantial productivity advances, which in turn require a more highly skilled labour force, a more efficient economic infrastructure and a more welcoming environment for technological innovation – all things that take money, including public money. This creates yet another long-term problem, for the appetite for more expansive public spending now seems very limited.

If, as is likely, it is economically or politically impossible to *both* sustain current levels of spending on social insurance, especially for retirement and health-care benefits, *and* increase spending on education and other productivity-enhancing public programmes, there is likely to be conflict between those on either side of this trade-off. The prospect is not a happy one, as we would all like to be able to satisfy both sets of needs; but the current financial and fiscal climate is such that we will undoubtedly have to make some hard choices along these lines. To some extent this involves intra-generational distributional issues (which retirees get what, which health-care benefits are cut) and to some extent it is inter-generational (whether we focus on care for the infirm and elderly now or on increasing future prosperity). The trade-off is not quite so stark, and most western societies are rich enough that they can do both, but still there are choices to be made – which implies that there are political conflicts ahead.

Indeed, the political challenges are daunting. In the short run, governments need to stimulate economies with monetary and fiscal policies, and to undertake an aggressive restructuring of sovereign and household debts, whether by negotiation or inflation. In the long run, governments need to cover the large and increasing costs of their generous retirement and health-care programmes, and to expand expensive public programmes to enhance education and economic infrastructure. None of these policies presents insurmountable technical difficulties. However, all of them face extraordinary political obstacles, which may indeed prove insurmountable.

Attempts to pursue more stimulative fiscal policies are running up against opposition from wealthier taxpayers, who have been much less seriously affected by the crisis and who understand that they will bear the principal burden of future taxation to service the debts that are incurred. Measures to restructure debts, whether by negotiation or by inflation, are confronting the hostility of creditors in the financial community and more broadly among the (largely wealthier, largely older) saving segments of the population. Western political systems indeed appear gridlocked over these issues, with little prospect of a clear, progressive way forward.

In the longer run, conflicts of interest are also likely to pervade future plans. Inasmuch as fiscal stringency is likely to be the order of the day, we will have to make hard choices between the generosity of retirement, health-care and other social programmes on the one hand, and public investment in human capital formation, infrastructure and other productivity-enhancing activities on the other. There are powerful supporters – and powerful arguments – for both sets of policies, and no easy decisions to be made.

Avoiding another Lost Decade

In this context, those who want to keep progressive ideals alive in these difficult times should focus on three important goals. First, in the short run, the primary imperative is to ensure a rekindling of economic growth. This requires maintaining stimulative fiscal and monetary measures for as long as they are needed. A government that imposes austerity too soon will only prolong, and worsen, the agony – after all, the longer the downward portion of the economic cycle lasts, the harder it will be for the public and private sectors to service their debts.

Second, in the medium run, governments need to make reasoned decisions about their fiscal positions. Almost all western governments face serious challenges as populations age, pension obligations come due and health care becomes more expensive. Many of our tax systems are in need of reform to make them more effective and less prone to abuse by special interests. But it is almost certainly the case that adjusting to the new demographic and economic realities will require some increased taxation and some reduced expenditures. These tasks can be accomplished in a way that shares both the pain and the gain, or their cost can be shunted onto those least able to protect themselves. The job for progressives is to try to make sure that whatever fiscal adjustments need to be undertaken are both justified and just.

Third, in the current environment, in which all attention is focused on short- and medium-term issues (recovery and fiscal retrenchment), we need to assert the importance of ensuring the quality of the future. This means, first and foremost, safeguarding or upgrading our societies' educational systems. The economic, intellectual, political and social demands of modern society require an ever-better-educated populace. This is an expensive undertaking, but the return on this investment in human capital formation well justifies the expense. Many of our societies also need an extensive programme to renew the physical and economic infrastructure, from bridges and railways to telecommunications. Again, this will be expensive, but it is the only way to avoid a deterioration of the quality of modern life. One way or the other, industrial societies will have to address three sets of tasks: recovery, fiscal adjustment and socio-economic renewal. Our job is to make sure that these tasks are accomplished in a way that benefits all rather than a select few.

Can the west avoid a second lost decade? It will be difficult – not for technical or purely economic reasons, but because the measures necessary to rekindle growth and make it sustainable will be resisted by powerful interests. In the short run, stagnant economies need stimulative fiscal and monetary policies; but these will be opposed by those less affected by the crisis, as well as by wealthier taxpayers, creditors, savers and those on fixed incomes. In the longer run, our economies need substantial public investments to improve our human and physical capital stock; but these will be opposed by those who want less government and lighter taxation.

Nonetheless, our goals should be clear. If we are to stave off another lost decade and prepare for a better future, we need macroeconomic policies to restore acceptable levels of economic activity and public investment to power sustained and productive growth. All dimensions require balance – balancing macroeconomic expansion with prudence, long-term growth with fiscal responsibility and fiscal responsibility with social responsibility. The balancing act is not simple, and the opposition is powerful, but the stakes are very high.

Note

1. For a more detailed analysis, see Menzie D. Chinn and Jeffry A. Frieden, *Lost Decades: The Making of America's Debt Crisis and the Long Recovery* (New York: Norton, 2011).

CHAPTER 4

The Fall-Out from the Eurozone Crisis
Turning EU Integration into a Positive-Sum Game

Loukas Tsoukalis

We are in the fifth year of a crisis originally caused by the bursting of a big bubble. What began as the biggest financial crisis of the west since the 1920s later transformed itself into a European crisis, and a crisis of the eurozone in particular, as markets and policy-makers began to realise what a currency without a state really implies when the going gets rough.

The crisis of the eurozone has three main components: a banking crisis and a sovereign debt crisis, which are not unique to Europe but which acquired a totally different dimension because of the high degree of interdependence between countries, plus an internal competitiveness component, which can no longer be dealt with through currency realignments. We are still living with the manifold and intricate consequences, including persistently low growth (indeed, negative in several countries); high, and still rising, rates of unemployment; a big increase in economic divergence across Europe; the rise of populism within countries; and a gradual loss of trust between them. European solutions to Europe-wide problems have become increasingly difficult as a result.

We have learned some hard lessons in the process of trying to manage the adjustment to a post-bubble world, especially inside the eurozone, where we discovered that we had neither the institutions nor the instruments to deal with a major crisis – and some people suspected we did not have the political will either, and they betted accordingly. Luckily, they did not win their bet, because they had underestimated once again the overall importance of the European project for most of those directly involved: economic and monetary union, as agreed at Maastricht, as a kind of post-modern construction that attempted to defy the forces of gravity. With some delay, those forces of gravity began to take their revenge, and we have been grappling with them ever since.

Fiscal Consolidation and Monetary Squeeze

When the financial crisis broke out, many people realised that the self-regulation of financial markets had been a bad joke. Alas, it was a kind of joke that many politicians on the centre-left had taken seriously in their effort to be modern, as a result of which they had often acted as missionaries for deregulation and free capital markets. The cost in terms of political capital and credibility has been big, and it is still being paid. Now we know (or have just been reminded) that moral hazard, inherent in the 'too big to fail' notion, is a real problem that needs to be addressed through regulation, or more drastic measures. We have also learned through bitter experience that retail banking needs to be insulated from high-risk betting, and also that the problem in financial markets goes far beyond asymmetrical information, as acknowledged long ago in the literature. Too frequently for comfort, the problem boils down to sheer manipulation of markets through cartel behaviour. Furthermore, pay compensation for those employed in the sector can be a matter of public concern, while the way the finance industry has so far been taxed (or not been taxed) raises important questions of equity.[1] There is a difference between democratically regulated markets and market-driven democracies – and we have come very close to the latter in Europe and North America. This is bad for economic stability and social cohesion; it is also bad for democracy.

Although almost all agree that over-indebtedness is a key factor behind the outbreak of the crisis, multiplied several times in a world where financial markets have tended to resemble the operations of a casino, deleveraging of the public and/or private sector needs careful monitoring. There is no doubt that fiscal consolidation is required in many (most?) European Union (EU) countries and further afield. Ageing populations, rapidly rising health costs and a large increase in sovereign debt burdens resulting from efforts to deal with the consequences of the crisis do not leave governments with much of a choice. Yet, there is a question of timing and aggregation, and also one about priorities at a time when Europe is faced with the dim prospect of a prolonged double-dip recession,[2] with the weakest members of the eurozone today leading a desperate suicide dance.

If many countries resort to fiscal contraction while the private sector is simultaneously trying to reduce its debt exposure, the probability of ending up in a vicious circle of austerity and recession is very high. Fiscal consolidation in a liquidity trap can be self-defeating, as Keynes pointed out many years back. This is precisely where much of the eurozone finds itself today. The combination of front-loaded fiscal consolidation, as part of adjustment programmes monitored jointly by the European Commission, the European Central Bank (ECB) and the International Monetary Fund (IMF), and the monetary squeeze resulting from bank undercapitalisation and sizeable premiums on interest rates because of the country risk perceived by markets, has forced the countries on the European periphery through a process of slow strangulation. And they have no exchange-rate instrument to resort to any more. This is a hellish combination indeed. The IMF has belatedly discovered that the so-called fiscal multipliers are much bigger than originally expected.[3] But output lost today cannot easily be regained tomorrow. The unemployed become long-term unemployed. Unemployment rates in countries with adjustment programmes have reached levels that nobody would have imagined possible, at least during peacetime. Economies implode and the risk of social explosion rises in the worst-hit countries.

Distributional Politics

The bursting of financial bubbles leaves behind a debt overhang. History teaches us that some of it is usually written off and some is eaten away through inflation.[4] The sooner we draw the line between debt (public or private) that is sustainable and debt that is not, the better it will be for all concerned and also the quicker economic recovery will follow. The restructuring and recapitalisation of financial institutions is a necessary precondition for recovery. The moment of truth has been unduly delayed in Europe, in comparison to the US, because a highly decentralised political system cannot easily cope with a crisis that criss-crosses national borders, and more specifically because it is extremely difficult to agree on how, in the adjustment to a post-bubble world, to distribute pain between debtors, bank stakeholders and taxpayers, and even more so between countries. Distributional politics has always been highly controversial: no doubt about it. For the EU, a still-half-baked political system at best, it is much more so given the narrow limits of solidarity across borders.

We know from the Bretton Woods negotiations and also from the early history of European monetary integration that it is difficult to agree on how to distribute the burden of adjustment between surplus and deficit countries in a world of fixed exchange rates. When there are no rules, the will of those with longer staying power in the game is likely to prevail. And these are normally surplus countries. In the long period of European monetary integration leading to Maastricht and the Economic and Monetary Union, repeated attempts were made to establish rules that would ensure symmetry between surplus and deficit countries.[5] Judging from experience, they were in vain.

Structural reforms are long overdue in many EU countries. Contrary to the expectations of those who invested much political capital in the so-called open method of co-ordination, the Lisbon Strategy has not delivered much. And it is not yet clear whether the strategy of Europe 2020 will fare any better. Insufficient progress in implementing reforms that have been officially endorsed at the European level matters even more for members of the eurozone, because the exchange rate is no longer available. More flexible markets, especially the labour market, are needed for the proper functioning of a currency union. But flexibility without security in times of high unemployment looks to those directly concerned like a bargain with few winners and many losers, at least for the immediate future. Reforms always meet resistance, and we know from experience that structural reforms are politically very difficult when the economy is shrinking. In the short term, they may even make the recession worse. How does one explain all that to well-paid technocrats with strong views drawn from economic theories that concentrate too much on efficiency and too little on equity?

Steps to Steer Europe Out of the Crisis

The first priority is to restore and further strengthen confidence in the irreversibility of Europe's currency union: easier said than done, as the experience of recent years painfully demonstrates. This, in turn, presupposes that we design a set of conditions and measures that deals effectively with a dual problem: the fear of moral hazard prevalent in the creditor countries on the one hand (meaning that, without adequate reforms and fiscal adjustment, money lent to countries in difficulty may go into a bottomless pit); and the convertibility (or country) risk in debtor countries on the other (a risk translated into capital flight and high-interest-rate premiums, fed in turn by self-sustaining market perceptions and leading to the disintegration of banking and financial sectors across national boundaries). There is a risk that a zero-sum mentality will take over in Europe, and the fear of 'transfer union' in the creditor countries hitting against the perception of the EU as the police-man of austerity in the south. If it becomes established, it could cause a big political explosion. Meanwhile, economic divergence continues to grow between creditor and debtor countries. European integration as a convergence machine was a key element of success in the past. Will it be no longer?

Greeks, Spaniards, Italians and others (including the French, we may add) need to take full ownership of a wide-ranging programme of reforms. And they need leaders of their own to articulate such a programme and defend it against vested interests and the forces of inertia. Conditionality attached to bail-out programmes is unavoidable, if not desirable. But successful reforms require domestic ownership; they cannot simply be imposed from outside, from Brussels or Berlin. This is one side of the bargain. The other is that countries going through painful adjustment also need time, money and an external environment more propitious to growth. Europe can provide all three as part of a new grand bargain that will take regional integration to a new stage, with firm commitments and conditions attached for all parties concerned. In designing this new grand bargain for Europe, the role of Germany will be absolutely crucial. Germany has, after all, become the indispensable country for any European agreement to deal with the crisis.

In trying to fill the lacunae left by economic policy, which is decided in a more intergovernmental setting, the ECB has resorted to meas-ures that had erstwhile belonged to the category of 'unthinkables': unprecedented measures for an unprecedented crisis. The mere intention of resorting to 'outright monetary transactions' (OMTs), publicly announced by the governor of the ECB, proved enough, for some time at least, to pacify the animal spirits in financial markets in relation to the beleaguered periphery of Europe. But it is all terribly fragile: many problems remain unsolved.

We need a more differentiated approach to fiscal stabilisation as well as different sequencing. Adjustment should not be borne exclusively by deficit countries. Creditor countries should make better use of the margin of manoeuvre available. We need a different mix of structural reforms, fiscal stabilisation and growth measures in Europe today, with more emphasis on growth as a necessary complement to reform and stabilisation. Growth policies should be investment-led, with particular emphasis on education and infrastructure. This requires both a national and a European component.

The EU multiannual financial framework (in other words, the EU budget package for 2014–20), small though it is, sends a mixed message at best: a smaller overall budget in times of recession; more money on research, education and innovation; less money than expected on EU-wide infrastructural projects; and new money to combat youth unemployment. True, an annual budget of about 1 per cent of the combined GDP of the EU-28 can only have a limited impact, but we are told this is all that was politically feasible. Things may, however, be increasingly different for the group of 17 countries inside the eurozone for the very simple reason that the stakes are much higher: this is now the core of European integration. Money committed to individual members of the eurozone during the crisis through bail-out programmes (programmes that dare not speak their name because they were not supposed to be there) are already a multiple of annual EU-28 budgets. Admittedly, they are loans, not transfers, but we have certainly not seen the end of this story as yet.

Despite continuing differences about the appropriate mix of policies and the sequencing of measures, there is growing consensus that the survival of the euro requires a banking union and fiscal (and economic) union. The latter should include close and effective co-ordination of national economic policies coupled with partial mutualisation of debt and, perhaps also, a separate budget for the eurozone as well as further advances in terms of political union. Of course, the devil lies not only in the details but also in the way decisions taken in Brussels are implemented in member countries. Politically difficult decisions are usually left for later: it happens to the best of families. A resolution mechanism for banks should be an integral part of banking union. But who should pay and how? And should the new mechanism apply to past failures (and debts) or only to those that may crop up in the future? On the other hand, a European guarantee for bank deposits and the issuing of Eurobonds are apparently not for tomorrow; perhaps for the day after? Debt sustainability for at least some countries remains the elephant in the room. It will surely not go away on its own, especially if growth prospects remain as bleak as they are now. In some cases, creditors may indeed be faced with a choice between mutualisation of debt and debt forgiveness: it is a choice that most refuse to even contemplate today.

Given the globalised nature of the financial sector, the effectiveness of regulation, supervision and taxation depends largely on the will and capacity to co-ordinate those functions at the level of the G-20, EU-28 and Euro-17. But waiting for all tax havens and offshore centres, big and small, to agree cannot be used forever as an excuse for doing nothing in the meantime. The eurozone, if not EU-28, is big and integrated enough to serve as a springboard for new initiatives that may gradually extend further. The introduction of an international financial transactions tax, the so-called Tobin tax, is a good example. In the days when there was more optimism about the European project, leading by example was meant to be a key element of the overall strategy.

Economics dictates, but the political appetite is lacking. We want to be virtuous, but not yet. To be fair, those politicians who may want to go down the road of further integration find it difficult to generate domestic support for it – perhaps because many of them have consistently failed to engage citizens in a proper dialogue on what European integration is all about and the benefits associated with it. Perhaps, also, it boils down to a lack of trust: we are reluctant to keep our side of the bargain because we are not at all sure that others will do the same. This lack of trust has grown considerably because of the crisis. Still, the stakes are high and time is running out. Piecemeal or half measures prolong the crisis and make exiting from it more costly. The key challenge is about restoring confidence in the capacity of our institutions, national as well as European, to take control of an admittedly very difficult situation. It is also about restoring trust between countries and regaining the conviction that there are benefits for all in this common project.

We also need to address the fairness–equality deficit in our countries. Before the bubble burst, inequalities had grown rapidly within many countries, especially those where the finance-dominated model of capitalism was strongest. The situation has deteriorated in several countries since then, largely because of the increase in unemployment. Growing inequality within our societies is undermining social cohesion and the political consequences are felt more intensely on the left side of the political spectrum. There is a strong feeling of unfairness as people understand that a small minority became very rich while the party was on, and now the rest are being called upon to pay a heavy price in the name of adjustment. Distributional politics is back in a big way, while the legitimacy of the political system is being eroded, with anti-establishment parties gaining strength in several countries.

There is also a strong intergenerational dimension to the unequal distribution of gains and losses before and after the crisis. Having often been the 'outsiders' in dual labour markets, young people are now the principal victims of recession and unemployment in the hard-hit countries of the European periphery. Young people are becoming increasingly alienated from politics. Dealing more effectively with equity concerns and offering a credible vision for the future to young people, without resorting to populism, constitutes a major political challenge today.

Distributional issues are the preserve of national governments, and can only remain so. The European component can only be an add-on, and hopefully also an incentive or catalyst for action at the national level. But, in times of declining popular support for European integration, especially among those who perceive themselves as losers in the opening of markets and competition in Europe and globally, the EU cannot afford to be identified mainly as a driver for liberalisation and stabilisation. Cohesion policies catering for the less developed countries and regions will not suffice as compensation in these difficult times.

The Transition from Policy to Politics

A new item has been added to future EU budgets, albeit with small sums involved, to address the problem of youth unemployment. Several years back, the European Globalisation Adjustment Fund (EGF) was set up with losers from globalisation in mind. Although its scope has increased over the years, the EGF has remained mostly in the domain of symbolism. What about enlarging its terms of reference by introducing an EU component of benefits paid to those who have become unemployed because of the crisis, as part of a broader European economic strategy? Conditionality attached to the deal would prevent moral hazard. It would be a redistributive and counter-cyclical measure that would be especially significant in the context of monetary union. It would also serve as a political message addressed to those who feel left out of a Europe without borders: a good example of *intégration solidaire*. Solidarity with good measure, linked to common projects and with conditions attached, is the best we can hope for at present. We should make good use of it.

One of the few positive developments during the crisis is that it has generated a lively public debate about ways and means of dealing with it at the European level. It has not been a mere juxtaposition of national debates going on almost independently of one another and limited to a small number of cognoscenti, which used to be the usual pattern with EU-related issues. As with so many other debates in a democracy, it has contained elements ranging all the way from the sublime to the ridiculous and nasty. There are signs of a European public forum emerging. We should nurture it.

We need to turn European integration back into a positive-sum game. And we need institutions to match the level of market integration (not only of financial markets) already reached. Those institutions cannot be created simply by fiat. They must have the legitimacy that can only be gained through democratic processes. It is expected that the big political families represented in the European Parliament, including most notably the group of socialists and democrats, will present joint candidates for president of the European Commission at the May 2014 elections. These should be people with broad appeal beyond national borders. Their selection will require thinking outside the box. This is an opportunity not to be wasted at a time when the legitimacy of institutions and the political process in Europe and individual countries is being tested. The 2014 elections could be a big step in the necessary transition from policy to politics in the EU.

Notes

1. FSA, *The Turner Review: A Regulatory Response to the Global Banking Crisis* (2009). Available at www.fsa.gov.uk/pubs/other/turner_review.pdf (accessed 1 May 2013).
2. Giancarlo Corsetti (ed.), *Austerity: Too Much of a Good Thing?* (2012). Available at www.voxeu.org/sites/default/files/file/austerity_ecollection.pdf (accessed 1 May 2013).
3. IMF, *World Economic Outlook, Coping with High Debt and Sluggish Growth* (2012). Available at www.imf.org/external/pubs/ft/weo/2012/02 (accessed 1 May 2013).
4. Carmen M. Reinhart and Kenneth S. Rogoff, *This Time Is Different: Eight Centuries of Financial Folly* (Princeton: Princeton University Press, 2009).
5. Loukas Tsoukalis, *What Kind of Europe?* (Oxford: Oxford University Press, 2005).

CHAPTER 5

Social Solidarity and Transformative Politics

Values, Tradition and Renewal

Sheri Berman

The current crisis is the worst since the Great Depression. Yet, despite it being largely caused by a neo-liberalism that forgot the dangers and downsides of markets in a mad embrace of their upsides, there was, at least initially, no upsurge in support for the left. Why has the left been unable to respond more forcefully to the current crisis? Why is it, more generally, so disoriented and rudderless, lacking the ideological and intellectual vitality that underpinned its strength during earlier eras?

This essay argues that the dire state of the contemporary left is not caused by any inherent weakness in or obsolescence of its principles. Indeed, just the opposite is the case. This is because the challenge at the heart of the contemporary crisis – reconciling capitalism with democracy and social stability – is not new at all, but very old. It is, in fact, the central challenge of modernity and one to which only social democracy has had an answer.

Indeed, up to the middle of the twentieth century, observers on both the right and left believed that this challenge could not be overcome – that capitalism simply could not be reconciled with democracy and social stability. From J.S. Mill to Alexis de Tocqueville to Friedrich Hayek, liberals have lived in constant fear of the 'egalitarian threats of mass society and democratic [...] politics, which, in their view, would lead, by necessity, to tyranny and "class legislation" by the property-less as well as uneducated majority'.[1] Karl Marx, meanwhile, expressed scepticism about whether the bourgeoisie would actually allow democracy to function (and workers to take power), but felt that, if it did, democracy might contribute to bringing about an end to capitalism – a potential, of course, that he, unlike his liberal counterparts, welcomed. And, indeed, such pessimism found ample support in European history.

Up to the early twentieth century, Europe underwent several democratic waves, all of which were failures. The social dislocation, atomisation and unease caused by capitalism contributed to the rise of extremism, social conflict and large-scale violence, culminating during the inter-war period in the emergence of the most brutal dictatorships the world had ever known. Yet, after 1945, Europe underwent a 'great transformation', finally managing to combine stable, consolidated democracy with well-functioning capitalism and social stability. There are many reasons for this, but a critical and underappreciated one was the social democratic shift in the relationship between states, markets and societies that occurred during the postwar years. Since we are today once again facing the challenge of reconciling capitalism with democracy and social stability, it is worth reviewing what this earlier transformation entailed and the principles upon which it was built. But, to do this, we need to take a brief detour into history.

The People's Home? Capitalism and the Left

The left's fate has always been inextricably intertwined with capitalism.[2] The emergence of capitalism in the eighteenth and nineteenth centuries led to unprecedented economic growth and personal freedom, but also brought dramatic inequality, social dislocation and atomisation. Soon after capitalism began transforming Europe, accordingly, a backlash against the new order began. However, by the end of the nineteenth century, capitalism had developed renewed vigour and did not seem to be heading towards the inevitable collapse that Marx and others had predicted. This raised the question of 'what was to be done?' If capitalism was not going to disappear on its own, how should socialists bring a better world into existence?

Some argued that, if the old order was not going to disappear on its own, the left should eliminate it by force. Lenin was the most important advocate of this view, and his heirs became the communists of the twentieth century. Most leftists, however, were unwilling to accept the Leninist answer and remained committed to a peaceful, democratic path to socialism. The democratic camp, however, was split as well. One group believed that, while Marx and others might have been wrong about the imminence of capitalism's collapse, they were basically right that it could not persist indefinitely. Because of its internal contradictions and human costs, it would ultimately give way to something fundamentally different.

Another democratic faction rejected the view that capitalism was bound to collapse in the foreseeable future, and argued instead that it was both possible and desirable to take advantage of its upsides while addressing its downsides. They argued that, rather than working to transcend capitalism, the goal should be to harness its immense productive capacity while at the same time striving to make sure it worked towards progressive rather than destructive ends. The real story of the democratic left over the past century has been the story of the battle between these two factions – between, say, democratic socialism and social democracy.

This battle reached its climax during the interwar years as European socialists confronted a political landscape transformed by World War I and growing economic problems, which culminated in the Great Depression. One critical consequence of the economic chaos of the period was the increasing popularity of nationalist right-wing movements, which drew on the anger, frustration and desperation of rising numbers of Europeans. In response to these trends, social democrats argued that clinging to the left's traditional programme would doom it to oblivion. Instead, they argued that, especially once the Great Depression hit, the left's first and most important goal was to use the state to reform, and perhaps even transform, capitalism.

Orthodox Marxists, communists and democratic socialists – not to mention most liberals – refused to accept that this *could* or *should* be done, since they did not believe there was much value in or point to interfering with markets. But, since taking over the state would require majority support, social democrats also argued that the left needed to reach out to groups outside the traditional working class. This type of cross-class strategy was important not only for electoral reasons, but also because social democrats recognised the dangers – both for democracy in general and the left in particular – of ignoring the anger and frustration that were feeding the rise of extremism. During the interwar years, budding social democrats therefore embraced communitarian appeals to the 'people', the 'little man' and the 'common good' in contrast to the emphasis on class struggle favoured by many of their colleagues. Versions of these appeals or programmes appeared in many parts of Europe, but this new social democratic approach had its fullest flowering in Sweden, where it was embraced by a unified party, which explains how this country came to hold such an iconic status for the left.

During the interwar years, the Swedish Social Democratic Party developed a new view of the relationship between the state and capitalism, culminating in their famous championing of 'Keynesianism before Keynes'. What made the Swedes so special, however, was not merely that such economic policies were fully embraced by a party of the left, but also that they were joined with a new type of political appeal that stressed the party's commitment to the common man and common good. The party's leader, Per Albin Hansson, popularised the theme of Sweden as the people's home – *folkhemmet* – an idea he stole from the Swedish right. In Germany, Italy and other parts of Europe it was the nationalist-populist right that appeared willing to tackle capitalism's problems, and defend the common man and the nation against the forces buffeting them. In contrast, in Sweden, it was the social democrats who had inspirational plans for dealing with capitalism's crisis and who were committed to recreating a sense of solidarity and fellow-feeling among Sweden's citizens, and thus were able to convince voters that they were best prepared to help the *entire* nation.

By the mid-1930s, therefore, social democrats had a clear political profile and a set of policies of their own. They favoured an emphasis on the ordinary or 'little' people, the 'community' and the collective good, and were committed to state intervention in the economy to correct the failures of capitalism. During the interwar years, social democrats generally lost the battle to transform their parties, except in Sweden. World War II, however, profoundly changed Europe and, when the dust settled in 1945, Europeans in general and the left in particular had a new-found appreciation for many of the principles long championed by social democrats.

The Postwar Era and the Onset of Neo-Liberalism

It was only after the most destructive war in history that western Europe was finally able to put an end to the long-standing political and national struggles that it had suffered through since 1789. How did this remarkable transformation happen?[3]

The answer, of course, lies in changes that occurred after 1945, one of the most critical of which was a widespread recognition by actors across the political spectrum that making democracy work would require not merely a change in political forms and institutions but crucial social and economic changes as well.[4] This shift to a 'social democratic' understanding of the relationship between states, markets and societies was based on a recognition that, for democratic consolidation to finally succeed in western Europe, the social conflict and divisions that had helped scuttle democratic experiments in the past would have to be confronted head on. In addition, the experience of the Great Depression – in which capitalism's failures produced social chaos, conflict and a widespread embrace of extremism – led many to accept that finding a way to ensure both economic prosperity and social peace was necessary if democracy was going to succeed in Europe after 1945.[5]

Accordingly, after 1945, western European nations began constructing a new order, one that could ensure economic growth while at the same time protecting societies from capitalism's destructive and destabilising consequences. This order represented a decisive break with the past: states would not be limited to ensuring that markets could grow and flourish; nor would economic interests be given the widest possible leeway. Instead, after 1945, the state was to become the guardian of society rather than the economy, and economic imperatives would sometimes have to take a back seat to social ones.

Across Europe, in short, the postwar order represented something historically unusual: capitalism remained, but it was capitalism of a very different type than had existed before the war – one tempered and limited by the power of the democratic state and often made subservient to the goals of social stability and solidarity, rather than the other way around. As we know, this social democratic order worked remarkably well; despite fears after the war that it would perhaps take decades for

Europe to recover economically,[6] by the early 1950s most of Europe had easily surpassed interwar economic figures and Europe's fastest period of growth ever was from 1945 to 1975. The restructured political economies of the postwar era seemed to offer something to everyone and this in turn helped to eliminate the belief – long held by liberals, Marxists and others – that democratic states could not or would not protect particular groups' interests. As a result, both workers and employers (and the organisations and parties that catered to them) underwent a remarkable deradicalisation after 1945 and became more willing to work together to achieve what came to be seen as many common interests. As Claus Offe noted:

> What was at issue in class conflicts [after 1945] was no longer the mode of production, but the volume of distribution, not control but growth, and this type of conflict was particularly suited for being processed on the political plan through party competition because it does not involve 'either/or' questions, but questions of a 'more or less' or 'sooner or later' nature. Overarching this limited type of conflict, there was a consensus concerning basic priorities, desirabilities and values of the political economy, namely economic growth and social [...] security.[7]

In short, by reshaping the relationship between states, markets and society, the social democratic postwar order helped to underpin the consolidation of democracy in western Europe after 1945. It helped to prove the falsity of liberal fears that democracy would lead to tyranny by the property-less and irrational 'masses'; of Marxist assertions that giving the poor and workers the vote would lead inexorably to the end of bourgeois society; and of fascism's and National Socialism's claim that democracy stood in direct contradiction to national cohesion and social solidarity. Under 'social' democracy, in other words, western Europe was finally able to achieve that elusive combination of consolidated democracy, well-functioning capitalism and social stability.

But, despite this historic achievement, the social democratic consensus of the postwar period eventually frayed. On the left, the very success of the postwar order led many to forget that reforms, while important, are simply a means to an end – that end being taming capitalism and reconciling it with democracy and social stability. Many on the left instead became content with merely managing the existing order and stopped thinking about its rationale or how the world was changing. Others in the democratic socialist tradition never really accepted the loss of a post-capitalist future and viewed the postwar social democratic order as 'second best'. Although the role of this group diminished over time, it played a significant part among the movement's intellectuals and within certain parties. Because democratic socialists believed that true justice and democracy could only come with capitalism's elimination, they implicitly and sometimes explicitly denigrated efforts to tame it and devoted little effort to coming up with the types of policies and reforms that could do this.

Yet another group on the left, disgusted by the loss of a post-capitalist future and bored by what they saw as the banality and materialism of the social democratic order, neglected analyses of capitalism entirely, focusing their intellectual energy instead on things like post-modernism, multiculturalism, feminism, post-colonialism and a variety of other intellectual trends that were cultural rather than economic in nature.[8] These trends, however, had little relevance to or resonance with average people and served in any case to fragment citizens rather than unite them, thus helping to render the formation of progressive coalitions increasingly difficult. The consequence of all this was that, during the last decades of the twentieth century, the left did not devote enough intellectual energy or strategic thought to the changing nature of capitalism and what needed to be done about it.

The consequences of this had became clear by the 1970s as a growing neo-liberal right had begun organising and thinking about what it viewed as the drawbacks of the postwar order. When the crisis hit in the 1970s, the right had explanations for the west's problems as well as solutions to them. It was therefore able to capture the ideological high ground on economic issues during the last decades of the twentieth century and help to transform late-twentieth-century capitalism, freeing it from many of the restrictions that had been placed on it during the postwar era.[9]

Now the pendulum has swung back, and the very ideas and policies trumpeted by the neo-liberal right since the 1970s are to blame for the mess we are in currently. This is the moment for which the left should have been waiting and preparing. For a consequential swing to the left to happen, the left would have had to be ready with well-considered plans, not merely for getting economies moving again but also for rewriting the rules of the game in a progressive manner. And, for the most part, no such strategy existed.

Taking on the Conservative Left

The left today stands at a critical juncture. Europe and much of the rest of the world face a number of challenges, the most important of which is repairing and reinvigorating capitalism so that it can generate economic growth, and be rendered compatible with democracy and social stability. This challenge is not of course new; it is the central challenge of modernity and one only social democracy has been able to answer.

The social democratic left has been distinguished by a few distinctive principles or insights. First, despite its many failures and downsides, capitalism is here to stay; it is therefore a waste of time to bemoan its existence or base plans for the future on its transcendence. Social democrats instinctively believe that it is both possible and desirable to reform and even improve capitalism. Today, as in the past, vigorous and sustained recovery will require recognising capitalism's strengths and weaknesses, and coming up with a coherent long-term programme to reconcile these two halves of the 'capitalist beast'. This may seem straightforward, but in practice it has not been the way much of the left has operated over the past years.

There is, of course, an active anti-globalisation left that sees capitalism as a curse to both the developed and developing world. Many on the left peddle fear of the future, fear of change and fear of the other. Too many leftists remain committed to policies that may have worked or made sense decades ago but are no longer relevant or effective.[10] (There should be nothing more depressing for social democrats than watching members of the left defend welfare states that stymie growth, create divisions between labour-market 'insiders' and 'outsiders', and keep young people and women out of the labour force.) If we examine the European countries that have fared best over the past years, it is clear that they have done so by helping their citizens manage and change capitalism rather than fight it. Many analysts have remarked on the success that countries like Denmark and Sweden have had in managing globalisation; these cases show that social welfare and economic dynamism are complementary rather than contradictory. Not surprisingly, surveys show that it is in precisely these countries that optimism about the future and opinions of globalisation are the highest. In the US and other parts of Europe, on the other hand, fear of the future is pervasive and opinions of globalisation are low.

Of course, managing contemporary capitalism is a challenge that must be dealt with not just at the domestic but also at the international and European levels. The current crisis has made clear that, despite the hopes and fears of some, the European Union (EU) has not pushed Europe in a social democratic direction. In fact, over the past years, the EU has acted as a force for neo-liberalism and austerity. This is not only because of the design of key institutions, such as the Central Bank, but more fundamentally because the Union was constructed without the requisite social solidarity that makes social democratic solutions possible. During the current crisis it has become clear that, while northern Europeans remain willing to pay 50 per cent of their income in taxes to support their fellow citizens, they are unwilling to pay anything resembling that to help what they view as profligate, lazy and even dishonest southern Europeans. This is a dynamic that progressives in the US find all too familiar and it is absolutely impossible to reconcile with successful left politics.

Social Solidarity and the Challenge of Diversity

If the first challenge facing the contemporary left is therefore reforming capitalism so as to make it once again compatible with democracy and social stability,[11] another (and related) challenge is diversity; or, rather, recreating a strong sense of social solidarity in the face of increasing domestic diversity and Europeanisation. Until fairly recently, the left has responded to the challenge of diversity either by ignoring it or, especially among the intellectual left, via 'multiculturalism', neither of which has stemmed social conflict or electoral flight from the left, especially on the part of the working class.[12] Here too, the contemporary left has something to gain from a re-examination of social democratic principles; in this case, communitarianism.

Communitarianism, in the social democratic view, is both a means and an end. Both strong interventionist states and generous welfare policies depend on a citizenry characterised by a high degree of solidarity and a sense of shared purpose. But communitarianism is also necessary to counteract the unease, confusion and frustration that accompany rapid social and economic change. In an increasingly diverse Europe, basing a call for social solidarity on shared ethnic or religious background is no longer a viable or attractive strategy. The left's refashioned communitarian appeal will therefore have to be built upon more inclusive grounds – namely, shared values and responsibilities.

The left needs to make clear, in other words, its commitment to a type of multiculturalism that involves embracing the growing diversity of European societies while making equally clear its rejection of the type of multiculturalism that segregates and divides citizens. In Britain, for example, multiculturalism for too long meant dealing with Muslim immigrants not as individuals or citizens but rather as members of particular groups or communities. As Kenan Malik put it:

> The claims of minorities upon society were defined less by the social and political needs of individuals than by the box to which they belonged [...]. Rather than appealing to Muslims as British citizens, politicians preferred to see them as people whose primary loyalty was to their faith and who could be politically engaged only by other Muslims.[13]

Financial resources and political power were distributed to leaders and groups that claimed to represent particular ethnicities or religions rather than on the basis of individual need. Immigrants were encouraged to turn to their ethnic/religious group rather than broader social and political institutions for help and support, which in turn encouraged other British citizens to believe that immigrants felt they belonged to their own group rather than to British society as a whole. The result has been 'subsidised segregation' and the growth of 'parallel societies'.[14]

The left must couple a rejection of these trends with a renewed commitment to better integration policies. Realistically, the left will probably also have to accept that more-concerted integration efforts will have to be accompanied by future limits on immigration. In the past, too many European societies allowed overly generous amounts of immigration but made only miserly efforts at integration.[15] The result has been massive and extremely rapid shifts in demographic patterns, combined with relatively little real effort devoted to helping both old and new citizens to adjust. European societies must therefore devote themselves to making citizens of recent origin feel more at home and better incorporated into and accepted by their new countries. Especially in times of economic crisis, when labour markets are weak and citizens stressed, this is more likely to succeed if the pace of change is slowed down and thus more easily managed. And finally, the left must insist that certain principles are non-negotiable and must be accepted by all – for example, democracy, rule of law, freedom of speech, equality between the sexes and non-discrimination on the basis of religion, ethnicity, sexual orientation and so on. Allowing groups to 'opt out' of values and responsibilities that the left has long fought for and that (finally) helped Europe to consolidate well-functioning liberal democracies during the twentieth century would be a disaster for Europe as a whole and for recent immigrants in particular.

Rekindling the Communitarian Leg of Social Democracy

The communitarian 'leg' of social democracy is probably as difficult for the contemporary left to come to terms with as its economic one. Many on the left may not like it and it may smack of nationalism or exclusivism, but the fact is that, if you want an order based on social solidarity and the priority of social goods over individual interests, a strong sense of fellow-feeling is required to get that order into place and keep it politically sustainable. Members of the left who cannot accept and deal with this will end up ceding political ground to the radical right and populists, who will step in to supply the communitarian cravings that publics continue to display. This is obviously risky territory to tread on, since the dark side of communitarianism can be very dark indeed. The left cannot peddle 'fascism-lite' nor accept nativism or prejudice. But ignoring the desire for some sort of community in a world where long-standing political, social and cultural traditions are being constantly questioned is a recipe for disaster, as the success of far-right parties in many parts of Europe makes clear.

In short, the traditional principles of social democracy – a belief in the reconcilability of capitalism, democracy and social stability, and communitarianism – are still the best basis upon which to formulate policies to deal with contemporary and future challenges. But a reinvigoration of traditional principles might also be able to help the left regain optimism and vision. Without principles and goals, the left is rendered directionless and uninspiring. Today, we have a left that can win some elections but does not inspire much hope for the future. Given the history of the left, this is simply astonishing. Traditionally, the left has been driven by the conviction that a better world was possible and that it was the left's job to bring it about. Social democracy in particular is based on a belief in the 'primacy of politics', a belief that people acting collectively via the democratic state can and should help determine the nature and evolution of both capitalism and society. But, over the past decades, the left has largely lost its transformative faith and this has been profoundly damaging, not just for progressive politics but also for a wider sense of public engagement with the political process. While the challenges of the twenty-first century are clearly varied and difficult, they are not more daunting than those the left has overcome in the past. Perhaps re-examining and reinvigorating the principles on which those accomplishments rested can provide both practical guidance and inspiration for the future.

Notes

1. Claus Offe, 'Competitive party democracy and the Keynesian welfare state: factors of stability and disorganization', *Policy Sciences* 15 (1983), pp. 225–6.
2. This section draws heavily on my book: Sheri Berman, *The Primacy of Politics: Social Democracy and the Making of Europe's Twentieth Century* (New York: Cambridge University Press, 2007).
3. Sheri Berman, 'The past and future of social democracy and the consequences for democracy promotion', in C. Hobson and M. Kurki

(eds), *The Conceptual Politics of Democracy Promotion* (London: Routledge, 2011).

4. Even the Americans recognised that their commitment to stability and democracy in Europe meant that there was no going back to the socio-economic status quo ante. Reflecting this, in his opening speech to the Bretton Woods conference, US Treasury Secretary Henry Morgenthau noted, 'All of us have seen the great economic tragedy of our time. We saw the worldwide depression of the 1930s [...]. We saw bewilderment and bitterness become the breeders of fascism and finally of war.' To prevent a recurrence of this phenomenon, Morgenthau argued, national governments would have to be able to do more to protect people from capitalism's 'malign effects'. See G. John Ikenberry, 'A world economy restored', *International Organization* 46/1 (1992), pp. 289–321; Ethan B. Kapstein, 'Workers and the world economy', *Foreign Affairs* 75/3 (1996), pp. 16–37.

5. Or, to put it another way, many came to accept (echoing the insights of T.H. Marshall) that, without certain social and economic rights, neither political nor civil liberties could be truly realised. See T.H. Marshall, *Class, Citizenship and Social Development* (Garden City: Anchor Books, 1965); Thomas Meyer with Lewis Hinchman, *The Theory of Social Democracy* (Cambridge: Polity Press, 2007).

6. German residents polled in the American zone after World War II expected that it would take at least 20 years for the country to recover. De Gaulle had similarly informed French citizens that it would take 25 years of 'furious work' before France would be back on its feet again (Tony Judt, *Postwar* (New York: Penguin, 2005), p. 89).

7. Offe, 'Competitive party democracy', p. 237.

8. Some have referred to this as a shift from the politics of redistribution to the politics of recognition. See Charles Taylor et al., *Multiculturalism: The Politics of Recognition* (Princeton: Princeton University Press, 1994); Joseph Schwartz, *The Future of Democratic Equality* (New York: Routledge, 2009).

9. Mark Blyth, *Great Transformations: Economic Ideas and Institutional Change in the Twentieth Century* (New York: Cambridge University Press, 2002).

10. For example, Gøsta Esping-Andersen, *Social Foundations of Post-Industrial Economies* (New York: Oxford University Press, 1999); Gøsta Esping-Andersen with Duncan Gallie, Anton Hemerijck and John Myles (eds), *Why We Need a New Welfare State* (New York: Oxford University Press, 2001).

11. For example, in the *New Left Review* and elsewhere, Wolfgang Streeck has argued that there is an inherent conflict between capitalism and democracy, and that 'a lasting reconciliation between social and economic stability in capitalist democracy is a utopian project'. See Wolfgang Streeck, 'The crises of democratic capitalism', *New Left Review* 71 (2011), pp. 5–29; Wolfgang Streeck, 'Markets and peoples', *New Left Review* 73 (2012), pp. 63–71.

12. See, however, *Exploring the Cultural Challenges to Social Democracy* (London: Policy Network, 2011).

13. Kenan Malik, 'Assimilation's failure, terrorism's rise', *New York Times* (7 July 2011), p. A23.

14. Timothy Garton Ash, 'Freedom & diversity: a liberal pentagram for living together', *New York Review of Books* (22 November 2012). Available at www.nybooks.com/articles/archives/2012/nov/22/freedom-diversity-liberal-pentagram/?pagination=false (accessed 1 May 2013).

15. This was largely because too many European societies viewed migrants as temporary workers, or *gastarbeiter*, and believed they would eventually return to their countries of origin. Such policies, for example, brought millions of Turks to Germany in the space of a generation. Meanwhile, other European countries that had no modern history of immigration (e.g. in Scandinavia) accepted in the last decades proportionally similar numbers of immigrants to those who came to the US during its most open periods.

CHAPTER 6

Value Shifts in European Societies
Clashes between Cosmopolitanism and Communitarianism

Onawa Promise Lacewell and Wolfgang Merkel

G lobalisation has changed the world. It has been driven by techno-logical change in worldwide communication and the respective decrease of the cost in communication and transport, but also by conscious political decisions such as Margaret Thatcher's and Ronald Reagan's early neo-liberal agenda, the Washington Consensus in 1990, and progressing deregulation, privatisation and denationalisation. The dismantling of borders and barriers has been the dominant economic, cultural and political paradigm since the 1980s.[1] National borders have increasingly become permeable, with risks and opportunities distrib-uted unequally among citizens. Although globalisation has altered the Westphalian system of sovereign nation states in international relations, it has paradoxically manifested itself above all in domestic politics.[2] It has created proponents and adversaries, pros and cons, winners and losers, and the formation of normative and ideological belief systems. The main ideological camps can be described as (neo-)liberal and paro-chial-national. The former argue for the further opening of economic, cultural and political borders, while the latter opt for demarcation, border closure, and the primacy of local and national communities as normative and political points of reference.

However, these traditional labels do not grasp the more complex reality of the values and beliefs that have been emerging since the 1980s. Those who advocate the lifting of national borders are not simply neo-liberals ruthlessly seeking their own economic benefits; they may also advocate for international guarantees of human rights and for equality of sex, religion, race and ethnicity on a global scale. However, it cannot be overlooked that these 'cosmopolitans' care more for cultural rights than socio-economic equality; they defend the equal recognition of cultures but not so much economic equality between social classes. For this reason, we do not term these groups neo-liberals and parochial-nationalists, but instead refer to the two groups as cosmopolitans and communitarians. One of the internationally renowned proponents of this split into two groups, Thomas Pogge,[3] argues that three principles define the normative core of cosmopolitanism:

1. Individualism: 'The ultimate units of concern are human beings, or persons – rather than say, families, lines, tribes, ethnic, cultural, or religious communities, nations, or states.'
2. Universality: 'The status of ultimate unit of concern attaches to every living human being equally.'
3. Generality: 'This special status has global force'; it applies to every-one, 'not only […] their compatriots'.

Cosmopolitans advocate open borders, liberalised migration, easy access to citizenship and cultural inclusion, but also global responsibility for human rights and ecological necessities. Cosmopolitans particularly recognise the opportunities of globalisation.

Communitarianism can be seen as an early philosophical and political reaction to the dominance of liberalism.[4] Communitarians criticise abstract individualism and the decontextualised 'unencumbered self'.[5] Above all, individuals' existence depends on 'communities'. Therefore, communities are of intrinsic value and human dignity and happiness cannot be seen separately from their constitutive communities. Three communitarian principles allow us to distinguish communitarianism from cosmopolitanism:

1. Community: Constitutive communities such as family, ethnic and religious groups and nations are important units of concern.
2. Particularity: Culture is an important value, and it cannot simply be subordinated to universal norms and principles.
3. Contextuality: Special group rights have to be granted to members of special communities.

Communitarians tend to opt for the control of borders (to restrict immi-gration and citizenship), to argue for demarcation and to emphasise the value of social cohesion and economic as well as social protection. Communitarians, in particular, emphasise the risks of globalisation.

Philosophical debates are one thing and political conflicts another. What potential do these juxtaposed values, norms and interests have to be translated into a social conflict or even a new political cleavage within the economically advanced OECD world?

A New Political Cleavage?

The political and philosophical debate over globalisation has advanced to the point that scholars now speak of a new political cleavage[6] and a new pattern of political conflict in western Europe, specifically. The proposed cleavage, between those actors who wish to retain the sanctity of national borders and those who wish to open these borders even at the cost of national sovereignty, is most starkly displayed in the context of the European Union (EU). The denationalisation process surrounding European integration is perhaps the clearest example of how traditionally conceptualised nation states can be moulded into integrated, globalised, denationalised actors.[7]

The puzzle, however, is whether this moulding and reforming constitutes a new socio-political cleavage or whether it is simply a redefinition of a traditional conflict or cleavage. More importantly, how do traditional parties respond to such underlying changes in the social structures of their countries and what effect does this have on their future? This question is, perhaps, most salient for traditional mass-based or catch-all parties, such as social democratic parties and Christian democratic parties, as shifts in the underlying structural divides within populations tend to pressure these parties to reformulate traditional methods of mobilising their constituencies. This is especially important as many of these key parties have been organised around existing cleavage structures, such as the capital–labour cleavage. Changing these underlying foundations could have an especially disruptive impact on the parties' ability to mobilise new constituencies, respond to outside pressures such as globalisation and fully represent the interests of new social groups. Altering social cleavages forces political parties to react. And the political reactions of the big parties determine whether social cleavages transform into persistent political cleavages.

Cleavages, Parties and Party Systems

Political cleavages structure political competition. They shape party systems and electoral alliances, and they serve to divide or unite diverse social groups under a single banner. Through the clarification and simplification of complex political issues, cleavages facilitate preference aggregation. Furthermore, the clear choices and camps articulated in cleavages stimulate involvement of citizens in politics.[8] Because of the dual impact of cleavages on parties and voters, we can speak more broadly of how cleavages structure the demand side (voters) and the supply side (parties) of political competition.

On the demand side, cleavages serve to align voters' preferences on either side of issues and they serve to help shape the preferences of voters, parties and other social actors towards important policy issues. Parties, on the other hand, mobilise voters by supplying clear policy choices between sets of issues related to the cleavage. In *Political Man*, S.M. Lipset wrote of cleavages as the democratic translation of the class struggle.[9] In 1967, Lipset added the specific conflicts from his earlier work to the writing of Stein Rokkan, which resulted in the well-known and much cited theory of voter alignments and frozen cleavage structures for western democracies from the beginning of the twentieth century.[10] This theory outlines the causal chain stretching between societal conflicts and the emergence of cleavages, while simultaneously specifying the roles of both parties and citizens in the emergence of social–structural divides and their crystallisation into political cleavages. Citizens, or groups of citizens (e.g. workers, small business owners, farmers), form political preferences in relation to this divide and political parties mobilise voters by offering clear policy choices on issues central to the conflict.

Political parties, then, are key as they provide a critical link between voters and governments by mobilising and representing the sides of the conflict. Because of party actions, the conflict becomes institutionalised in the context of party competition, which transforms the social conflict into a true political cleavage. Catch-all parties and their mass-based predecessors have an express role in this tale, as these parties represent heterogeneous groups of citizens, aggregate these diverse preferences into clear policy goals and maximise their vote shares by ascribing to broad programmatic profiles.[11] Thus, the role of the party, and of the catch-all party specifically, is key to the continuity of these traditional political cleavages.

It is precisely this critical link between parties and citizens that is pressured by globalisation and denationalisation. As citizens' underlying structural interests shift due to changing preferences related to newly arising issues, parties may be able neither to fully mobilise citizens nor to fully represent new citizen interests without undertaking major changes to party programmatic supply and mobilisation strategies. Therefore, during periods of underlying structural change, there is a high risk of inadequate representation of citizens' interests, which, in turn, may lead to high levels of apathy and disillusionment, which consequently can trigger a weakening of democracy in general.

Increasingly, non-partisan groups, such as interest groups, international organisations, social movements and charismatic individuals, fulfil this representative role,[12] showing that, in many party systems, parties have not responded adequately to these underlying structural changes. The decline of traditional, mainstream mass parties, such as Christian democratic or social democratic parties, accompanies a corresponding rise in popularity for parties at the left and right of the political spectrum during the past three decades. One reaction to the perceived negative ecological or distributional effects of globalisation, then, may be the increase in popularity of ecology parties and right-wing or left-wing populist parties, as we have witnessed in many European democracies. Taken together, the symptoms of cleavage change the resulting instability and further fragmentation of the party system. This is coupled with continued disillusion of traditional voter groups and disparity between representatives and the represented, which present major challenges to the future of western democracies and mass-based parties generally.

Where Does Social Democracy Stand?

There are signs of a new social cleavage between cosmopolitans and communitarians, between winners and losers of globalisation within the European party systems. Smaller parties (e.g. environmental, post-materialist or parties of the New Left on the cosmopolitan side and right-wing populist or anti-European parties on the communitarian side) mobilised voters along the cosmopolitan and communitarian divide. By doing so they began to translate social conflicts into a political cleavage, thereby forcing the big mass or catch-all parties to also take positions on the new cleavage. But this was not only triggered by exogenous pressures; there were also internal pressures that confronted big parties, such as the increased pluralisation of various member and voter groups within their own organisations. This was observed most visibly within social democratic parties starting in the mid-1970s, when well-educated, often post-materialist-oriented middle-class citizens joined these parties' traditional blue-collar electorate. As a consequence, the once traditionally working-class parties lost much of their previous social homogeneity.[13] This cleavage is still alive and it may be widened and deepened by the new cosmopolitan–communitarian divide.

The cosmopolitan and communitarian conflict itself can be divided into economic and cultural dimensions. The cultural dimension includes political questions such as immigration, citizenship, multiculturalism and environmental issues. An open and positive approach to these questions characterises the better-educated middle classes, who, en masse, joined European social democracy in the mid-1970s. Many of these new constituents can be seen as winners of globalisation and Europeanisation since they often dispose of the kind of human capital that enables them to deal with cultural differences and cross-national mobility requirements. The lower strata are less mobile and educated, and therefore more critical towards open borders, immigration and multiculturalism. They are the losers of globalisation. They can often be found among the traditional electorate of social democratic parties and stand in contrast to the new social democratic constituency. The social democratic electorate, then, is more divided along cultural lines than New Left ecological parties and liberal parties (which are rather homogeneously cosmopolitan) or right-wing populist parties (with their barbaric version of communitarianism, incorporating exclusion, xenophobism and nationalism).

The economic dimension of the new cleavage also divides social democratic sympathisers into potential winners and losers. Again, the better educated, especially those working in the private sector of business or information technology, are the winners, whereas those working in mass production or in sheltered or public sectors often consider themselves the losers of opening borders. These 'losers' fear competition from immigrants and they are justifiably afraid of becoming victims of privatisation, of the reduction of public employment and of the relative decrease of public wages. For them, globalisation and Europeanisation have led to a global tax race to the bottom, and have consequently resulted in a reduced capacity of the state to finance public goods, services and employment.

The 'objective' communitarian–cosmopolitan cleavage cuts across the social democratic electorate. The party leaders are left between a rock and a hard place: they cannot placate either constituency without losing voters from the other. Therefore, the divide between blue-collar workers and white-collar employees of the early 1970s has been deepened by the effects of globalisation. In more recent decades, social democratic elites were therefore condemned to reconcile the values and interests of the two camps. And they have partly succeeded, at least as far as the cultural side is concerned. A traditional worker today is not necessarily against multiculturalism or environmental policies. However, where economic issues are concerned, the situation becomes more difficult. Domestic workers can be and have been convinced that immigrant workers are not necessarily competitors for their jobs but may contribute to more productivity, especially where there is a shortage of domestic human capital. But globalisation has proved that there are strong counter-arguments for opening economic borders if doing so leads to privatisation, deregulation and a tremendous increase of socio-economic inequalities, to the disadvantage of many workers and low-skilled private and public employees. If these negative distributional effects are linked to economic globalisation – and often they are – the natural reaction is more protectionism, more national regulation and, in the last instance, more demarcation against the global economic opening of the nation state.

Let us take a closer look at what empirical research tells us. We examine two relevant issues: one belonging to the cultural and one to the socio-economic dimension of the cosmopolitan and communitarian cleavage. The first concerns the question of immigration and cultural integration, and the second social stratification and inequality.[14] The empirical evidence is based on a voter survey in 25 EU countries between 2002 and 2010. The survey compared the opinions of social democratic and Christian democratic/conservative voters. With regard to the immigration and cultural-integration issues shown in Figure 6.1, the differences are clear. Social democratic voters see both immigration and European integration much more positively than Christian democratic/conservative voters do. More generally, one can argue that social democratic voters are much more cosmopolitan than conservative/Christian democratic voters when it comes to cultural matters. This contradicts, to some extent, the long-standing opinion that there is still a strong strand of working-class authoritarianism that includes intolerant opinions and attitudes vis-à-vis multiculturalism.

If we look at the socio-economic dimension, we again see a divide between social democratic voters and Christian democrats. When asked whether 'it is important to be rich' or 'it is important to be successful', conservative/Christian democratic and social democratic voters do not

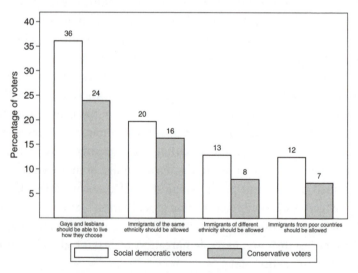

FIGURE 6.1   European citizens: tolerance and immigration. Percentage of those who 'strongly' agree with each statement (on the following scale: 'strongly agree', 'agree', 'neither agree nor disagree', 'disagree' and 'strongly disagree').
Source: European Social Survey 2002–10. Sample: EU-25 (excluding Latvia, Lithuania and Malta, and including Norway); weighted data.

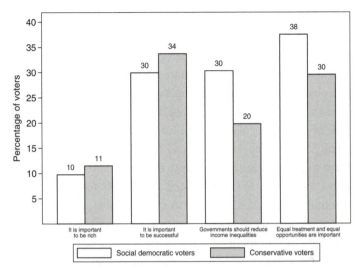

FIGURE 6.2   European citizens: social stratification and inequality. Percentage of those who 'strongly' agree with each statement (on the following scale: 'strongly agree', 'agree', 'neither agree nor disagree', 'disagree' and 'strongly disagree').
Source: European Social Survey 2002–10. Sample: EU-25 (excluding Latvia, Lithuania and Malta, and including Norway); weighted data.

show much of a difference. However, the differences becomes more pronounced when the voters are asked about 'equal opportunities' or whether 'governments should reduce income inequalities'. Social democratic voters are more communitarian than Christian democratic voters. However, what Figure 6.2 also shows is that the differences in socio-economic issues are slightly less pronounced than in cultural matters. Thus, all things being equal, one can argue that the cultural issue has become at least as important as the socio-economic issue.

Cosmopolitanism and Communitarianism in the German Party System

Changes in underlying cleavage structures pressure political parties to respond. Turning from the European level to the specific case of Germany, we know that, for traditional mass-based parties, this pressure may be even greater as these parties have long-established programmes and established constituencies that may resist mobilisation based on new issues. 'Programmatic supply' refers to the types of issues highlighted by parties in their electoral manifestos; naturally, such documents do not capture the full complexity of party responses to underlying structural changes. However, as Budge states: 'Election programmes occupy a unique position as the only fully authoritative statement of the party policy for an election. They constitute the only medium-term plans for the whole of society regularly produced by any organisation.'[15]

We will next look at data collected from the electoral programmes of the five main German parties between 1949 and 2009, and at how the parties responded to issues linked specifically to cosmopolitanism and communitarianism.[16] In order to measure how globalisation pressures affect underlying cleavages, we identified five key issues where we expected that cosmopolitan and communitarian ideologies would come into particularly stark conflict: environment, trade, migration, human rights and regional integration.

Environment

The first key contested issue related to globalisation and the possible rise of a new cleavage is the environmental issue. Starting with the rise of ecology parties in the late 1970s, matters relating to global warming and climate change quickly became some of the most noticeable issues separating the cosmopolitan and communitarian camps. While in some countries, such as the US, the debate over global warming and climate change centres on the very existence of the phenomenon, in western European democracies this debate has progressed much further across the political spectrum, with actors accepting that environmental issues are important and that climate change is a real threat. Therefore, in the context of the German case, we expect that cosmopolitan actors will prefer responses to environmental issues that are carried out independent of traditional nation-state structures. Preferences, then, for a global response to environmental issues, or for a response from the EU over nation states, will be common to cosmopolitans. Communitarians, however, are expected to advocate for responses to such issues within the context of traditional nation-state boundaries and for national governments to take a leading role in combating environmental issues.

Trade

Much as with environmental issues, the divide over trade in the context of globalisation is expected to fall along the lines of an open borders–closed borders argument. Cosmopolitans, according to our conceptualisation, should favour more globalised responses to trade issues. Steps such as decreasing trade restrictions, removing stringent national tariffs and preferring regulation of trade at the level of the EU or United Nations will characterise the positions of cosmopolitan actors. Communitarian actors, on the other hand, will prefer traditional nation-state-dependent trade models and will favour closing borders in order to protect the trade sovereignty of their individual nations or specific social classes over a globalised setting of trade restrictions.

Migration

Migration issues are some of the key factors in the debate over globalisation and Europeanisation. As globalisation and Europeanisation make the movement of people across national boundaries easier, some of the most polarised debates between cosmopolitans and communitarians have been around preserving or opening borders to migrants. It is in relation to migration issues, especially, that we see much more of a positive–negative split in responses along the cosmopolitan–communitarian divide. Often, cosmopolitans are seen as the 'good' actors who prefer opening borders to immigrants and weakening existing regulations regarding immigrant assimilation into society, and view multiculturalism as a boon for society. Communitarians, on the other hand, often take more nationalistic and occasionally xenophobic positions regarding migration and call for stricter regulations in order to limit outside immigrant groups entering the host country. Such actors often discuss preserving cultural homogeneity (e.g. the Swiss People's Party, the Freedom Party of Austria, the True Finns) and setting stricter rules for immigrant assimilation into the host society. Despite the often highly controversial nature of such issues, however, we can again link both sides of the debate to questions concerning the preservation of traditional nation-state boundaries versus the loosening of the importance of such boundaries.

Human Rights

Another key issue that is highly contested in the context of globalisation is that of human rights. We measure human rights via non-discrimination rights and freedoms ranging from traditional religious freedoms to post-materialist values. We predict that cosmopolitan actors will take generally open stances regarding women's rights and the rights of other groups, such as homosexuals, children or ethnically defined subgroups. Communitarians, on the other hand, are expected to take a traditional view of society and moral values even at the cost of decreased rights for women and other groups. While this definition of human rights is far from perfect – and does not account for rights concerning civil liberties or due process, or physical integrity rights generally – it does account for pressures that have arisen at times when globalisation and modernisation have come into direct conflict with traditional views of societies.

Regional Integration

Regional integration is the last of the five chosen contested issues and is, in some ways, a meta issue, as all four other issues deal, to some extent, with the opening or closing of borders and the traditional sovereignty of the nation state. In our conceptualisation, however, the contestation of regional integration goes above and beyond these underlying issues – especially in the European context. This issue deals directly with the giving up of national sovereignty in favour of regional or global sovereignty. It represents the crux of globalisation pressures: cosmopolitan actors are more willing to support regional or global sovereignty over national-level sovereignty, and communitarian actors take the directly opposite position.

Cosmopolitan Futures?

Taking the five contested issues and operationalising them using matched categories from the manifesto data (see Table 6.1), we were able to see what percentage of each party's manifesto was devoted to cosmopolitan or communitarian issues.

TABLE 6.1   Contested issues and their operationalisation.[17]

Contested issue	Manifesto categories	
	Cosmopolitan	Communitarian
Environment	Globally sustainable development	Traditional economic growth
Trade	Economic protectionism: negative	Economic protectionism: positive
Migration	Multiculturalism: positive Nationalism/patriotism: negative	Multiculturalism: negative Nationalism/patriotism: positive
Human rights	Traditional morality: negative	Traditional morality: positive
Regional integration	Internationalism: positive European Union: positive	Internationalism: negative European Union: negative

After calculating the manifesto percentages devoted to each of the five contested issues for each party in each election year, we examined how the parties have addressed these issues since 1949 by party family. As there have been some changes to party labels in the German party system since 1949, the analysis was conducted within five party families: ecological (Die Grünen), left-socialist (Die Linke), social democrats (SPD), Christian democrats (CDU-CSU) and the liberals (FDP). Figure 6.3 shows this calculation, with the percentage of manifesto statements attributed to either cosmopolitan categories or communitarian categories on the y-axis and election year on the x-axis. The ecological party family was the most cosmopolitan in the German party system, followed by the socialist/left parties. As was also expected, the more conservative Christian Democrats had the highest levels of communitarian policy statements in their manifestos; however, they also had a more or less equal weight of cosmopolitan orientations over time. One could even argue that the Christian Democrats succeeded in integrating both trends into their programmatic outlook without producing major rifts among their party membership or electorate.

Some findings that were less expected came from the liberal parties and the social democrats. Both showed an increase in cosmopolitan manifesto statements beginning in the mid-1970s. The FDP sustained this increase through the late 1980s and then followed it with a small

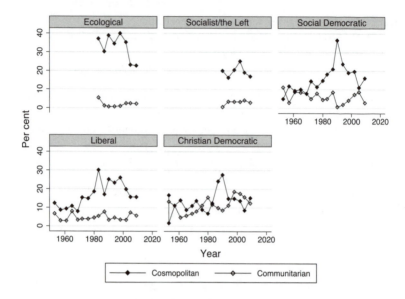

FIGURE 6.3   Cosmopolitanism and communitarianism by party family membership.

decline in cosmopolitanism in the 2000s. However, it did not simultaneously focus more on communitarian issues during this period. The SPD had an almost equal representation of communitarian and cosmopolitan positions until the early 1970s. Thereafter cosmopolitan issues gained ground and were better represented than communitarian positions. After the fall of the Berlin Wall, cosmopolitanism experienced its peak within the SDP, and it has remains better represented in the party's electoral manifesto up to the present.

Looking across party families, the last two election periods point towards a possible convergence of the party system to a moderate level of cosmopolitanism weighted by a decreased salience of communitarian policies (with the exception of the CDU-CSU). While the point of convergence is lower than the previously high levels of cosmopolitanism experienced in the late 1980s and the 1990s, such a convergence is actually a good indication that cosmopolitanism and communitarianism are one step closer to representing a truly new cleavage between German parties. As expected, Die Grünen is the most cosmopolitan German party, while the CDU-CSU is the most communitarian. By the mid-2000s, Die Linke and the FDP had both become more cosmopolitan than the SPD. However, by 2009 there had been a rather stark shift among German parties towards more cosmopolitanism. Even the CDU had become largely oriented towards cosmopolitanism, albeit to a lesser extent than the other four parties.

Political Positioning in an Age of Globalisation

It is clear that the processes of globalisation and denationalisation have put traditional parties under extraordinary pressure. It is also clear that social democratic parties have felt these pressures above and beyond their competitors. The question then becomes: how should social democratic parties position themselves in relation to globalisation issues in order to decrease the loss of traditional voting groups to competing parties? Additionally, how can social democratic parties position themselves to better represent the diverse groups of constituents on such issues?

The optimal mix of social democratic programmes and policies seems to be cautious re-regulation of markets, strengthening of the tax state and improvement of public educational programmes. Such policies will not completely stop the loss of voters to right-wing populists and left-wing environmentalists but they can contain it. They also could provide a smart programme for the future that deals selectively with the economic risks and cultural opportunities globalisation can provide. Surprisingly, social democrats are considerably more cosmopolitan than other parties in cultural issues of multiculturalism, immigration and the deepening of the EU. And, even more surprisingly, the difference between social democrats and other parties concerning the reduction of socio-economic inequality is less pronounced. There seems to be strong empirical evidence that the cultural divide between cosmopolitan social democrats and communitarian conservatives is visibly wider than it is in matters of socio-economic inequality. The Third Way and its remnants in many social democratic parties in western Europe may have contributed to this socio-cultural turn. This is the most surprising aspect, since socio-economic inequality has increased in almost all European countries.

Needless to say, the social democrats cannot give up their programmatic image as parties of social justice and advocates of the social needs of the lower classes. However, it seems to be at least as important to also pursue their new image as progressive parties of multiculturalism that are pro-immigration. Otherwise, they will lose culturally progressive voters of the middle classes.

Nevertheless, even if social democratic parties or political parties in general choose to pursue such an optimal strategic mix, it will not bring them back to the high time of postwar party politics. There are signs that the organisational patterns of political mobilisation through large collective organisations that characterised the twentieth century may become increasingly obsolete in the post-industrial societies of the twenty-first century. Specifically, big parties will have to compete with smaller parties – at least in proportional-representational electoral systems – and above all specialised non-governmental organisations. In times of declining voter turnout, the quasi-monopoly of political parties on representing citizens in parliament will be seriously challenged on democratic grounds.

Appendix: Method of Coding the Party Manifestos

The Comparative Manifesto Project (CMP/MARPOR) data collection provides content-analytical data derived from human coding of political-party manifestos. The German data begins in 1949 and continues through the 2009 election. The manifesto coding scheme is based on a saliency theory of party position-taking and the subsequent coding scheme reflects this nature. (Saliency theory proposes that parties will highlight those issues they favour while not discussing those issues they do not favour, rather than speaking negatively about unfavoured issues. Therefore, in the context of manifestos, it may be difficult to discern whether unmentioned issues are unfavoured or simply not of interest to the party in the first place.)

The coding of manifestos requires breaking each manifesto down into composite parts using 'quasi-sentences' that are defined, by the project, as an individual policy argument. Usually quasi-sentences coincide with natural sentences, but sometimes natural sentences contain multiple policy statements and these are coded individually. This process, referred to as unitising, is then combined with the process of code allocation, in which each individual quasi-sentence is given one of 56 policy codes. These 56 codes, called 'categories' in the project parlance, cover a wide variety of policy areas in seven loosely defined domains: external relations, freedom and democracy, political system, economy, welfare and quality of life, fabric of society, and social groups. Each domain includes specific policy categories, such as: military: positive/negative; freedom and human rights; labour groups: positive/negative; nationalism/patriotism; and free enterprise. The coding process is strictly controlled by a training supervisor and the collected data go through multiple quality-control checks before publication. After coding, the data are offered to users in either raw form (frequency of category use) or as an aggregated index of a party's left–right ideological positioning (RILE) (developed by Laver and Budge[18]). For the purposes of this analysis, we use the raw data only and therefore do not go into the controversy surrounding the use of the RILE score.

Notes

1. Michael Zürn, 'Democratic governance beyond the nation–state: the EU and other international institutions', *European Journal of International Relations* 6/2 (2000), pp. 183–221; Axel Dreher, Noel Gaston and Pim Martens, *Measuring Globalisation: Gauging its Consequences* (New York: Springer, 2008).
2. Hanspeter Kriesi, Edgar Grande, Romain Lachat, Martin Dolezal, Simon Bornschier and Timotheos Frey, *West European Politics in the Age of Globalisation* (Cambridge: Cambridge University Press, 2008), p. 3.
3. Thomas W. Pogge, 'Cosmopolitanism and sovereignty', *Ethics* 103/1 (1992), p. 48.
4. Michael J. Sandel, *Liberalism and the Limits of Justice* (Cambridge: Cambridge University Press, 1982); Michael Walzer, 'Liberalism and the art of separation', *Political Theory* 21/3 (1984), pp. 315–30; Alasdair MacIntyre, *Whose Justice? Which Rationality?* (London: University of Notre Dame Press, 1988); Michael Walzer, 'The communitarian critique of liberalism', *Political Theory* 18/1 (1990), pp. 6–32.
5. Sandel, *Liberalism and the Limits of Justice*.
6. Hanspeter Kriesi, Edgar Grande, Romain Lachat, Martin Dolezal, Simon Bornschier and Timotheos Frey, 'Globalisation and the transformation of the national political space: six European countries compared', *European Journal of Political Research* 45/6 (2006), pp. 921–57; Kriesi et al., *West European Politics*; Hanspeter Kriesi, Edgar Grande, Martin Dolezal, Marc Helbling, Dominic Höglinger, Swen Hutter and Bruno Wüest, *Political Conflict in Western Europe* (Cambridge: Cambridge University Press, 2012).
7. Michael Zürn and Gregor Walter-Drop, 'Democracy and representation beyond the nation state', in S. Alonso, J. Keane and W. Merkel (eds), *The Future of Representative Democracy* (Cambridge: Cambridge University Press, 2011).
8. Pieter de Wilde, 'No polity for old politics? A framework for analysing the politicization of European integration', *Journal of European Integration* 33/5 (2011), pp. 559–75.

9. Seymour M. Lipset, *Political Man: The Social Bases of Politics* (Garden City: Doubleday, 1960), p. 50.

10. Seymour M. Lipset and Stein Rokkan, *Party Systems and Voter Alignments* (New York: Free Press, 1967).

11. Otto Kirchheimer, 'The transformation of the Western European party systems', in J. LaPalombara and W. Weiner (eds), *Political Parties and Political Development* (Princeton: Princeton University Press, 1966).

12. Philippe C. Schmitter, 'On the way to a post-functionalist theory of European integration', *British Journal of Political Science* 39/1 (2009), pp. 211–15.

13. Wolfgang Merkel, Alexander Petring, Christian Henkes and Christoph Egle, *Social Democracy in Power: The Capacity to Reform* (London/New York: Routledge, 2008), p. 19.

14. In our project 'Cosmopolitanism and Communitarianism: A New Cleavage?' (Social Science Research Center Berlin), we investigate the base of elite and mass surveys, party manifestos and analyses of media claims in the following five countries: the US, Germany, Poland, Turkey and Mexico. Here we present some figures from the German case, which served as a pilot project.

15. Ian Budge, 'A new spatial theory of party competition: uncertainty, ideology and policy equilibria viewed comparatively and temporally', *British Journal of Political Science*, 24/4 (1994), p. 443.

16. For methodological details concerning the coding and analysis of party programmes, see the appendix to this chapter.

17. As Table 6.1 shows, some issues are represented better in the manifesto data than are others. For instance, there is no manifesto coding category for negative statements concerning the environment. However, the economic growth category is generally used, for instances where parties support economic growth as the dominant goal (as opposed to economic growth in the context of sustainable development). Generally, however, the operationalisation of the five issues is plausibly based on the manifesto coding scheme.

18. M.J. Laver and Ian Budge, *Party Policy and Government Coalitions* (London: Sage, 1992).

CHAPTER 7

The Electoral Performance of Centre-Left Parties

Putting 'Decline' in Perspective

Pippa Norris

S ocial democratic parties might have been expected to benefit politically from the most recent global financial downturn, the resurgence of debate about the politics of inequality, and the Occupy movement and backlash against cuts in public services that swept through down-town capitals.[1] Far from being rewarded politically in the wake of the financial crisis, however, centre-left parties suffered several resounding defeats at the ballot box and, with a few exceptions, have been electorally underwhelming in the post-crisis era.[2]

In the light of all these events, some commentators have speculated that social democratic parties face severe threats. The core electoral problem has commonly been diagnosed as arising from the long-term erosion in the core working-class and trade-union base, where socioeconomic trends are thought to make prospects for future recovery bleak for left-leaning parties.[3] Others detect a deep-seated *cultural* challenge, where it is believed that the spread of self-expression values has undermined support for collectivist values.[4] Commentators argue that the public has lost faith in the capacity of governments to manage the economy in hard times.[5] Some suggest an ideological crisis, where it is thought that parties on the centre-left have failed to offer any clear and distinctive progressive vision following the end of the Third Way debate.[6]

Nevertheless, grim prognostications detecting a fatal 'crisis' facing the centre-left are hardly novel; even before the recent global financial crisis, many commentators have seen social democracy as 'exhausted',[7] in 'irreversible decline',[8] a 'threatened species',[9] in retreat from a supposed 'golden age'[10] or simply 'dying'.[11] In each case, the published obituaries proved premature. Observers have often proclaimed that a particularly dramatic election defeat represented a realigned party system within a country, only to find the restoration of the status quo ante in subsequent contests. Some contemporary accounts have also challenged the popular 'crisis thesis', recognising a complex patchwork of multiple centre-lefts in Europe, with some progressive forces doing well and others facing serious challenges.[12]

Another interpretation suggests that the severe financial crisis could have triggered an anti-incumbency electoral reaction directed against all governing parties, not merely the centre-left; for example, parliamentary elections in some of the meltdown European economies saw modest improvement in the centre-left share of the vote.[13] Nevertheless, the electoral performance of centre-left parties in Britain, France, Germany and Sweden – the historical heartland of social democracy – has triggered renewed speculation that social democracy in western Europe has suffered from a sustained, enduring and long-term erosion in its social and ideological base from which these parties are unlikely to recover.

The Electoral Performance of Centre-Left Parties

This chapter considers the electoral performance of centre-left parties in the light of structural and cultural theories emphasising changes in mass society. It briefly considers the background to these theories, and the implications, before reflecting on evidence documenting long-term trends in the proportion of votes and seats held by centre-left parties in national parliamentary elections since 1945.

A useful starting point is to consider social and cultural theories seeking to explain changes in the mass electorate in post-industrial societies as 'demand-side' sociological perspectives, emphasising the electoral impact of long-term processes of societal modernisation and economic development occurring in post-industrial societies.

It should be stressed, however, that these theories differ in their diagnoses of the expected consequences. *Structural* accounts emphasise that modern societies have weakened the salience of class-based subjective identities and sapped the link between these identities and left–right party preference, and have also eroded the size of the working-class and trade-union populations living in European societies.[14] Alternatively, *cultural* theories focus upon the way development is thought to have transformed social and political values within affluent nations, reducing support for traditional collectivist appeals as a result of the growth of self-actualisation values.[15]

While they differ in certain important regards, the logic of both these accounts implies that common and persistent trends have undermined the electoral performance of centre-left parties across similar post-industrial societies and across established democracies. Thus, aggregate electoral results demonstrating a steady and sustained erosion in the share of votes and seats among social democratic and centre-left parties across similar post-industrial societies would be *prima facie* evidence that social forces are probably at work, although this strategy by itself would be unable to determine whether any such downwards trajectory were due to transformation of the labour force or of cultural values. By contrast, trendless fluctuations would point to alternative causes.

For evidence, to test these arguments, the second part of this chapter analyses long-term trends in the proportion of votes and seats held by centre-left parties in national parliamentary elections in post-industrial societies since the end of World War II.[16] The evidence suggests that, far from there having been a simple, steady decline in western European social democratic electoral support over successive decades (as social and cultural theories posit), in fact, far more complex fluctuations are evident, and substantial regional and cross-national variations can be observed.

The results suggest, although they cannot prove, that party policies, government performance and institutional conditions are more plausible explanations for varying centre-left electoral performance than the long-term impact of socio-economic and cultural forces. Speculation about a steady secular decline threatening the electoral fortunes of social democratic parties exaggerates the challenges they face.

In other words, the results suggest that the most plausible candidate comes less from political economy and political sociology than from politics itself, and thus from complex cocktails of events, leaders, policies, issues and other 'supply-side' factors that generate volatility in party fortunes. 'Supply-side' explanations focus on what parties offer to the electorate.

Indeed, the comparison of aggregate centre-left voting performance over successive decades since the mid-twentieth century disguises considerable underlying volatility within each state. Moreover, the main beneficiaries of any erosion of social democratic support in western Europe are not simply the major parties on the centre-right. Christian democracy has also lost substantial ground, as others have noted.[17] Voting gains are most often registered by a mélange of radical right, green, territorial and ethnic parties throughout Europe. Studies of electoral behaviour focused upon individual-level voting choices need to understand the broader context of party competition and candidate choices presented to citizens. This suggests, although of course it is unable to prove, that scholars should instead use multilevel analysis exploring voting behaviour, party strategies and institutional contexts. The conclusion considers the implications of the main findings for understanding party competition and the future of social democracy.

Theories of Social Democratic Electoral Performance

The extensive research literature on the electoral performance of centre-left parties offers three alternative theoretical perspectives:

- accounts focusing upon the broader *institutional context* regulating party competition in the electoral market place (exemplified by the impact of the voting franchise, ballot-access laws, electoral systems and party-funding regulations);
- theories stressing *supply-side* factors, determined by the decisions of strategic political actors (such as the effect of the choice of party policies, the selection of leaders, governments' management of public goods and services, and the impact of party organisations, campaign spending, mass media, opinion polls and political marketing);
- accounts emphasising the *demand side* of the mass electorate and the impact of long-term processes of societal modernisation and economic development occurring in post-industrial societies (including the social and ideological bases of voting behaviour).

Within the third of these, two related mainstream perspectives have long dominated. These focus on the effect of *structural* and *cultural* changes in mass society.

Structural Change

Considerable debate surrounds changing patterns of class voting in established democracies, with some scholars detecting long-term class dealignment and others seeing trendless fluctuations.[18] European political sociology has traditionally been dominated by theories of class voting, originating in the classic work of Lipset and Rokkan.[19] This perspective was subsequently developed, theoretically and empirically, by numerous scholars.[20] Lipset and Rokkan emphasised the impact of traditional social cleavages (including social class, religion and cultural regions) that divided European societies and European party politics during the late nineteenth and early twentieth centuries (the industrial era when the mass franchise was extended and mass political parties organised and mobilised their grass-roots support base). The working class and trade unions formed the historical bedrock of labour, social democratic and socialist party organisations, providing funds, members and voters. The traditional cleavages of class, religion and region were theorised to have a strong impact upon voting preferences in industrialised European societies, since social groups shared a common sense of identity and set of interests, and they supported political parties that reflected their identities and defended their interests. The process of socialisation encourages children to adopt parental party preferences, and thus early cleavages were fixed from generation to generation.

The classic structural explanation of centre-left electoral decline, arising from this influential perspective, builds upon Daniel Bell's notion that modern post-industrial economies have been transformed by growing societal complexity and a series of fundamental social changes.[21]

New cross-cutting social cleavages have also arisen, not least due to the entry of women into the workforce and the substantial waves of population migration into post-industrial societies. Europe has hosted the largest number of international migrants, who are estimated by the OECD to constitute almost one-tenth of Europe's total population.[22] The rapid settlement of Muslim migrants into European societies, in particular, has raised important challenges for how European policy-makers manage cultural diversity, maintain social cohesion and accommodate minorities.[23]

Contemporary multicultural European societies (especially urban areas) are characterised by cross-cutting cleavages where social identities based on the industrial cleavages of farm, factory or office work, as well as gradations of socio-economic status (and thus income, wealth and education), have become fractured by alternative multiple identities arising from religion and religiosity, nationality, race and ethnicity, gender and sexuality, age and generation, territorial region and language.

Structural theories of social dealignment have long suggested that these processes have several important political consequences in post-industrial societies, by (first) weakening the salience and strength of class identities as the primary driver of party preferences, and (second) shrinking the relative size of the traditional working-class and the trade-union base of centre-left parties.[24]

If changes in the occupational class structure, and weakening class identities, have indeed undermined the social foundations of centre-left parties in post-industrial societies, then long-term secular and glacial erosion in voting support for these parties should be observable throughout western Europe. Moreover, the growth in the size of the professional and managerial middle class within the service sector could also be expected to expand electoral support for the centre-right in affluent societies.

Cultural Change

Yet processes of societal modernisation could change values as well as the structure of the economy. Alternative demand-side explanations seek to explain the electoral performance of centre-left parties by emphasising enduring cultural shifts in public opinion that are believed to have occurred in post-industrial societies. The most comprehensive theoretical framework of cultural change has been developed in an extensive series of publications by Ronald Inglehart.[25] Inglehart argues that a long-term process of cultural change has reduced the salience of 'industrial' variables for voting behaviour, notably the impact of social class.

Growing affluence and security have simultaneously expanded a wide range of 'self-actualisation' and 'self-expression' values in post-industrial societies, Inglehart argues, especially among the younger generation. These values include growing social tolerance and trust, secularisation, permissive attitudes towards sex and sexuality, respect for human rights, and support for environmentalism and related quality-of-life issues. This process is thought to have either eroded support for or reduced the salience of universal welfare states and the traditional post-World War II values of collectivism, state ownership, economic redistribution and social equality. This is especially true among the younger generation and has stranded 'Old Left' parties in the ideological wilderness.

Cultural change is thought to have increased the salience of polarising issues – including policy debates about globalisation, climate change and environmentalism, gender and sexuality, population migration, multiculturalism, nationalism and minority rights. In turn, this process is believed to have fragmented public issues and weakened traditional social identities, limiting the capacity of Old Left parties to respond to their core constituencies.

Divisive issues reflecting 'morality' issues can be seen as zero-sum games; delivering to one constituency can alienate another.[26] In this regard they differ from distributive or regulatory policies towards bread-and-butter concerns about economic performance, national security and managing delivery of core public goods and services, including health, education and social security, where public preferences are distributed as more of a normal bell-shaped curve. Issue polarisation is thought to have encouraged new social movements and protest politics directed against governing parties, providing opportunities for diverse minor parties that appeal to both the populist right and green and ethnic-regional parties on the 'New Left'.

If cultural shifts are at the heart of changes in party systems, this should be understood as a broader phenomenon that should be evident in collapsing voting support for both the centre-left *and* the centre-right of the political spectrum. The cultural thesis would also be confirmed if the European public expressed less support today for many core principles of social democracy (via attitudes towards the welfare state, unemployment, health care, social benefits and services) or if the balance of public opinion now favoured neo-liberal values.

Trends in Party Votes and Seats, 1945–2009

Several signs indicate that centre-left parties, especially in western Europe, if they have not yet experienced an electoral 'crisis' are at least under growing pressure. Recent years have witnessed the defeat of several

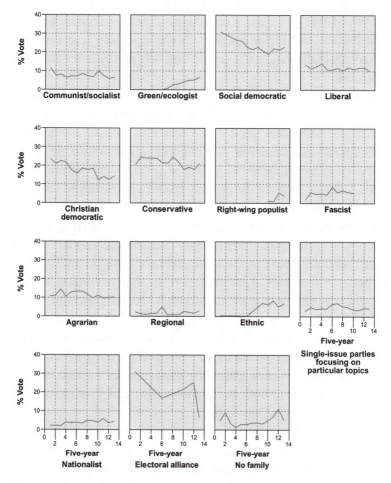

FIGURE 7.1   Vote percentage by party family, 1945–2009, in national parliamentary elections in 34 post-industrial societies. The year is coded: 1, 1945–9; 2, 1950–4; 3, 1955–9; 4, 1960–4; 5, 1965–9; 6, 1970–4; 7, 1975–9; 8, 1980–4; 9, 1985–9; 10, 1990–4; 11, 1995–9; 12, 2000–5; 13, 2005–9.

Source: Calculated from Holger Döring and Philip Manow, 'ParlGov spring 2010 preview release' (25 February 2010). Available at http://parlgov.org (accessed 1 May 2013).

major centre-left parties among the G8 powers. In 2007, Ségolène Royal for the Parti Socialiste (PS) was defeated in the French presidential elections by Nicolas Sarkozy, despite staging a 10-percentage-point recovery for the PS share of the vote compared with 2002. In 2009, across the border

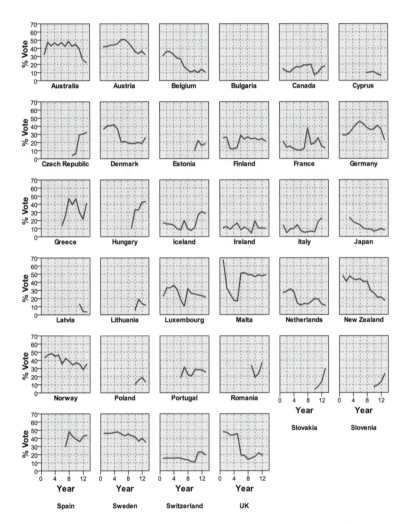

FIGURE 7.2 Vote percentage for social democratic parties, 1945–2009, by nation, in national parliamentary elections in 34 post-industrial societies. The year is coded as in Figure 7.1.

Source: Calculated from Holger Döring and Philip Manow, 'ParlGov spring 2010 preview release' (25 February 2010). Available at http://parlgov.org (accessed 1 May 2013).

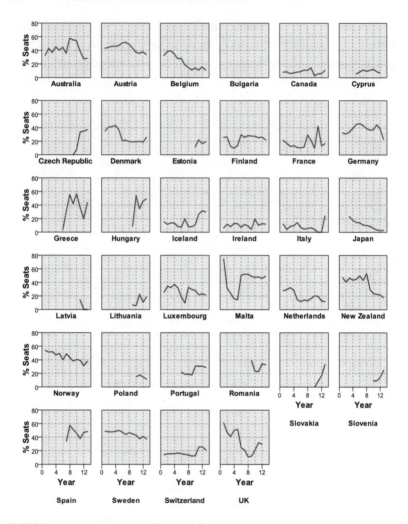

FIGURE 7.3   Seat percentage for social democratic parties, 1945–2009, by nation, in national parliamentary elections in 34 post-industrial societies. The year is coded as in Figure 7.1.

Source: Calculated from Holger Döring and Philip Manow, 'ParlGov spring 2010 preview release' (25 February 2010). Available at http://parlgov.org (accessed 1 May 2013).

in Germany, the Sozialdemokratische Partei Deutschlands won 23 per cent of the Bundestag vote, their lowest share ever in a postwar federal election. Then, under the leadership of Gordon Brown, after 11 years in power, in the 2010 British general election the Labour government

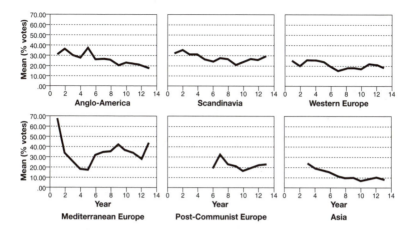

FIGURE 7.4 Vote percentage for social democratic parties, 1945–2009, by region, in national parliamentary elections in 34 post-industrial societies. The year is coded as in Figure 7.1. See text for regional classifications.
Source: Calculated from Holger Döring and Philip Manow, 'ParlGov spring 2010 preview release' (25 February 2010). Available at http://parlgov.org (accessed 1 May 2013).

returned to the opposition benches with just 29 per cent of the UK vote, their second worst share since 1918. Nevertheless, the outcome was close, generating a hung parliament; the Liberal Democrats, under Nick Clegg, entered a coalition with David Cameron's Conservative party. In the 2010 Swedish elections, the broad left opposition, led by the once dominant Sveriges Socialdemokratiska Arbetareparti, suffered its worst result since 1921. In the same year, in the US mid-term elections, the Republicans gained 63 seats in the House of Representatives, which was the largest seat gain in any mid-term election since 1938.[27]

Do the results in these countries represent outcomes related to particular events, leaders and issues in specific contests, exemplified perhaps by the Tea Party backlash against the Obama administration in the US and the end of an extended period of Blair–Brown Labour governments in the UK? Or has a broader long-term trend systematically eroded centre-left support across many countries? Data from the European Union Democracy Observatory (EUDO) allows us to compare five-year averaged trends since the end of World War II (1944–2009) in the share of the vote and seats won by parties and party families in 35 post-industrial societies (see Figure 7.2).[28]

TABLE 7.1 Vote percentage for social democratic parties, by region, 1945–2009. Mean percentage vote and number of multi-party elections per region. See text for regional classification.

Year	Anglo-America		Scandinavia		Western Europe		Mediterranean Europe		Post-Communist Europe		Asia		All	
	%	N	%	N	%	N	%	N	%	N	%	N	%	N
1945–9	31.2	9	32.4	9	24.8	15	67.1	2					30.8	35
1950–5	36.5	11	35.3	8	20.1	15	32.7	6					29.5	40
1956–60	30.1	7	30.9	11	25.5	13					23.2	3	28.0	34
1961–5	28.0	9	31.0	7	25.9	12	17.5	3			18.2	2	26.4	33
1966–70	37.2	8	26.2	11	24.0	12	16.8	3			16.1	4	26.0	38
1971–5	26.1	14	24.6	21	19.2	21	32.2	2	19.3	4	14.4	2	22.7	64
1976–80	26.5	8	27.6	10	15.7	22	34.1	4	31.5	7	10.2	8	21.6	59
1981–5	25.4	10	26.5	11	17.4	19	35.1	6	22.4	7	9.1	3	22.7	56
1986–90	20.1	12	20.7	11	18.5	22	42.0	6	20.5	8	9.1	6	20.7	65
1991–5	22.8	7	24.2	10	17.0	18	35.8	4	15.8	23	6.6	3	19.0	65
1996–2000	21.6	11	26.9	6	21.9	11	33.4	8	18.5	24	7.9	2	22.0	62
2001–5	20.5	13	26.0	8	20.7	15	27.8	5	21.4	21	9.7	4	21.4	66
2006–9	17.8	7	29.0	6	18.1	11	43.6	4	22.5	14	7.9	2	22.8	44
Total	26.2	126	27.3	129	20.1	206	34.3	53	20.3	108	11.6	39	23.3	661
Change 1945–9 to 2006–9	–13.4		–3.4		–6.7									

Source: Calculated from Holger Döring and Philip Manow, 'ParlGov spring 2010 preview release' (25 February 2010). Available at http:// parlgov.org (accessed 1 May 2013).

In short, the wisest conclusion based on the comparison across a range of diverse post-industrial societies, including older and younger democracies, is to be extremely cautious in assuming any steady and uniform erosion of support for parties on the centre-left. A more complex picture emerges that requires further exploration with survey evidence captured at the individual level.

To summarise the longitudinal trends, the electoral performance of the centre-left parties in the 35 post-industrial societies under comparison were compared by global region, to see whether there are common or divergent trends. If structural changes in the basis of social class are at the heart of any erosion of social democratic support (notably the shrinkage in the proportion of blue-collar workers in the labour force), then this structural change should be evident as a steady decline in centre-left votes across similar affluent economies that have gradually shifted from manufacturing-industry to service work (e.g. in the banking, insurance and educational sectors), irrespective of their global region.

Nevertheless, Table 7.1 and Figure 7.4 display some contrasting regional patterns. The sharpest decline in social democratic support has occurred in the Anglo-American societies, where votes for the centre-left have fallen on average by 10 percentage points from 1945 to date. A parallel slide is evident in Japan, which has also experienced massive social and economic change during the postwar era. The aggregate trends in these nations are therefore consistent with the story of class change. By contrast, however, mean voting support for social democracy fell in Scandinavia from 1945 to the early 1990s and then recovered across the region. Moreover, even less consistently with the structural change narrative, western European states have seen a pattern of trendless fluctuations in centre-left votes around the mean – and more complex fluctuations are evident in Mediterranean Europe and in post-Communist Europe.

Rejecting Declinism

The descriptive evidence tracing the postwar electoral performance of European social democracy provides some important insights into demand-side explanations of this phenomenon. The results presented here certainly suggest that a more complex story is required, rather than any simple narrative concerning inevitable erosion (still less a crisis) of electoral support for the centre-left and social democratic parties.

Three key findings of this study deserve to be highlighted. First, within contemporary post-industrial societies, centre-left parties govern more than a dozen states. It is true that the social democratic mean share of the vote across post-industrial societies fell by about a dozen percentage points from 1945 to the early 1990s, and this is a substantial drop that cannot be easily dismissed. Since the early 1990s, however, centre-left support has recovered slightly. Moreover, cross-national trends show complex fluctuations characterised by rises and falls rather than simple and steady secular decline.

Second, any erosion in social democratic support needs to be understood in the context of broader patterns of European party competition and electoral volatility, since the overall share of the Christian democrat vote also declined by an equivalent amount. As a result, electoral competition among the major governing parties remains on a roughly equal footing. This is equivalent to both Coke and Pepsi losing market share to bottled water; but it is not the case that only the left is losing ground to its primary competitor. The main challenge to the status quo and to catch-all parties in the centre of the political spectrum has arisen from the success of the diverse minor-party contestants, notably the greens, the radical right and ethnic-minority parties. These diverse contenders have made substantial gains in recent years, although more in terms of their share of votes than their seats, due to the constraints of vote thresholds in electoral systems. Some surges in popularity for the radical right have proved fleeting while others have been more long-lasting.[29]

Volatility is certainly a challenge as parties can no longer rely so heavily upon their own supporters through economic good times and bad; instead, they have to work harder to mobilise support and engage participants. Populism by the radical right – especially the heated mix of immigration, unemployment and anti-tax rhetoric – is certainly a threat to social democratic values in Europe. Similarly, in America, in spite of the fact that public support for them is failing, Tea Party true believers in the House of Representatives are threatening to push the

Republican Party towards extremist fiscal policies, with potentially disastrous consequences for the US economy. Nevertheless, it should be remembered that populist appeals are not merely a tool for the right; progressive politics can also use them, as exemplified by the late Hugo Chávez's appeal in Venezuela.

Lastly, the centre-left vote displays trendless fluctuations across regions and nations, more than a consistent secular decline. Thus these patterns suggest, although they cannot prove, that supply-side and institutional factors are more plausible explanations for varying centre-left electoral performance across different societies than is the impact of long-term structural and cultural forces on the mass electorate. That is, citizens face different choices today from those they faced 50 years ago; not surprisingly, they make different decisions. During the postwar era, European consumers faced displays of carrots, onions and cabbage; today they can choose from a bewildering array of lemongrass, bok choy, plantain, daikon and organic kohlrabi. Not surprisingly, like our menus, our voting behaviours and election outcomes have become less predictable and more colourful. This process may prove challenging for the major parties of the left and right, but greater electoral choice is to be celebrated in a democracy.

The results documented in this chapter lend credence to alternative institutional and supply-side accounts, emphasising that any sustained shifts in social structure and public opinion that have occurred will not necessarily *determine* the fate of social democracy. Rational-choice theories suggest that political parties can choose to either reinforce the strength of group–party ties (through issuing bonding appeals) or decide to weaken these links through bridging strategies. These ideas were developed by Adam Przeworski and John Sprague and subsequently expanded by other scholars.[30] Strategic theories emphasise that parties can respond to social and cultural developments by shifting policy positions, social appeals and ideological locations within the electoral market.

Centre-left parties can thus decide to widen their strategic appeals to attract other social sectors, such as professional and managerial public-sector employees, and they can aim to mobilise broader and more heterogeneous electoral coalitions; for example, by emphasising issues that appeal to women, younger voters and ethnic minorities. Hence, many contemporary centre-left parties now strongly espouse progressive principles, emphasising environmentalism, feminism, human rights, multiculturalism and racial equality, while retreating from traditional socialist notions of state control of the economy and income redistribution.

From this perspective, the erosion in the size of the working-class base, the weakening of subjective class identities and party loyalties, and the subsequent growth of electoral volatility are all factors that make it more difficult, but far from impossible, for social democratic parties to regain power. Cultural and social changes have made the electoral challenge harder for centre-left parties; essentially, social democrats have to race uphill to recover support against a downward-moving escalator. Minor parties are commonly favoured by institutional changes that lower the hurdles to attaining elected office, especially reforms to make electoral systems more proportional, to establish multilevel and decentralised elected bodies, and to implement inclusive forms of public funding of parties and campaigns.[31] Speculation about an inevitable *secular* decline that is threatening social democratic parties today, based on the transformation of mass society, thus exaggerates the complex global challenges they face; they can still succeed and often do.

Notes

1. It should be noted that throughout this paper the terms 'social democracy' and 'centre-left' are used interchangeably. However, 'social democratic parties', whatever their official title, are defined by full-membership affiliation with the Socialist International.

2. Progressive parties have lost elections in France (2007), Germany (2009), Britain (2010), Sweden (2010), Canada (2011) and Italy (2013).

3. Gerassimos Moschonas, 'Historical decline or change of scale? The electoral dynamics of European social-democratic parties (1950–2009)', in J.E. Cronin, G.W. Ross and J. Shoch (eds), *What's Left of the Left: Democrats and Social Democrats in Challenging Times* (Durham: Duke University Press, 2011).

4. Ronald Inglehart, *The Silent Revolution: Changing Values and Political Styles Among Western Publics* (Princeton: Princeton University Press, 1977).
5. Peter Kellner, *The Crisis of Social Democracy* (London: Demos, 2010).
6. Magnus Ryner, 'An obituary for the Third Way: the financial crisis and social democracy in Europe', *Political Quarterly* 81/4 (2010), pp. 554–63.
7. Ralf Dahrendorf, *After Social Democracy* (London: Liberal Publication Department, 1980).
8. Christiane Lemke and Gary Marks, *The Crisis of Socialism in Europe* (Durham: Duke University Press, 1992).
9. Jonas Hinnfors, *Reinterpreting Social Democracy* (Manchester: Manchester University Press, 2006).
10. John T. Callaghan, *The Retreat of Social Democracy* (Manchester: Manchester University Press, 2000); John T. Callaghan (ed.), *In Search of Social Democracy: Responses to Crisis and Modernization* (Manchester: Manchester University Press, 2009).
11. Ashley Lavelle, *The Death of Social Democracy: Political Consequences in the 21st Century* (Aldershot: Ashgate, 2008).
12. Wolfgang Merkel, Alexander Petring, Christian Henkes and Christoph Eagle, *Social Democracy in Power: The Capacity to Reform* (London: Routledge, 2008); James Cronin, George Ross and James Shoch (eds), *What's Left of the Left: Democrats and Social Democrats in Challenging Times* (Durham: Duke University Press, 2011).
13. Parties that fall into this category include the Icelandic Social Democratic Alliance (2009), the Greek Pannhellenic Socialist Movement (2009) and the Irish Labour Party (2011).
14. See Seymour M. Lipset and Stein Rokkan, 'Cleavage structures, party systems and voter alignments', in S.M. Lipset and S. Rokkan (eds), *Party Systems and Voter Alignments* (New York: Free Press, 1967).
15. See Inglehart, *The Silent Revolution*.
16. Pater Mair, 'In the aggregate: mass electoral behaviour in Western Europe, 1950–2000', in H. Keman (ed.), *Comparative Democracy* (London: Sage, 2001).

17. Duncan Fraser, 'A decade of Christian Democratic decline: the dilemmas of the CDU, OVP and CDA in the 1990s', *Government and Opposition* 45/4 (2006), pp. 469–90.

18. Geoffrey Evans (ed.), *The End of Class Politics?* (Oxford: Oxford University Press, 1999).

19. Lipset and Rokkan, 'Cleavage structures, party systems and voter alignments'.

20. Stefano Bartolini and Peter Mair, *Identity, Competition and Electoral Availability* (Cambridge: Cambridge University Press, 1990); Mark N. Franklin, Thomas T. Mackie and Henry Valen (eds), *Electoral Change: Responses to Evolving Social and Attitudinal Structures in Western Countries* (Cambridge: Cambridge University Press, 1992); Paul Nieuwbeerta, *The Democratic Class Struggle in Twenty Countries 1945–90* (Amsterdam: Amsterdam Thesis Publishers, 1995); Geoffrey Evans, 'The continued significance of class voting', *Annual Review of Political Science* 3 (2000), pp. 401–17; Evans (ed.), *The End of Class Politics?*; Maria Oskarson, 'Social structure and party choice', in J. Thomassen (ed.), *The European Voter* (Oxford: Oxford University Press, 2005); Mark N. Franklin, 'Epilogue', in M.N. Franklin, T.T. Mackie and H. Valen (eds), *Electoral Change: Responses to Evolving Social and Attitudinal Structures in Western Countries, Classics in Political Science Edition* (Colchester: ECPR Press, 2009).

21. These rapid social changes include rising education levels, globalisation, population migration, changes in family structures and marriage, and the entry of more women into the workforce. The growth of the white-collar service sector (clerical, sales and administrative areas, as well as professionals and managers), in particular, eroded the number of skilled and unskilled manual workers employed in manufacturing industries, transforming the occupational structure across OECD states. See Daniel Bell, *The Coming of Post-Industrial Society* (New York: Basic Books, 1973); Colin Crouch, *Social Change in Western Europe* (Oxford: Oxford University Press, 1999).

22. OECD, *International Migration Outlook* (2008). Available at www.oecd.org/els/mig/internationalmigrationoutlook2008.htm (accessed 1 May 2013).

23. Joel S. Fetzer, *Muslims and the State in Britain, France, and Germany* (New York: Cambridge University Press, 2004); Friedrich Heckman, 'National modes of immigrant integration', in W. Bosswick and C. Husbanded (eds), *Comparative European Research in Migration, Diversity and Identities* (Bilbao: University of Duesto, 2005).

24. Russell J. Dalton, Scott Flanagan and Paul A. Beck (eds), *Electoral Change in Advanced Industrial Democracies: Realignment or Dealignment?* (Princeton: Princeton University Press, 1984); Ivor Crewe and David Denver (eds), *Electoral Change in Western Democracies: Patterns and Sources of Electoral Volatility* (New York: St Martin's Press, 1985); Franklin et al., *Electoral Change*; Jeff Manza and Clem Brooks, *Social Cleavages and Political Change: Voter Alignments and U.S. Party Coalitions* (New York: Oxford University Press, 1999); Franklin, 'Epilogue'.

25. Inglehart, *The Silent Revolution*; Ronald Inglehart, *Culture Shift in Advanced Industrial Society* (Princeton: Princeton University Press, 1990); Ronald Inglehart, *Modernization and Postmodernization: Cultural, Economic and Political Change in 43 Societies* (Princeton: Princeton University Press, 1997); Ronald Inglehart and Christian Welzel, *Modernization, Cultural Change and Democracy* (New York/ Cambridge: Cambridge University Press, 2005).

26. Ted J. Lowi, 'Foreword: new dimensions in policy and politics', in R. Tatalovich and B.W. Daynes (eds), *Moral Controversies in American Politics* (New York: M.E. Sharpe, 1998); Kevin B. Smith, 'Typologies, taxonomies, and the benefits of policy classification', *Policy Studies Journal* 30/3 (2002), pp. 379–85.

27. The Democratic Party in the US is not officially a social democratic party, as defined by affiliation with the Socialist International, though it shares many core ideas with the centre-left.

28. EUDO classifies 89 parties as part of the social democratic family; examples include the Norwegian Labour Party, the SDP in Germany and the Socialist Party in France. The EUDO dataset includes election results from multi-party contests in all five nations in Scandinavia (Denmark, Finland, Iceland, Norway and Sweden), seven nations in western Europe (Austria, Belgium, France, Germany, Luxembourg, the Netherlands and Switzerland), six from

Mediterranean Europe (Cyprus, Greece, Italy, Malta, Portugal and Spain), five Anglo-American Westminster democracies (Australia, Canada, Ireland, New Zealand and the UK), one Asian post-industrial society (Japan) and nine consolidated democracies in Central Europe (Bulgaria, the Czech Republic, Estonia, Latvia, Lithuania, Hungary, Poland, Romania and Slovenia). Thus, the comparison allows us to examine trends in the 'old' region of western Europe as well as the contemporary boundaries of modern Europe. For details, see Holger Döring and Philip Manow, 'ParlGov spring 2010 preview release' (25 February 2010). Available at http://parlgov.org (accessed 1 May 2013).

29. Pippa Norris, *Radical Right* (New York: Cambridge University Press, 2005).

30. Adam Przeworski and John Sprague, *Paper Stones: A History of Electoral Socialism* (Chicago: University of Chicago Press, 1986); Thomas Koelble, 'Recasting social democracy in Europe: a nested games explanation for strategic adjustment in political parties', *Politics and Society* 20 (1992), pp. 51–70; Herbert Kitschelt, *The Transformation of European Social Democracy* (New York: Cambridge University Press, 1994); Herbert Kitschelt, *The Radical Right in Western Europe* (Ann Arbor: University of Michigan Press, 1995); Herbert Kitschelt, 'Linkages between citizens and politicians in democratic polities', *Comparative Political Studies* 33/6–7 (2000), pp. 845–79; Pippa Norris, *Electoral Engineering* (New York: Cambridge University Press, 2004).

31. Joseph M. Colomer, *Handbook of Electoral System Choice* (New York: Palgrave Macmillan, 2004); Norris, *Electoral Engineering*; Michael Gallagher and Paul Mitchell (eds), *The Politics of Electoral Systems* (Oxford: Oxford University Press, 2005); Anika Gauja, *Political Parties and Elections* (Farnham: Ashgate, 2010).

CHAPTER 8

Predistribution and Institutional Design

Making Markets Work for the Middle

Jacob S. Hacker

W hat does it mean to be middle class? Economic experts talk about levels of income: between two and four times the poverty level, for example, or the middle three quintiles of the income distribution.

When you ask Americans, though, you get a very different answer. First, most Americans believe they *are* middle class; only a small share say they are poor or rich. Second, what defines the middle class for them – according to decades of polling, focus groups and public discourse – is much broader than income: a job with reasonable pay and benefits, the ability to raise a family without undue hardship, basic economic security grounded in the ownership of homes and other assets, and the opportunity to rise up the economic ladder through education and hard work.

All these core aspects of the middle class are under siege in the US and, increasingly, the UK as well. The most unmistakeable sign of trouble is the stagnation of median wages that has occurred over the past generation as income gains have accrued overwhelmingly to the richest.[1]

But the income squeeze associated with rising inequality is only the most visible tip of a much larger iceberg of middle-class strain. As wages have stagnated, families have gained economic ground mostly by relying on both parents working more – which has created a 'care squeeze' as they juggle paid work and caring for young children or ageing parents. As job-based benefits such as health insurance and traditional defined-benefit pensions have eroded or disappeared, middle-class families have borne greater economic risk despite little in the way of greater economic rewards. And the private safety net of savings and wealth on which these families depend has become much more threadbare, especially after the market crisis of 2007.

In short, the ideal and reality of the middle class are increasingly distant. Yet political leaders have been slow to respond to this growing gap and, in crucial ways, have actually made it worse. In this essay I examine why, focusing on the US and its lessons for the UK.

The Middle Class and Its Discontents

The past generation has witnessed a remarkable turnaround in American economic outcomes. In the generation after World War II, the economy and the earnings of all income classes grew roughly in tandem. Since the 1970s, the economy has slowed modestly, but the big change has been where the rewards of growth have gone. In a word, they have gone to the top. Over the past generation, the share of pre-tax national income received by the richest 1 per cent of Americans has more than doubled. The share received by the richest 0.1 per cent has more than *quadrupled*, rising from less than 3 per cent in 1970 to more than 12 per cent in 2007 – the highest proportion since the creation of income tax in 1913.[2]

This is not mainly a story of stagnant productivity or general economic malaise. It is mainly a story of the decoupling of aggregate productivity and most workers' wages. Even a college-educated entry-level male worker earns barely more than such a worker did a generation ago.[3] Middle-class families filled the wage gap with two difficult-to-sustain strategies – more work hours and more borrowing. While the 1990s' economic boom temporarily reduced the pay–productivity gap, the gap returned with a vengeance in the 2000s. Indeed, the 2000s expansion was the first on record in which a typical family's income was lower at the end than at the close of the prior business cycle.[4]

As job security has eroded and gains have shifted towards the top, other pillars of security and opportunity have also come under strain.

Education and Social Mobility

Class lines have hardened. American inequality is sky high; American social mobility is below the advanced industrial norm.[5] The US has gone from being the world leader in college completion to a middling performer. More and more of the rapidly rising college costs are financed through loans, burdening students and their parents – except for children of the rich, who gain a huge head start.[6]

Pensions and Social Insurance

America's job-based framework of economic security has gone from basic to broken. Defined, secure pensions that promise a guaranteed benefit in retirement – once the hallmark of a good job – are vanishing. 401(k) retirement-savings plans and other tax-deferred retirement accounts are not filling the gap. As medical costs continue to outstrip inflation, employment-based health-insurance benefits are becoming rarer and less protective.[7]

Housing and Economic Assets

Besides their homes, most middle-class families have strikingly little in the way of private assets to cushion economic shocks or build their futures. And, of course, those homes look far less secure than they once did. The traditional strategy of gradually accumulating wealth through housing has taken a perhaps-fatal hit, with implications for the economic security not just of the middle aged but also of the young aspiring middle class.

Balancing Work and Family

With families increasingly needing two earners to maintain a middle-class standard of living, their economic calculus has changed in ways that accentuate many of the risks they face. What happens when a parent leaves the workforce to care for children, when a child is chronically ill, when one spouse loses his or her job, or when an elderly parent needs assistance? Precisely because it takes more work and more income to maintain a middle-class standard of living, events that require the care and time of family members produce special strains. This 'care squeeze' creates new risks alongside traditional job concerns.

The Political Roots of Middle-Class Strains

Who killed the old middle-class social contract? Most explanations focus almost exclusively on the unstoppable forces of technology and globalisation. Computers and automation have reduced the rewards for routine skills and encouraged outsourcing and offshoring. The entry of hundreds of millions of literate low-wage workers into the global workforce has undermined the earning power of middle-class Americans, especially those without a college degree. This conventional wisdom suggests that American politics and policy have played only a bit role – and can do only a limited amount to reclaim the 'American dream'.

Technological change and globalisation matter immensely, of course. But their effect in the US (and other nations) has been heavily shaped by whether and how governments have responded to them. After all, these shifts have affected all rich nations – most more so than the US – and yet few have seen anything like America's sharp upward shift of economic rewards, erosion of economic security or breakdown of social benefits.

Moreover, in many nations where inequality and insecurity have risen, policy-makers have pushed back through active labour-market policies, taxes and public spending. Not so in the US. Despite the 'earned income tax credit' for the working poor and the expansion of Medicaid health-insurance coverage for low-income families and children, low-wage workers have continued to fall behind. According to the Congressional Budget Office, even after all public and private benefits and federal taxes are taken into account, almost 40 per cent of all household income gains between 1979 and 2007 accrued to the richest 1 per cent of Americans – more than the bottom 90 per cent combined.[8]

Another clue that politics and policy have been crucial is that America's newly unequal and insecure economy developed hand in hand with a new politics. As Paul Pierson and I have argued in our book *Winner-Take-All Politics*, corporate America organised on an unprecedented scale in the late 1970s to influence government policy, not just through campaign giving but also vast lobbying efforts. At the same time, with campaign costs shooting up, money became a far more important resource for politicians – and, as we have seen, a far more unequally distributed resource in American society.

The rising role of money and the increasing imbalance between business and other organised interests fundamentally changed Washington. For the contemporary Republican Party, these changes were welcome and encouraged the party to shift ever rightward on economic issues. Democrats, by contrast, found themselves increasingly torn between their historical commitment to the 'little guy' and the pull of money from the big guys, including, for much of the 1990s and early 2000s, the ascendant titans of Wall Street. The result was an ever more polarised economic debate in which a significant faction of one party, the Democrats, repeatedly proved willing to cut bargains that undermined the middle class' standing.

The recent string of large tax cuts for the richest of Americans has highlighted the long-term role of the tax system in abetting inequality. Far more important and less recognised have been ways in which public policies have remade markets to the advantage of the top. Failure to enforce federal laws that empower workers to form unions undermined organised labour as a force for good pay and benefits. Corporate governance rules all but asked top executives to drive up their own earnings. Financial deregulation brought great riches for some while pushing many ordinary families into unaffordable loans, ultimately crashing the economy.

Perhaps the least visible policy changes were passive-aggressive in nature – deliberate failures to address changing economic and social conditions, such as the need for people to balance work and family. Entire categories of support that have become essential to middle-class life, such as good child-care, are simply not a public responsibility in the US. Meanwhile, responsibilities that corporations once shouldered are shifting back onto families. Uniquely among industrial nations, the US came to rely on employers as mini-welfare states, providing health insurance, pensions and other benefits that elsewhere enjoyed state sponsorship. But, as employers have pulled back, government has not filled the gap, leaving families more vulnerable.

Perhaps it is not surprising then that so many middle-class Americans feel abandoned. Asked in mid-2010 whom government had helped 'a great deal' during the downturn, 53 per cent of Americans said banks and financial institutions and 44 per cent fingered large corporations.

Just 2 per cent thought economic policies had helped the middle class a great deal.[9]

Lessons for the UK

To what extent has the UK experienced similar trends? In one respect, the parallels are striking. The share of income accruing to the richest cohort in the UK has risen almost as sharply as it has in the US. In 2005, the last year for which data is available for both nations, the proportion of pre-tax income that went to the top 1 per cent (excluding capital gains, which cannot be easily compared across the two countries) was 14.25 per cent in the UK, compared with 17.42 per cent in the US.[10]

In the UK, however, this upward shift of income has not occurred alongside stagnation at the middle as it has in the US – at least not until recently. The main explanation appears to be public policy: direct government transfers to the middle and the bottom of the economic ladder. In a careful comparative analysis, the sociologist Lane Kenworthy has found that the income gains of low-income citizens in the past three decades have depended heavily on changes in public taxes and transfers. He notes:

> The New Labour governments under Tony Blair and Gordon Brown increased benefits and/or reduced taxes for low earners, single parents, and pensioners. […] [T]hese were big policy shifts, even if not always high-profile ones. They produced a significant rise in the real disposable incomes of poor households.[11]

In addition, the continued strong role of the National Health Service in providing universal – and comparatively affordable – services stands in stark contrast to the American experience of runaway health costs and declining private coverage. These policy differences may in turn reflect the stronger role of labour unions and the greater commitment to the welfare state evidenced by the Labour Party as compared with the Democratic Party. Whatever the cause, the substantial decline in economic security and painfully slow median income growth seen in the US does not appear to be the UK story.

Nonetheless, the US experience is looking more and more relevant. In the past decade, the British middle class has begun to experience the same wage and income stagnation that the American middle class has confronted for years. What's more, the economic crisis and subsequent austerity policies have simultaneously increased economic hardship and encouraged an American-style stagnation in policies, as public and employment-based benefits have been cut or held steady in the face of rising needs, and initiatives to deal with new risks (such as the care needs of an ageing population) have been pushed off the agenda. For all these reasons, the American experience offers increasingly salient lessons for the UK.

Lesson 1: Pay Attention to 'Predistribution'

When we think of government's effects on inequality, we think of 'redistribution' – government taxes and transfers that take from some and give to others. And redistribution is certainly a major part of what government does to reduce inequality and insecurity. As noted, the UK has done more to offset the growth in inequality in the market through taxes and transfers than has the US.

Yet there is good reason to look beyond redistribution in thinking about how to tackle inequality and insecurity. In the US, many of the most important changes have been made in what might be called 'predistribution' – the way in which the market distributes its rewards in the first place. Policies governing financial markets, the rights of unions and the pay of top executives have all shifted in favour of those at the top, especially the financial and non-financial executives, who make up about six in ten of the richest 0.1 per cent of Americans.[12]

The moral is that reformers need to focus on market reforms that encourage a more equal distribution of economic power and rewards even before government collects taxes or pays out benefits. This is not just because predistribution is crucial. It is also because excessive reliance on redistribution fosters backlash, making taxes more salient and feeding into the conservative critique that government simply meddles with 'natural' market rewards. And, lastly, it is because societies in which market inequality is high are, ironically, ones where creating common support for government action is often most difficult. Regulation of markets to limit extremes and give the middle class more voice is hardly easy – witness the fight over financial reform in the US. But it is both more popular and more effective than after-the-fact mopping up.

A predistribution agenda should have several elements. First and most obvious, it must involve a commitment to high levels of employment – a necessary but hardly sufficient condition for broadly shared growth. To tackle hyper-concentration of income at the top and protect against financial instability, effective regulation of financial markets and corporate governance are essential – starting with greater transparency and accountability in executive pay-setting. At the high end of the income scale, policies should be designed to encourage countervailing pressures against self-dealing and pay-without-performance from watchdog organisations and shareholder collectives (such as large institutional shareholders). In the middle range, policies should be focused on facilitating the organisation of workers and creating opportunities for a voice in the workplace, including not just more aggressive protection of those seeking union representation, but also institutional reforms (such as 'right to request' laws) that give workers protected institutional channels through which to seek better employment arrangements.

Because growing top-heavy inequality creates threats to equality of opportunity as well, special emphasis should be placed on ensuring that small-scale enterprises and start-up entrepreneurs have the access to capital and legal protection necessary to enter into markets and expand. Similarly, ensuring that educational opportunities are broadly distributed – with a special emphasis on early childhood education and adequate support for college completion for less-advantaged students – is also a pressing priority, even if not a panacea for addressing the deep inequality that so threatens basic equality of opportunity today.

Lesson 2: 'Drift' is Dangerous

Over the past generation, across a wide range of areas, American public officials have deliberately failed to update policy in the face of changing economic circumstances, allowing outcomes to 'drift' away from a more equal equilibrium.[13] Although particularly pronounced in the US, drift seems characteristic of many rich democracies today as they confront a rapidly changing economy and society and grapple with persistent fiscal constraints. If this is so, preserving existing policies is not the only challenge. The welfare state as traditionally understood remains deeply rooted. But the broader environment of the welfare state – a mixed economy characterised by a healthy civil society – is much more vulnerable. It has become abundantly clear that well-functioning markets are not natural or inherently self-correcting; they require continuing public-policy updates in a highly dynamic economic world.

To be sure, British policy-makers face nothing like the institutional hurdles faced by their American counterparts – who must cope with the extreme fragmentation of US governing authority, including the rise of the Senate filibuster as a routine hurdle to the passage of laws that lack three-fifths support in the Senate. Still, it is worth remembering that many of the most severe causes of drift in the US (such as the filibuster) are extra-constitutional, and thus potentially relevant to British developments. Partisan polarisation – which in the US at least has involved the conservative pole of the debate moving steadily further to the right – presents inherent barriers to policy updating, reducing the chance of agreement even when there is broad public support for it. Fiscal constraints are another cause of drift, and the tightness of these constraints depends very much on the policy choices of the past. Large shifts in the fiscal constitution of the state, such as major changes in the visibility or source of tax revenues, can powerfully influence the tendency of the political system towards drift.

To protect and restore a well-functioning market democracy, therefore, those worried about inequality and insecurity must preserve an effective capacity for robust governance. They should resist institutional reforms that abet gridlock and ensure that the policies put in place retain the capacity for adjustment over time, whether automatically (as in benefits indexed to wages or prices) or structurally (through the preservation of basic regulatory, tax and spending powers that are too often sacrificed on the conservative altar of privatisation and delegation).

Lesson 3: Increase the Organisational Might of the Middle

As documented at length in *Winner-Take-All Politics*, the transformation of America's political economy over the past generation has had far less to do with the shifting demands of voters than with the changing organisational balance between concentrated economic interests and the broad public. Indeed, the sharp shift of policy towards the affluent and business occurred despite remarkable stability in public views on many economic issues – including views on government redistribution, progressive tax policy and the importance of key programmes of economic security. The agenda disconnect that we see today, as politicians ignore Americans' concerns about the lack of jobs in favour of cutting programmes that the public likes and preserving tax reductions for the rich that it doesn't, is not new. It has characterised the politics of much of the past generation.

The root of the problem, once again, is organisational. As Theda Skocpol has argued, middle-class democracy rested on organisations, such as unions and cross-class civic organisations, that gave middle-class voters knowledge about what was at stake in policy debates and political leverage aiming to influence these debates.[14] Without this organisational grounding, voters simply have a very hard time drawing connections between the strains they face in their lives and what politicians do, and even more so formulating a broad idea of how those strains could be effectively addressed.

A revival of middle-class organisations will necessarily require moving beyond the traditional base of such movements (namely, organised labour and old-line fraternal organisations) to encompass new social movements and the harnessing of new technologies. Where such initiative will come from is inherently difficult to foresee, but three trends give at least some cause for optimism. The first is that the start-up costs of organisational development have dramatically fallen over the past generation. The second is the widespread dissatisfaction with existing policy seen in the US and other wealthy nations. The third – and most up for grabs – is the typical pattern of new leaders emerging out of crisis moments to galvanise citizens around shared concerns.

Ironically, since the economic crisis, these trends have mostly benefited conservative movements. In the US, the most effective organising has taken place not on the left but on the right, with the rise of the loose organisation of conservative voters, right-wing media figures and corporate-funded ideological activists that travel under the 'Tea Party' banner. But there is good reason to believe that many of the forces that impelled these developments also have the potential to galvanise progressive movements in the coming years, especially as the Tea Party agenda moves from gauzy ideals to concrete (and deeply unpopular) policies.

Indeed, the Tea Party's success should be instructive for all organisational reformers. It rests on the combination of champions inside government and organisers working at the grass roots. It has a clear agenda (scale back government) and enemy (President Obama). And it has effectively utilised both old-style organising through local chapters and new communications technologies (and, yes, has also benefited from lavish financing from deep-pocketed donors, including many from corporate quarters). While the Tea Party cannot and should not be simply emulated by those seeking to reconstruct middle-class democracy, its three key features – grass-roots organising linked to national reform leaders, a forward-looking vision that is directed against a perceived contemporary threat and the use of flexible participatory modes enabled by new media – are contemporary preconditions for effective organising.

Rebuilding the Organisational Foundations of Democratic Capitalism

This diagnosis is both encouraging and challenging. It is encouraging because there is nothing natural about the harsh divisions that have arisen in the US. They are rooted in politics and policy, not the inexorable forces of globalisation or technological change. In many cases, moreover, they require not major programmes of redistribution – never easy to enact – but measures to reshape the market so that it distributes its rewards more broadly in the first place.

The challenge, however, is that reforms to tackle middle-class strains will require using a broken political system to fix a broken political system: the main obstacle to change and the main vehicle for change are one and the same. This Catch-22 affords no easy resolution. But it does suggest where reformers' energies should be directed, and it points to opportunities that are too often missed by those narrowly focused on rhetorical messages and strategic moves.

Perhaps the most important implication is that those seeking to achieve a new governing economic philosophy will have to rebuild the organisational foundations of democratic capitalism. An inspiring economic vision will be grounded in an institutional blueprint for using active democratic government to meet the challenges facing American society – challenges that are increasingly facing America's great ally across the Atlantic.

Notes

1. Larry Mishel and Heidi Sherholz, 'A lost decade, not a burst bubble: The declining living standards of middle-class households in the U.S. and Britain', in Sophia Parker (ed.), *The Squeezed Middle: The Pressure on Ordinary Workers in the United States and Britain* (Bristol: The Policy Press, 2013), pp. 17–30.
2. Jacob S. Hacker and Paul Pierson, *Winner-Take-All Politics: How Washington Made the Rich Richer – And Turned Its Back on the Middle Class* (New York: Simon & Schuster, 2011), pp. 11–40.
3. Ibid., p. 36.
4. Robert Greenstein, Sharon Parrott and Arloc Sherman, *Poverty and Share of Americans Without Health Insurance Were Higher in 2007 – And Median Income for Working-Age Households Was Lower – Than at the Bottom of Last Recession* (Washington: Center on Budget and Policy Priorities, 2008). Available at www.cbpp.org/cms/?fa=view&id=621 (accessed 1 May 2013).
5. OECD, *A Family Affair: Intergenerational Social Mobility Across OECD Countries* (Paris: OECD, 2010). Available at www.oecd.org/dataoecd/2/7/45002641.pdf (accessed 1 May 2013).
6. College Board Advocacy and Policy Center, *Trends in Student Aid* (2010). Available at http://trends.collegeboard.org/student-aid (accessed 1 May 2013).
7. Jacob S. Hacker, *The Great Risk Shift: The New Economic Insecurity and the Decline of the American Dream* (New York: Oxford University Press, 2008).

8. Congressional Budget Office, *Average Federal Taxes by Income Group* (2010). Available at www.cbo.gov/publication/42870 (accessed 1 May 2013).

9. Pew Research Center, *Gov't Economic Policies Seen as Boon for Banks and Big Business, Not Middle Class or Poor* (2010). Available at http://pewresearch.org/pubs/1670/large-majorities-say-govt-stimulus-policies-mostly-helped-banks-financial-institutins-not-middle-class-or-poor (accessed 1 May 2013).

10. Paris School of Economics, *Top Incomes: A Global Perspective* (2011). Available at http://g-mond.parisschoolofeconomics.eu/topincomes (accessed 1 May 2013).

11. Lane Kenworthy, 'Has the rise in income inequality been Rawlsian?' (2010). Available at www.u.arizona.edu/~lkenwor/hastherisein incomeinequalitybeenrawlsian.pdf (accessed 1 May 2013); Lane Kenworthy, 'Has rising inequality been bad for the poor?' (Consider the Evidence, 2011). Available at http://lanekenworthy. net/2010/12/14/has-rising-inequality-been-bad-for-the-poor (accessed 1 May 2013).

12. Hacker and Pierson, *Winner-Take-All Politics*, p. 46.

13. Jacob S. Hacker, 'Privatizing risk without privatizing the welfare state', *American Political Science Review* 98/2 (2004), pp. 243–60.

14. Theda Skocpol, *Diminished Democracy: From Membership to Management in American Civic Life* (Norman: University of Oklahoma, 2004).

CHAPTER 9

The New Politics of Production
A Progressive High-Growth Strategy

Will Marshall

The US is struggling to find a way out of overlapping economic crises. One is cyclical: a painfully slow, jobless recovery from a recession magnified by the 2008 financial crash. The other is structural: US economic output and job growth have fallen well off the pace of previous decades. Although liberal commentators seem preoccupied with rising inequality, America's fundamental economic problem is slow growth.

Even before the recession struck, the once-mighty American job machine was sputtering. Between 2000 and 2007, the US posted its worst job creation record in any decade since the Great Depression.[1] Not only have many good jobs vanished, but also real wages have fallen or turned stagnant for all but the top US earners.

Overall economic growth has been declining steadily since the halcyon years after World War II, when the babies boomed and GDP grew at a robust average of 4 per cent per year. National output fell to 3 per cent during the 1970s and 1980s, before picking up in the late 1990s. Since 2000, the economy has downshifted again, averaging under 2 per cent growth per year.[2] Research from the Kauffman Foundation also suggests a loss of entrepreneurial verve. The number of business start-ups, which Kauffman says generate most of US net job growth, has plummeted by about a quarter since 2006.[3]

If there is a bright spot in the US economy, it is the rebound of corporate profits and stock prices since 2009. Yet these gains also highlight a stark inequity: returns to capital are up, but returns to labour are down.

In President Kennedy's day, US prosperity really did lift all boats. Today, however, productivity gains do not automatically translate into higher pay for workers, especially people with middling skills. 'This is America's largest economic challenge', says the economist Robert J.

Shapiro. 'People can no longer depend on rising wages and salaries when the economy expands.'[4]

Amid such dismal conditions, Obama's re-election by a comfortable margin (5 million votes) was an astounding political feat. Despite Republican challenger Mitt Romney's claims that Obama fumbled the recovery, swing voters credited the president with having prevented the economy from capsizing during the perfect storm of 2008–9. It helped too that Romney offered no theory of his own for rekindling growth beyond hackneyed calls for lower taxes and regulation.

Unfortunately, little has happened since Obama's victory to dispel the pall of economic pessimism that hangs over America. A late spring poll,[5] for example, found that nearly 60 per cent of Americans worry about 'falling out of (their) current economic class over the next few years'. No doubt subpar job growth is chiefly responsible for such unwonted gloom. According to preliminary figures, the number of people with jobs grew by only 28,000 (0.02 per cent) during Obama's first term.[6]

And there is little relief in sight. The Congressional Budget Office forecasts weak GDP growth and abnormally high unemployment persisting to the end of Obama's second term. America is stuck in a slow-growth rut. While liberal Keynesians are calling for more short-term spending to kick-start the pace of recovery, what progressives really need is a bolder plan for overcoming structural impediments to more robust growth.

Instead of devising one, Obama is bogged down in Washington's endless trench warfare over taxes, spending and debt. True, the president won a tactical victory in averting the 'fiscal cliff' and forcing Republicans to swallow higher tax rates on wealthy households. Yet this modest blow for tax fairness did little to fix the nation's debt or stimulate growth. In fact, distributional politics distracts progressives from a truly historic opportunity to lay new foundations for US prosperity in the twenty-first century.

To inspire hope for such a change, the US president must broaden his message from fairness to growth: he must put America back on a high-growth path. By setting audacious goals – say, doubling the growth rate and halving unemployment by the end of his second term – Obama would convey the requisite sense of national urgency.

A clarion call for renewed growth would create political space for progressive initiatives – public investments in training and education, broad tax reform – intended to spread economic gains more widely. And, by fanning hopes for a reversal of America's economic decline, such a call could help Democrats make inroads among white working-class voters.

These voters, once the backbone of Democrats' New Deal–Great Society coalition, have since defected en masse to the Republican camp. A conscious campaign to start winning them back, while retaining the Democrats' strong advantages with young and minority voters, is the key to building a durable progressive majority and ending the 50:50 polarisation that has paralysed Washington.

The Consumption Bias

Setting out a new progressive growth narrative must begin with an accurate diagnosis of America's core economic dilemma. Many liberals believe it is weak economic demand, and they prescribe more government spending to stimulate consumption. This is the standard Keynesian remedy, but it is inadequate at best because it does not deal with the US economy's structural weaknesses: lagging investment and innovation, a paucity of workers with technical and middle-level skills, and unsustainable budget and trade deficits. None of these problems can be fixed by boosting consumption.

We should not be misled by analogies between the present predicament and the Great Depression. In the 1930s, the issue was overproduction and under-consumption; now it is the reverse. Over the past decade especially, Americans have consumed far more than they have produced, borrowing heavily to make up the difference. This model of debt-fuelled consumption brought the country anaemic growth, a shrinking job base, recurrent financial bubbles and crippling deficits.

Progressives must disenthral themselves from the notion that consumption drives US prosperity. There are few economic factoids more misleading than the claim that consumer spending accounts for 70 per cent of US economic activity. Of course, consumer spending creates economic activity, but the question is, where? If you buy a shirt or television, you stimulate manufacturing jobs in China, or perhaps Mexico.

Progressives in the US do not begrudge these countries opportunities to grow. But the problem with borrowing massively to buy imports is that it does not encourage domestic investment. Business investment in the US is a stunning 25 per cent below its long-term trend.[7] America's job drought is in fact an investment drought.

Making production rather than consumption the organising principle of US economic policy will not be easy. For a generation, Washington has relentlessly increased subsidies for consumption, assuming that the productive base of the economy will take care of itself.

For example, around 44 per cent of the federal budget today goes to the big three social-insurance programmes: Medicare, Medicaid and Social Security. Automatic spending on these programmes is expected to double by 2050 as America ages. For every five dollars it spends to support consumption by retired people, Washington invests just one dollar in the health, well-being and future productivity of America's children. Federal spending on non-defence tangible and intangible investment – in science and technology, in education and workforce skills, in public goods such as transportation – amounts to less than 10 per cent of budget outlays.[8]

The consumption bias pervades government and society. It is evident in the growing federal deficits, which have swollen America's national debt; in monetary policies that drive the cost of borrowing towards zero; in tax policies that put greater burdens on labour and capital investment than consumption spending; and in trade policies that encourage a deluge of low-cost imports, even at the expense of domestic production and jobs.

We see it at work at the household level as well. Americans are digging out from under mountains of debt amassed during the speculative binge that saw household savings rates dip into negative territory. The bursting of speculative bubbles in stocks and housing triggered the previous two recessions, leaving millions of homeowners 'underwater' (they owe more than their houses are worth) and devastating the construction industry.

Americans today collectively owe over $11 trillion, or about 95 per cent of the country's disposable income.[9] Leveraged to the hilt, they can no longer rely on cheap credit and low-priced imports to compensate for lost jobs, dwindling production and stagnant middle-class wages. In a world of cheap labour and rapidly narrowing technology gaps, advanced countries can thrive only by speeding the pace of innovation and capturing its economic value in jobs that stay at home.

For all these reasons, progressives need to replace the old growth model with a new strategy that stimulates production rather than consumption, saving rather than borrowing, and exports rather than imports. The goal should be to make America once again a global centre for production rather than the world's consumer of last resort.

Progressives for Production

This shift will require fundamental changes in policy that cut across conventional partisan and ideological lines and challenge entrenched interests. Liberals in the US, for example, are unquestionably right that America needs to boost public investment. But conservatives also are correct in calling for lower taxes on entrepreneurs and urging government regulators to take a light hand to encourage investment in innovative industries.

Political polarisation, in fact, may pose the most daunting obstacle to a high-growth strategy. The two parties are deadlocked in a witless 'government versus markets' argument even as it becomes blindingly obvious that both a more dynamic private sector and a more strategic public sector are necessary to create the right conditions for a US economic comeback.

Let's get specific. What policy changes are required, and what political adjustments do progressives need to make?

First, they must get serious about breaking the fiscal impasse in Washington. Liberals are right that, with the economy still weak and US interest rates hovering around zero, there is no need for austerity. But they are wrong to oppose controlling the growth of federal spending on health and retirement benefits for seniors.

Thanks to Republican support for the 'sequester', the budget axe has fallen instead on defence and domestic spending, imposing fiscal drag on the US economy at exactly the wrong time. Not only is the endless wrangling over deficits and debt hogging centre stage politically, but it is also undermining confidence in the federal government's basic competence. Most importantly, US prosperity cannot be rebuilt on the quicksand of chronic government and household borrowing, overconsumption and a soaring national debt.

A high-growth strategy requires a credible framework for long-term debt reduction that boosts public investment now while gradually raising revenues and cutting public spending on consumption. There is no way for America to create more jobs or hone its competitive edge without more investment in modern infrastructure, science and technology, and education and workforce development. Also essential are institutional innovations, such as a national infrastructure bank that would use federal dollars to leverage private capital investments in transport, energy and water projects that can generate measurable economic returns.

How to pay for new investment while also whittling down the nation's $16 trillion debt? By rebuilding the tax base and slowing the unsustainable growth rates of the big three entitlements: Medicare, Medicaid and Social Security. Health benefits especially are set to balloon as the number of Americans over 65 will double by 2030. But, just as conservatives have adopted a pigheaded stance against tax hikes, too many liberals are in denial about the need to rebalance the nation's massive social-insurance programmes.

Like some kind of fiscal doomsday machine, automatic, formula-driven spending on consumption by retirees is relentlessly crowding out space in the federal budget for future-oriented investments in things progressives ought to care about – early education for poor children, child nutrition and health, access to colleges, environmental protection, and more. The Congressional Budget Office projects that entitlement spending will more than double, from 7.3 to about 16 per cent of GDP, by 2037. Spending on everything else will fall from 11 to 7 per cent.[10]

The long battle for universal coverage has accustomed progressives to think in terms of health-care access. Now, as Obamacare is phased in, they must grapple with the systemic drivers of soaring health-care costs. To deal with the coming demographic tidal wave, Washington will need to trim benefits for the wealthy retirees who need them least. By spurring more efficient ways of delivering health care, injecting more competition into the big public programmes could also put downward pressure on prices. It is also crucial to raise productivity in the health-care sector, which will require more technological innovation, not less, as is commonly assumed by analysts who mistakenly blame health-care inflation on high-priced medical equipment.

Beyond the modest hike in tax rates Obama forced on Republicans in the fiscal cliff deal, progressives also should push for a sweeping reform of federal taxes. This is essential for restoring the government's revenue base, but, done properly, it could also be a powerful catalyst for economic growth.

Consider America's absurd corporate tax system. Its top rate (35 per cent) is well above global norms. It is riddled with loopholes that distort economic decisions and introduce mind-boggling complexity. And it leaves $1.7 trillion in profits earned by US companies stranded overseas. Can progressives overcome their habitual suspicion of big business and lead the long-overdue overhaul of corporate taxation? We will likely find out in 2013.

High-Tech Innovation and a Manufacturing Revival

In addition to reorienting fiscal policy around saving, investment and growth, the Obama administration needs a balanced strategy that fosters both high-tech innovation and a manufacturing revival.

The US leads the world in a crucial new category of economic activity: 'data-driven growth'.[11] According to Progressive Policy Institute economist Michael Mandel, the digital realm of internet publishing, search and social media has become one of America's fastest growing sectors, posting an 80 per cent gain in jobs from 2007 to the present. As US telecommunications companies invest heavily in high-speed mobile broadband, sales of mobile devices and data services are growing exponentially. Mandel's research shows that, since the first smartphone was introduced in 2007, 'app' developers have created 500,000 new jobs. Jacques Bughin of McKinsey & Company estimates that companies that make strategic use of 'big data' grow twice as fast as those that do not.[12]

Progressives should give high priority to protecting the innovation ecosystem responsible for the dramatic rise of the data-driven economy.

Yet they have often sided reflexively with self-styled 'consumer activists' who demand more regulation in the name of privacy, competition, low prices, or a general suspicion of big and successful companies such as Apple, AT&T and Google.

Since innovation is America's main comparative advantage in global competition, striking the right balance between innovation and regulation is crucial. This means recognising, for example, that the sheer accumulation of rules, regardless of their individual merits, imposes mounting compliance and opportunity costs on US entrepreneurs. The problem is not that government creates new regulations but that it almost never rescinds old ones. To rectify this problem, the Progressive Policy Institute has proposed a 'Regulatory Improvement Commission' that would meet periodically to retire or modify old rules.[13]

Of course, progressives must stand firm against right-wing attempts to roll back vital health and environmental regulations. But, if they are serious about growth, they will embrace a more strategic approach to economic regulation, one that stresses the impact of rules on innovation, productivity and competitiveness as well as traditional concerns about market power and consumer prices.

Innovation is also integral to expanding manufacturing jobs, another key element of a progressive growth strategy. There is promising news here. Thanks to a confluence of economic factors, some major companies (such as Apple, General Electric and Otis Elevator) are beginning to bring production back home. Such factors include rising wages in China (about 17 per cent a year); the higher productivity of US workers; automation that reduces labour's share of company expenses; rising transportation costs; and an influx of cheap natural gas in the US. Companies are also increasingly worried about intellectual property theft and leery of separating their research and production centres.

These trends raise workers' hopes for relief from wage compression and suggest an opportunity not to reverse globalisation but to rebalance it in favour of domestic production. Policies that encourage 'inshoring' of production could reverse the hollowing out of America's middle class by creating millions of good jobs for workers with both high- and middle-level skills.

All this, of course, implies rising consumer prices, since the US will be making more commodities at home and buying fewer cheap imports. But a modicum of inflation is a price worth paying to rebuild a diverse job base that offers opportunities to all workers, not just those with advanced degrees. After all, unless you are retired or on the dole, to be a consumer you first have to be a worker.

Finally, a high-growth strategy will also take advantage of America's shale gas and oil windfall. Since the 1970s, the idea that the US is running out of fossil fuels has been the planted axiom of the country's energy policy. Advances in drilling technology have turned this assumption of energy scarcity on its head, by unlocking vast reserves of natural gas and oil trapped in shale formations.

This truly is an economic game changer. In just a few years, the US has become the world's largest natural gas producer, and the International Energy Agency predicts America's oil production will overtake Saudi Arabia's by the end of the decade.[14] Already, the influx of cheap shale gas (and associated liquids) is cutting home heating bills, reviving the petrochemical industry and lowering US manufacturing costs. It has brought environmental benefits as well: in the power sector, fuel switching from coal to gas has cut US greenhouse gas emissions by 430 million tons over the past five years.[15] There is growing interest in using natural gas as a transportation fuel, which would lessen US reliance on imported oil and bring further carbon reductions.

Yet the shale boom has stirred deep unease among 'green' activists, who see it as prolonging America's addiction to dirty fossil fuels. Eco-fringe groups have launched a campaign to demonise 'fracking', despite scant scientific evidence that it is harming people or ruining the environment.

Americans deserve better than a false choice between the left's fantasies of a fossil-free world and the right's atavistic demands to 'drill, baby, drill' heedless of environmental consequences. A truly progressive alternative would tap all fuels – shale gas and oil as well as nuclear and renewable – to power robust economic growth, and also adopt a carbon tax or cap to steadily reduce greenhouse gas emissions.

No country, even one as wealthy and fundamentally sound as the US, can afford to consume more than it produces indefinitely. It is time for progressives to refocus the nation's energies on building a more productive version of democratic capitalism that leads the world in innovation, generates good jobs in abundance and raises returns to both labour and capital.

Notes

1. McKinsey Global Institute, *An Economy That Works: Job Creation and America's Future* (2011), p. 3. Available at www.mckinsey.com/insights/employment_and_growth/an_economy_that_works_for_us_job_creation (accessed 1 May 2013).
2. US Department of Commerce Bureau of Economic Analysis, *GDP & Personal Income* (n.d.). Available at http://bea.gov/iTable/index_nipa.cfm (accessed 1 May 2013).
3. E.J. Reedy and Robert E. Litan, 'Starting smaller; staying smaller: America's slow leak in job creation' (July 2011). Available at www.kauffman.org/research-and-policy/starting-smaller-staying-smaller-americas-slow-leak-in-job-creation.aspx (accessed 1 May 2013).
4. Jonathan Rauch, 'The no good, very bad outlook for the working-class American man', *National Journal* (6 December 2012). Available at www.nationaljournal.com/next-economy/the-no-good-very-bad-outlook-for-the-working-class-american-man-20121205 (accessed 1 May 2013).
5. Ronald Brownstein, 'Being in the middle class means worrying about falling behind', *National Journal* (25 April 2013). Available at www.nationaljournal.com/next-economy/solutions-bank/being-in-the-middle-class-means-worrying-about-falling-behind-20130425 (accessed 1 May 2013).
6. Floyd Norris, 'Four years later, 28,000 more jobs', *The New York Times* (4 January 2013). Available at http://economix.blogs.nytimes.com/2013/01/04/four-years-later-28000-more-jobs (accessed 1 May 2013).
7. Diana G. Carew and Michael Mandel, 'Investment heroes: who's betting on America's future?' (Progressive Policy Institute, 2012). Available at www.progressivepolicy.org/2012/07/investment-heroes-who's-betting-on-america's-future (accessed 1 May 2013).

8. Office of Management and Budget (US), *Fiscal Year 2013 Historical Tables: Budget of the U.S. Government* (2013), Table 9.1. Available at www.whitehouse.gov/sites/default/files/omb/budget/fy2013/assets/hist.pdf (accessed 1 May 2013).

9. Adam Davidson, 'What's it gonna be, 2013?', *The New York Times* (2 January 2013). Available at www.nytimes.com/2013/01/06/magazine/what-will-the-economys-new-normal-look-like-in-2013.html?ref=itstheeconomy (accessed 1 May 2013).

10. Jim Tankersley, 'Entitlements', *National Journal: The Next Economy* Winter (2012), p. 13.

11. Michael Mandel, 'Beyond goods and services: the (unmeasured) rise of the data-driven economy' (Progressive Policy Institute, 2012). Available at www.progressivepolicy.org/2012/10/beyond-goods-and-services-the-unmeasured-rise-of-the-data-driven-economy (accessed 1 May 2013).

12. Progressive Policy Institute, 'Conference report – the rise of the data-driven economy: implications for growth and policy' (2012). Available at www.progressivepolicy.org/2012/11/the-rise-of-the-data-driven-economy (accessed 1 May 2013).

13. Michael Mandel, 'Reviving jobs and innovation: a progressive approach to improving regulation' (Progressive Policy Institute, 2011). Available at www.progressivepolicy.org/2011/02/reviving-jobs-and-innovation-a-progressive-approach-to-improving-regulation (1 May 2013).

14. International Energy Agency, *World Energy Outlook 2012 – Executive Summary* (2012), p. 1. Available at www.iea.org/publications/freepublications/publication/English.pdf (accessed 1 May 2013).

15. Sherle R. Schwenninger and Samuel Sherraden, 'America's emerging growth story' (New America Foundation, 2012). Available at www.newamerica.net/publications/policy/america_s_emerging_growth_story (accessed 1 May 2013).

CHAPTER 10

Reclaiming the Supply-Side Agenda
Innovation, Redistribution and Labour-Absorbing Services

Wendy Carlin[1]

The past five years have transformed the way we think about short- and longer-run economic strategy. Short-term strategy means creating high levels of employment consistent with stable inflation, along with a sustainable external balance and public debt ratio. Longer-term strategy refers to the goals of improving environmentally sustainable living standards and providing opportunities for people with all kinds of talents to have satisfying working lives. I will concentrate on the latter – and, in particular, the interconnected issues of innovation, redistribution and labour-absorbing services – but begin with the former.

From a world in which the problems of stabilisation policy seemed to have been solved, government debt ratios were falling and poor countries were for the first time catching up with the rich, we have transitioned to a situation in which households face increased uncertainty about jobs and incomes and are burdened with debt in many countries, and in which the ability of the state to intervene creatively appears heavily circumscribed. In between the two phases was a brief moment culminating in the London G-20 Summit of April 2009 when governments acted in a co-ordinated way to avert disaster and public confidence in the constructive role of government was raised.

The years of crisis and extended recession have led to a much more critical appraisal of the achievements of the preceding Great Moderation period (from the mid-1990s to the eve of the financial crisis), for substantial periods of which progressive governments were in power in many countries. It is clear that in many countries the combination of high growth and low unemployment was not based on improved long-run prospects for the economy. In some like Spain and the UK, it was based on unsustainable patterns of domestic demand-led growth underpinned by appreciated real exchange rates, which artificially boosted real wages and allowed high employment to be maintained consistent with constant inflation. In these cases, buoyant growth rested on rising levels of private debt; elsewhere, growth was supported by rising public debt. During this period, the rapid growth of China as manufacturer to the world provided sustained downward pressure on inflation. In combination with the unregulated expansion of credit creation by banks, this allowed households to become accustomed to standards of living that were not based on realistic assessments of their future income prospects.

Less attention has been paid to countries where an opposite pattern developed. In Germany, demand at home was depressed. There was no boom in consumption, construction or government spending. On the contrary, the economy grew very slowly and the growth that took place mainly resulted from orders from abroad. This was a pattern of export-dependent growth. In contrast to the patterns of domestic-demand-led growth elsewhere, dependence on export markets for growth promoted supply-side restructuring by the private sector in Germany. However, it is striking that, as the fiscal position improved, the opportunity to implement reforms that would have set in place a more balanced growth model based on a progressive economic strategy was not taken.[2]

The German experience in the decade before the financial crisis provides an interesting perspective on the theme of this chapter – the interconnection between the dynamism of the tradable sector of the economy and the economy's ability to deliver high employment and good jobs outside tradables. Although the macroeconomic performance of Germany was very poor for a decade from the mid-1990s, medium and large companies succeeded in implementing deep restructuring of their production networks to meet the challenges of the emergence of new low-cost producers, and to take advantage of the opportunities of rapidly growing markets for capital goods and automobiles. This laid the foundations for the revival of Germany's traditional export sectors through the functioning of long-established but adaptable non-govern-mental institutions of co-determination, vocational education and co-ordinated wage setting.

However, Germany did not succeed in translating improved dynamism of the private sector into buoyant growth of domestic as well as external demand, with the result that its growth performance from 1999 to 2007 was on a par with that of Italy, the eurozone's laggard economy. New well-paid jobs were not created in the sheltered sectors of the economy. On the contrary, the welfare state reforms produced a new low-wage sector to which public-sector jobs in services were outsourced.[3] Increased job insecurity also appears to have led to a rise in precautionary savings, which further depressed domestic demand.

The reforms failed to increase flexibility in the labour market by removing penalties on second earners in the household and introducing incentives for women to combine employment with child rearing. In Germany, women lose substantially by having children and then returning to work, since they do so at greatly reduced earnings and often conditions. The two consequences are that young women with good career prospects are reluctant to have children and women who have children and are engaged in home-working are reluctant to return to the market; these consequences are, as is also well known, compounded by the absence of readily available high-quality childcare.

Where these problems do not apply, such as in the Nordic countries, it seems likely that the ability to move relatively costlessly between working at home and in the market acts as an additional mechanism to reinforce the standard insurance provided by the welfare state and thus to reduce the need for building up precautionary savings. The one-sided character of the German reforms during the run-up to the global financial crisis was reflected in an increasingly segmented labour market, with the prevalence of low-paid work rising to match that of the UK. This is reflected in the size of the wedge between the market and post-tax and transfer distribution of household incomes, to which I return below.

In their contrasting ways, the experiences of the domestic-demand-oriented countries (which neglected dynamism of the tradables sector) and of an export-oriented country like Germany (which neglected the chance to complement private-sector restructuring with policies to create good jobs in services) bring to the fore the failure of social democratic policy-makers to face up to the challenge of how to design and win political support for an economic strategy that achieves distributive justice, and is consistent with longer-run macroeconomic sustainability.

We now understand much better how it was possible for central banks to achieve successful inflation targeting consistent with the build-up of the major imbalances between deficit and surplus countries, and between the financial and non-financial sectors that eventually produced both the crisis and the particular shape of the post-crisis recessions. The institutions of the liberalised financial sector took advantage of the incentives to increase their leverage in what was widely viewed as a lower-risk macroeconomic environment. This interacted with increased lending for mortgage and consumption loans to produce house-price bubbles, and create the conditions for a financial crisis to occur when house prices began to fall and the assessment of lower risk became reversed. However, an under-explored aspect of the build-up to the crisis is the connections between central-bank interest-rate policy, rising inequality and weak investment (outside housing) in a number of important advanced economies.[4]

Patterns of increased inequality varied a lot across countries in terms of timing and intensity over the decades preceding the crisis. Common factors behind rising wage inequality were technical progress biased towards more highly educated workers, and globalisation. The weakening of unions was more important in some countries than in others. Little attention was paid to why the high and rising profits of the non-financial sector were not showing up in higher fixed investment. Instead, central banks were keeping interest rates low to support demand and keep inflation close to target through the extension of loans to less and less creditworthy households. It was new houses rather than new factories or workplaces that were being built. Ironically, in the UK, where new houses were needed, they were not being built.

From this perspective, one problem for progressive economic policy is finding a way not only to address the need to make the financial sector safer and to deal with the consequences for public debt of the clean-up of the banks and the depth of the recession, but also to engage with the causes of the lack of dynamism in the non-financial business sector before the crisis. Businesses were awash with profits they did not invest. Unlike in the Great Depression, when banks failed because of excessive lending to businesses, it was excessive lending to households and to other financial institutions that characterised this financial crisis. Opinions differ widely about the potential for new technologies to drive a revival of investment.[5] Unlike in the 1930s, there does not seem such an obvious set of new general-purpose technologies (in the 1930s these were based on electrification) that could form the basis of renewed capital accumulation in the advanced economies. In the aftermath of the 1930s, the left had good ways to stimulate economic dynamism: given that new technologies were ready to go, the implementation of aggregate demand stabilisation and the support for real wage growth through the establishment of the welfare state represented a viable strategy for growth and redistribution in the golden age of the 1950s and 1960s.

More recently, the left has less successfully addressed supply-side problems of productivity, investment and innovation. The traditional supply-side model relying on the incentive effects of market rewards and financial liberalisation did not create high investment and stability, and it drove up inequality. Where supply-side restructuring in the dynamic sector of the economy was brought about by co-operation between 'corporatist' institutions as in Germany, government reforms worsened the market distribution of income by increasing labour-market segmentation. The important lessons of successful supply-side egalitarianism (such as in the Nordic countries and in various ways in East Asia) were largely ignored.

Inequality and the Role of Economic Policy in Supporting Egalitarian Interventions

A progressive supply-side strategy recognises that there are policies that increase equality and innovation. To explore this argument it is necessary to focus on policies that reduce the inequality of the distribution of market incomes by affecting the distribution of human and material assets and by affecting market incomes.[6]

The crisis has raised interest not only in the fairness consequences of the secular rise in inequality over the 30 years before the crisis but also in its implications for efficiency. Higher inequality and profits seem not to have had their expected pay-off in terms of more risk-taking by entrepreneurs in the non-financial sector; this would have led to investment in new capacity in the advanced countries, producing new products with lower cost-production processes. There was plenty of innovation in the financial sector by the highly educated workers attracted there, but these innovations yielded private and not social gains. Reform of the financial sector to make jobs there more boring again will help to redress this misallocation of talent and should be good for innovation in the non-financial sector.

There has been recent debate in the UK about the balance between policies that support a reduction in inequality by interventions affecting the market distribution itself and those that affect the post-tax and transfer distribution (of income or assets). The unattractive word 'predistribution' refers to interventions to reduce inequality in the market distribution. Most of the discussion has been about *income* redistribution. Yet policies to make the distribution of assets or wealth more equal would directly affect the market distribution of income. One of the most obvious 'predistribution' interventions on the asset side, which also enhances efficiency, is to raise human capital among poor households (e.g. through the use of early childhood education programmes). Success in education policies (such as universal childcare and high-quality primary and secondary education) in the Nordic countries is seen to have contributed to the relatively egalitarian *market* distribution of income. This effect is even more marked in the East Asian countries, where reasonably egalitarian distributions of post-tax and transfer income are achieved without much redistribution by the state. This emphasises the role of political choice about egalitarian outcomes consistent with efficiency – in the Nordic cases, both the education policies and the very substantial post-tax and transfer redistribution require political consent.

There is great variety among rich countries around the world in both the primary (market) distribution of income and in post-tax and transfer distribution. Table 10.1 presents data for 21 OECD advanced economies for which there are comparable data on the Gini coefficient measure of inequality; a higher score indicates a less equal

TABLE 10.1 Market and disposable income distribution, advanced economies, data from the late 2000s.

	Rank in market distribution	Gini for market distribution	Gini for disposable income distribution	Redistribution ratio	Rank in redistribution ratio
Denmark	4	0.42	0.25	0.40	5
Norway	3	0.41	0.25	0.39	8
Sweden	6	0.43	0.26	0.39	7
Finland	12	0.47	0.26	0.44	3
Belgium	14	0.47	0.26	0.45	1
Austria	15	0.47	0.26	0.45	2
France	16	0.48	0.29	0.39	6
Netherlands	5	0.43	0.29	0.31	13
Germany	18	0.50	0.30	0.41	4
Switzerland	2	0.41	0.30	0.26	19
Greece	7	0.44	0.31	0.30	14
Korea	1	0.34	0.31	0.09	21
Spain	10	0.46	0.32	0.31	12
Canada	8	0.44	0.32	0.27	18
Japan	11	0.46	0.33	0.29	15
New Zealand	9	0.46	0.33	0.27	17
Australia	13	0.47	0.34	0.28	16
Italy	21	0.53	0.34	0.37	9
UK	19	0.51	0.34	0.32	10
Portugal	20	0.52	0.35	0.32	11
US	17	0.49	0.38	0.22	20

Note: The redistribution ratio is 1 − (Gini disposable ÷ Gini market).

distribution of income. The countries in the table are ranked according to the Gini coefficient for disposable income distribution in the late 2000s, with the most equal countries at the top. The Gini coefficient for the distribution of *market* income (i.e. pre-tax and transfer) is shown in the third column and the rank of countries (from 1 for the most equal in market distribution) is shown in the second column. By running your finger down the second column you can quickly see that a country's rank in disposable income distribution is not closely related to its rank in market distribution. The role of the government in redistribution can be captured by the 'redistribution ratio', which is calculated as:

$$1 - (\text{Gini for disposable income} \div \text{Gini for market income})$$

The redistribution ratio is shown in the fifth column and the ranking of countries according to the size of the redistribution ratio is shown in the final column.[7]

An important but insufficiently emphasised point is that countries with egalitarian post-tax and transfer distributions compete successfully in a globalised world. Countries with egalitarian market income distributions are also successful in global export markets: the top six for market income equality are Korea, Switzerland, Norway, Denmark, the Netherlands and Sweden.

Of the six countries with low post-tax and transfer inequality (four Nordic plus Austria and Belgium), three have market distributions that are more equal than the median (among 21 countries) and three have market distributions that are less equal than the median. A very interesting example is South Korea, which has the most egalitarian market distribution of all the economies in the table and almost no redistribution via taxes and transfers, which means South Korea ends up just below the median in terms of post-tax and transfer equality.

Given the debate about predistribution in the UK, it is interesting to note that the country is one of the most unequal in terms of market distribution (second bottom) and yet is at number ten in terms of the extent of redistribution. This still leaves it in the bottom five for post-tax and transfer equality.

What does this imply? Especially in countries with high disposable-income inequality that are already doing a lot of redistribution, like the UK, the palette of egalitarian policies needs to be extended to include those that address the market as well as the post-tax and transfer distribution. Thinking this way is helpful in systematising policy options (see Table 10.2) and also highlights the efficiency- and dynamism-enhancing potential of many egalitarian interventions.

TABLE 10.2 Examples of policy areas and instruments according to whether they affect market or post-tax and transfer distribution.

	Policies that affect the distribution of assets	*Policies that affect the distribution of income*
Affect market income distribution	Education, especially early childhood Improved access by poor households to borrowing for productive investment Reduced wealth inequality (inheritance tax)	Increased employment rate of women, disabled and older people Limited executive pay Raised low pay (e.g. minimum wage or living wage) Improved trade-union rights Competition policy to reduce exploitation of households (e.g. energy prices)
Affect post-tax and transfer income distribution		Usual tax and transfer policies Basic income guarantee

Since people think that they deserve their market incomes, attacking inequality through selective policies of asset redistribution that are consistent with widely held norms may incur less political resistance. Examples are policies that fall under the 'levelling the playing field' rubric, such as high-quality health and social care and schooling for all, and bequest taxation. Also, measures that target the market distribution of income directly – such as wage compression and eradicating discrimination in labour markets by, for example, increasing access of women to the labour market through changes to the tax code and provision of high-quality childcare – are likely to have more political support than measures that try to affect the post-tax and transfer distribution in countries with high redistribution ratios.

Living standards in an open economy depend on the economy's terms of trade – that is, the bundle of imports that can be bought for a given bundle of exports. This means that the competitiveness of the economy's tradable sector cannot be ignored in the design of policies that focus on redistribution. This underlines the importance of identifying policies that improve productivity by removing the constraints on the development and deployment of talent.

The Implications for Policy of Labour-Absorbing Services in the Economy

If productivity growth in the important service sectors of health, care of the elderly and disabled and education is systematically slower than elsewhere in the economy, then the relative price of these services will go up. In the American economist William Baumol's original example, the relative price of a live performance of a Mozart quartet goes up as productivity improves elsewhere in the economy.[8] The quartet still requires four people and 20 minutes as the centuries go by, but the number of minutes of work in the market that a concert-goer has to undertake to pay for a performance goes down. This highlights the fact that the benefits of productivity growth in the dynamic sectors of the economy allow us to enjoy more live concerts and meals in restaurants and better healthcare, *as well as* more manufactured goods and more leisure. A logical consequence of the existence of sectors with relatively low productivity growth (Baumol's stagnant services) is that their share in employment and in GDP goes up.

The argument is as follows. We consume bundles of goods and services from sectors of the economy with fast and with slow productivity growth. As we get richer, we want more of both of these bundles. To keep the argument simple, we assume that our demand for the two types of bundle remains constant as our living standards improve. The bundle produced by the dynamic sector of the economy (mainly industry) – that is, the sector with the faster productivity growth – falls in relative price and fewer people are needed to produce it. The bundle produced by the so-called stagnant services rises in relative price and more people are needed to produce it. If these services are publicly financed, the tax share of GDP rises. Finally, the faster that productivity growth is in the dynamic sector, the better off we are and the more of the labour-absorbing services we can afford.

Since demand for these so-called stagnant services at constant prices rises at least in line with demand for the output of the industry, these sectors absorb labour. If, as people get richer, they demand a higher share of stagnant services in their consumption bundle measured at constant prices, this will reinforce the tendency for the employment share of these sectors to grow. In the baseline case, where demand for the output of the two sectors grow in line, the stagnant services become a bigger share of the economy in terms of employment, and their share of value added measured at current prices rises as well. This is simply a feature of the characteristics of technology and preferences (i.e. of differential productivity growth and similar demand patterns in constant price terms). It does not reflect anything to do with efficiency (unless efficiency is confused with relative productivity growth).

Of course, there are all kinds of reasons why some activities in the economy are more likely to be affected by inefficiency than others. And there is every reason to ensure that a given quality of service is produced as efficiently as possible. In the case of the Mozart quartet, the notion of the quality of the service is clear: performing the quartet in half the time or with musicians half as qualified would represent a clear deterioration of the quality of the service. Performing the quartet beginning half an hour late would be less efficient than performing it on time. I do not pursue the issues related to quality and inefficiency further in this chapter as they are not intrinsically related to the character of Baumol's 'cost disease', where it is assumed that output is produced efficiently in both the dynamic and the stagnant sectors.

The cost disease has important implications for the financing of public services. It predicts a rising share of the stagnant services in GDP – properly interpreted, this is an indicator of the success of the capitalist economy in driving up productivity growth in other sectors. We can all become better off as a result of falling prices for the goods where productivity growth is fastest. Because of the cheapening of the products of industry, we can more easily afford the products of the stagnant services. But, if the stagnant services are financed through taxation, a higher tax burden is inevitable. Again, this is a sign of success not failure of the economy – the higher tax burden is paid for by the higher living standards that come from the higher productivity growth elsewhere.

The terms 'cost disease' and 'stagnant services' are very unfortunate – the political challenge is to refocus attention on the fact that a more dynamic economy (i.e. higher hourly productivity growth, measured properly in terms of environmental accounting) increases the share of employment in the stagnant services and increases the share of taxation, but raises welfare and living standards more broadly. If the stagnant services are not publicly financed, then, in the absence of offsetting redistributive policy, the cost disease feeds directly into higher inequality. Of course, with a very egalitarian *market* distribution of income, this effect would be mitigated.

A better way of referring to the stagnant services is as labour-absorbing or employment-intensive sectors. The care sector and early childhood education are obvious areas where human contact is intrinsic to the quality of service provided. These sectors could – if the political challenges are won – become thriving areas offering large and growing amounts of employment and decent jobs and careers to many people who do not have the aptitude for or interest in working in the knowledge-based sectors.

A Progressive Economic Strategy

A progressive economic strategy is envisioned as one that delivers a more dynamic, fair and stable economy that competes in open global markets, and where the labour-absorbing sectors both efficiently supply services that people want and are places of growing and rewarding employment. In such an economy, innovation and equality are promoted by asset redistribution and by level-playing-field policies that reduce market income inequality.

A way of looking at the challenges for a progressive economic strategy is to see the complementarity among policies that:

- boost innovation;
- reduce inequality in assets and in market income;
- foster the growth of good jobs in the labour-absorbing service sectors.

Competition policy is one lever that could be used for such ends – reducing monopoly profits by promoting new entry of businesses has the potential to reduce prices (boosting real incomes and reducing market inequality) and to stimulate innovation. The restructuring of the financial sector should not only make it safer, but also direct savings to investment projects in the real economy and encourage highly educated workers to look for fulfilling careers in the non-financial sector. Better-functioning banks should complement more effective competition policy by providing access to credit for business start-ups to a much wider talent pool. These examples highlight the supply-side character of egalitarian policies.

A thriving dynamic sector of the economy is crucial to providing the resources for high-quality labour-absorbing sectors. The dynamic sector is also the tradable sector and in many countries the ability of government policy to help uncover new sources of comparative advantage has been neglected.[9] In the UK, specialisation in tradable financial services has less potential for securing world export market share than was widely believed before the financial crisis. The disappointing response of exports to the substantial depreciation of the UK's real exchange rate in 2009 underscores the importance of policy interventions to restructure tradables. As the examples of the UK and Germany have illustrated, the nature and balance among co-ordinated policies for *innovation, redistribution and labour-absorbing services* will differ across countries.

The political challenge is threefold: to demonstrate the efficiency as well as the fairness benefits of lower inequality; to show that a growing tax share is a sign of success and not failure of the economy, reflecting the dynamism of the economy and its ability to supply care services, healthcare and education to citizens; and to value and welcome the expansion of good career jobs in the labour-absorbing services.

Notes

1. Without implicating them in the views expressed, I am grateful to Sam Bowles, Bob Rowthorn and Philippe Van Parys for useful discussions about these issues.
2. For more detailed discussion, see Wendy Carlin and David Soskice, 'Reforms, macroeconomic policy and economic performance in Germany', in R. Schettkat and J. Langkau (eds), *Economic Policy Proposals for Germany and Europe* (London/New York: Routledge, 2008); Wendy Carlin and David Soskice, 'German economic performance: disentangling the role of supply-side

reforms, macroeconomic policy and coordinated economy institutions', *Socio-Economic Review* 7/1 (2009), pp. 67–99.

3. In 2005, the German government implemented the so-called Hartz-IV reform. This reform was a major overhaul of the welfare system and reduced unemployment benefits substantially.

4. For more detailed discussion, see Raghuram G. Rajan, *Fault Lines: How Hidden Fractures Still Threaten the World Economy* (Princeton: Princeton University Press, 2011); Wendy Carlin, Robert J. Gordon and Robert M. Solow, 'Round table discussion: where is macro going?', in R.M. Solow and J.-P. Touffut (eds), *What's Right with Macroeconomics?* (Cheltenham/Northampton, MA: Edward Elgar, 2012).

5. For a pessimistic view, see Robert J. Gordon, 'Is U.S. economic growth over? Faltering innovation confronts six headwinds' (NBER Working Paper 18315, 2012).

6. For an extended analysis of these issues, see Samuel Bowles, *The New Economics of Inequality and Redistribution* (Cambridge: Cambridge University Press, 2012).

7. For a discussion about Nordic exceptionalism, including comparison with pre-capitalist societies, see Mattia Fochesato and Samuel Bowles, 'Nordic exceptionalism in world historic perspective'. Sante Fe Institute Working Paper, 2013.

8. See William J. Baumol, 'Health care, education and the cost disease: a looming crisis for public choice', *Public Choice* 77 (1993), pp. 17–28.

9. For an example of one way to think about this problem, see Wendy Carlin, 'Good institutions are not enough: ongoing challenges of East German development', *DICE* 9/1 (2011), pp. 28–34.

CHAPTER 11

Lifting Living Standards in an Open Economy

The Danger of Front-Loading Income Inequality

Lane Kenworthy

Over the past decade, the American left has directed a growing share of its attention at income inequality.[1] Indeed, for some, reducing income inequality seems to have become the central goal.

There are compelling reasons to object to America's high and rapidly rising level of income inequality.

One is fairness. Much of what determines a person's earnings and income – intelligence, creativity, physical and social skills, motivation, persistence, confidence, connections, inherited wealth, discrimination – is a product of genetics, parents' assets and traits, and the quality of one's childhood neighbourhood and schools. These aren't chosen; they are a matter of luck. A non-trivial portion of income inequality is therefore undeserved.

Second, income inequality may increase inequality of other valuable things, such as education, health and happiness. Even if we think greater inequality in the distribution of income is acceptable, we may feel that greater inequality in the distribution of health, schooling and subjective well-being is not.

Third, a rise in income inequality contributes to slower absolute income growth for those in the middle and at the bottom.[2]

These, however, are not the rationales commonly put forward for worrying about income inequality. Instead, the most common arguments are that inequality is bad for the economy, overall health, opportunity and democracy. 'Of all the competing and only partially reconcilable ends that we might seek', writes Tony Judt in *Ill Fares the Land*, 'the reduction of inequality must come first. Under conditions of endemic inequality, all other desirable goals become hard to achieve.'[3]

Is that true?

Income Inequality and Economic Growth

In *The Price of Inequality*, Joseph Stiglitz suggests:

> We are paying a high price for the inequality that is increasingly scarring our economy – lower productivity, lower efficiency, lower growth, more instability – and the benefits of reducing this inequality, at least from the current high levels, far outweigh any costs that might be imposed.[4]

Stiglitz outlines some reasonable hypotheses about why income inequality is bad for economic growth. For instance, the rich spend a smaller fraction of their income than the middle class and the poor, so rising inequality may reduce consumer demand. And people may not work as hard if they perceive the distribution of pay and income to be unfair.

What does the evidence say? 'The US grew far faster in the decades after the second world war, when inequality was lower', Stiglitz points out, 'than it did after 1980, since when the gains have gone disproportionately to the top.'[5] However, there are many other differences between these periods that could account for the difference in growth rates. Better to compare the American experience with that of some other countries where inequality did not increase. Denmark and France are good candidates. Neither has had a noteworthy rise in income inequality. The top 1 per cent has not separated from the bottom 99 per cent, nor has the income gap widened within the bottom 99 per cent.[6] From 1947 to 1973, the heart of the postwar golden age, GDP per capita grew at an average annual rate of 2.4 per cent in the US, 3.3 per cent in Denmark and 4.4 per cent in France. Between 1979 and 2007, the growth rate averaged 1.8 per cent in the US, 1.8 per cent in Denmark and 1.5 per cent in France. In other words, economic growth slowed more in the more egalitarian countries. That is not what we would expect to see if inequality is a significant obstacle to economic growth.

According to Stiglitz: 'The bottom line [...] that higher inequality is associated with lower growth – controlling for all other relevant factors

– has been verified by looking at a range of countries and looking over longer periods of time.[7] But in support of this claim he cites just one study, published nearly two decades ago. More recent research has reached varying conclusions about the effect of income inequality on economic growth in rich nations, with few finding that inequality is bad for growth.[8]

Faster economic growth would be a good thing (particularly if with it came a shift towards greener growth). But there is little evidence that the American economy will grow more rapidly if the US manages to reduce income inequality.

Income Inequality and the 2008 Economic Crisis

A related claim is that rising income inequality was a significant cause of the 2008 economic meltdown. Proponents cite three mechanisms, as summarised by Anant Thaker and Elizabeth Williamson:

> (1) sharp increases in debt-to-income ratios among lower- and middle-income households looking to maintain consumption levels as they fall behind in terms of income; (2) the creation of large pools of idle wealth, which increase the demand for investment assets, fuel financial innovation, and increase the size of the financial sector; (3) disproportionate political power for elite financial interests which often yields policies that negatively affect the stability of the financial system.[9]

It will be a while before the causes of the crisis are sorted out, but there are grounds for scepticism about income inequality's contribution.[10] Growing demand for loans by middle- and low-income households may have been driven more by the rising cost of homes and college, along with relaxed lending standards and the availability of second mortgages (home equity loans), than by slow household income growth. Risky lending may have been spurred by the creation of new financial instruments that appeared to spread risk and by an increase in pressure for profits in publicly owned investment firms. Finally, the Federal Reserve could have quashed the housing bubble, the proximate precipitant of the crisis, had it wanted to do so. That it chose not to arguably owed more to the ideological predilections of its chair, Alan Greenspan, than to the political influence of the rich.

Income Inequality and Health

A number of researchers, most prominently Richard Wilkinson and Kate Pickett in their book *The Spirit Level*, argue that income inequality is bad for life expectancy. Inequality is said to increase status competition, which increases stress, thereby shortening lifespan.

This hypothesis has been studied extensively, with the bulk of findings suggesting that income inequality is indeed associated with shorter life expectancy.[11] But virtually all of these studies are cross-sectional. They examine the association between the level of income inequality and the level of life expectancy across nations, regions, counties or cities at a single point in time.

A better approach is to analyse changes across countries.[12] None of the studies that have done so find evidence of a negative association between changes in income inequality and changes in life expectancy. Several relatively comprehensive reviews conclude that the empirical case for an effect of income inequality on life expectancy is very thin.[13]

Income Inequality and Other Social Outcomes

A similar conclusion holds for other social phenomena, including college completion, family stability, safety and happiness. Various claims have been made that income inequality is a key source of worrisome trends in these outcomes. But there is little supportive evidence.[14]

Income Inequality and Opportunity

Alan Krueger, Chair of President Obama's Council of Economic Advisers from 2011 to 2013, has suggested that rising income inequality in the US may have reduced intergenerational income mobility.[15] Krueger's inference is based on the fact that affluent nations with greater income inequality tend to have less mobility (they have a stronger correlation between the earnings of parents and their children). What does this cross-country association tell us about inequality's impact on mobility?

The goal is not high intergenerational mobility per se; it is low inequality of opportunity. Mobility serves as an indicator – not perfect, but not bad – of equality of opportunity. Money ought to be good for children's opportunity. Those growing up in households with higher incomes are more likely to have good health care, low stress, learning-centred pre-schools, good elementary and secondary schools, extracurricular activities that promote cognitive skills and earnings-enhancing non-cognitive traits, and access to a strong university. It would be surprising, therefore, if inequality of parents' incomes did not contribute to inequality of opportunity among their children.

But how large is the effect? After all, money is not the only thing that matters; our abilities and motivations when we reach adulthood also stem from non-monetary influences such as genetics, in-utero development, our parents' habits and behaviours, peers and schooling. In addition, there are diminishing returns to money; beyond a certain point, more parental income probably helps only a little, if at all.

The four Nordic nations – Denmark, Finland, Norway and Sweden – have low inequality and high mobility. At the same time, they have been providing affordable, high-quality early education to a substantial portion of children aged one to five for roughly a generation.[16] James Heckman and Gøsta Esping-Andersen, among others, argue that early education is perhaps the single most valuable thing a society can do to equalise opportunity.[17] The Nordic countries also feature late tracking (streaming) in K–12 schools and heavy subsidies to ensure that college is affordable for all. These public services, rather than low-income inequality, may be the chief reason the Nordic countries have such high intergenerational mobility. If we leave out the Nordic nations, the cross-country association between income inequality and intergenerational mobility remains, but it is quite weak.[18]

Income Inequality and Democracy

The most commonly voiced concern about income inequality in the United States is the fear that it has polluted our politics. Rising inequality is said to do four things: reduce trust in political institutions, reduce voter turnout, increase polarisation between the two parties and increase the influence of the rich on policy-making.[19]

The first two hypotheses do not square with the trends over time in trust and voting. According to data from the American National Elections Studies, trust in government and in the political process in the US began to decline in the 1960s and continued in the 1970s, but changed little during the period of rising income inequality since the 1970s. Voter turnout in presidential elections also declined beginning in the 1960s. But it reached a low point in 1996 and has increased since then. By 2008 it was back up to the level of the early 1960s. Voter turnout in off-year elections has not changed since 1974.

Party polarisation refers to the fact that elected Republican legislators have moved to the right on key economic issues while Democratic legislators have moved to the left. Here, too, the timing is a problem. According to the authoritative study of party polarisation, *Polarised America*, by Nolan McCarty, Keith Poole and Howard Rosenthal:

> In both chambers [the House and the Senate], the Republicans became more moderate until the 1960s and then moved in a sharply conservative direction in the 1970s. The pattern for the Democrats is almost exactly the opposite. Consequently, the two party means [average party positions] moved closer together during the twentieth century until the 1970s and then moved apart.[20]

But income inequality between the top 1 per cent and the bottom 99 per cent did not begin increasing until the 1980s.

What of inequality of political influence? Money clearly matters in American politics.[21] With the richest getting a larger and larger share of the country's income, it is sensible to hypothesise that they have greater success in swaying policy-makers to support their preferences. On the other hand, the influence of money in American politics occurs mainly via lobbying rather than campaign contributions, and lobbying is funded primarily by companies and other organisations rather than by individuals. The amount of money spent on lobbying has increased exponentially in the last few decades.[22] But much of that increase, if not all of it, might well have occurred in the absence of a rise in income inequality.

The most relevant evidence comes from studies by Larry Bartels and Martin Gilens.[23] For the period from 1989 to 1994, Bartels examined the association between senators' votes on proposed policy changes and the opinions of Americans in the lower third, middle third and upper third of income. He found that voting correlated much more closely with the views of those with higher incomes. Gilens extended Bartels' analysis by examining both the Senate and the House of Representatives, and by covering the presidencies of Lyndon Johnson, Ronald Reagan, Bill Clinton and George W. Bush. His finding echoes that of Bartels.

What we need to know, however, is whether this pattern of unequal influence has increased as income inequality has risen. According to Gilens, the association between affluence and influence was weak during the Johnson presidency, strong during the presidencies of Reagan and Clinton, and relatively weak during the presidency of George W. Bush. This is not what the inequality hypothesis predicts, though there may be some confounding factors, such as the 11 September 2001 terrorist attacks, that skew the pattern during the Bush years.

Now, this is by no means a full and complete test of the inequality hypothesis. After all, the well-to-do may exert their influence mainly by keeping proposed reforms from ever coming to a vote and behind-the-scenes shaping of legislation that does pass. It is possible that their growing income share has enhanced their ability to use these kinds of levers. But if this has in fact happened, it has yet to be effectively documented.

In their recent book *Winner-Take-All Politics*, Jacob Hacker and Paul Pierson detail a litany of policy initiatives since the mid-1970s that in their view have had a significant influence – some because they were passed, others because they were blocked – on the degree of income inequality in the US and on the living standards of ordinary Americans. But there is no indication in their account of a steady increase in the tendency of policy to favour the rich.

Reduce Income Inequality, but not Above All Else

I believe, as I said earlier, there are good reasons to object to the high and rising level of income inequality in the US. Yet I fear the American left's recent move to put income inequality reduction front and centre might be harmful rather than helpful. It may foster a conviction that the key to addressing America's social, economic and political problems is to reduce the top 1 per cent's share or the Gini coefficient. That could distract attention from more direct and effective efforts to address those problems.

Such efforts include fully universal health insurance; improvements in eligibility, duration and benefit level for various social-insurance and social-assistance programmes; wage insurance; early education; enhanced financial support for college; a minimum wage indexed to prices; an expanded earned-income tax credit indexed to average compensation; and monetary policy less tilted towards inflation avoidance. Policy changes like these would go a long way towards improving economic security, enhancing opportunity (and mobility) and ensuring shared prosperity in the US. Inequality of political influence could be lessened via direct reforms, such as reversal of the Citizens United decision, introduction of a strong transparency rule and public funding for congressional election campaigns.

Developments in the UK under the New Labour governments from 1997 to 2010 are illustrative. Among rich countries, the UK has one of the highest levels of income inequality, and inequality continued to rise under New Labour (though less rapidly than in prior decades). Yet, through a variety of new programmes and changes to existing policies, those governments achieved one of the best records of any affluent nation over the past generation in improving economic security, opportunity and living standards for middle-class and poor households.[24]

In the US, policy changes such as these will require more tax revenue. Here lies another troublesome consequence of a focus on inequality reduction: a sizeable portion of the American left has come to think of taxation solely in terms of its redistributive impact. The aim of tax reform, in this view, should be to reduce income inequality. The change many favour is higher tax rates on the top 1 per cent or 5 per cent. Yet while that may reduce income inequality, it will not provide the US government with anywhere near the money it needs to do the sorts of things I've just mentioned. Instead, the chief aim should be to increase revenues. In my estimation, the US ought to be thinking about how to get an additional 10 per cent of GDP in coming decades, and that cannot be done by increasing the taxes of just those at the top.[25]

Some of the programmes I've mentioned would help to reduce income inequality by boosting the incomes of households on the lower and middle rungs of the income ladder. Indeed, focusing on economic security, opportunity and rising living standards might be the most effective route to lessening income inequality. The American public has never shown much appetite for income redistribution. Even during the past three decades, as income inequality has shot up, the main detectable reaction among Americans has been a desire to expand programmes that focus on opportunity.[26] That does not mean it is impossible to take steps to reduce inequality in the market distribution or to increase redistribution. It means programmes that do this are more likely to be supported if they are not marketed as a means to achieve income-inequality reduction.

Other programmes I listed above are public services. Though child-care, schooling and health care do not reduce the measured degree of income inequality, since they do not change household incomes, they do reduce inequality of living standards.[27]

Income inequality is too high in the US. It would be good to reduce it. But it is a mistake, in my view, to put inequality reduction at the top of the agenda.

Notes

1.   Paul Krugman, 'For richer', *New York Times Magazine* (2002); Kevin Phillips, *Wealth and Democracy* (Broadway Books, 2002); Lawrence R. Jacobs et al., 'American democracy in an age of rising inequality', *Perspectives on Politics* 2 (2004); Robert H. Frank, *Falling Behind: How Rising Inequality Harms the Middle Class* (University of California Press, 2007); Paul Krugman, *The Conscience of a Liberal* (W.W. Norton, 2007); Robert B. Reich, *Supercapitalism* (Knopf, 2007); Larry Bartels, *Unequal Democracy* (Princeton University Press, 2008); Benjamin Page and Lawrence Jacobs, *Class War? What Americans Really Think about Economic Inequality* (University of Chicago Press, 2009); Jacob S. Hacker and Paul Pierson, *Winner-Take-All Politics* (Simon and Schuster, 2010); Robert B. Reich, *Aftershock* (Knopf, 2010); Rebecca M. Blank, *Changing Inequality* (University of California Press, 2011); Tony Judt, *Ill Fares the Land* (Penguin, 2011); Barack Obama, 'Remarks by the President on the

economy in Osawatomie, Kansas', 6 December 2011; Paul Pierson, 'Inequality and its casualties', *Democracy* Spring (2011); Lawrence Summers, 'We have to do better on inequality', *Financial Times* (20 November 2011); Jared Bernstein, 'Inequality, the middle class, and growth', *On the Economy* (30 January 2012); Heather Boushey and Adam S. Hersh, 'The American middle class, income inequality, and the strength of our economy', Center for American Progress (2012); James Galbraith, *Inequality and Instability* (Oxford University Press, 2012); Alex Gibney, *Park Avenue: Money, Power, and the American Dream* (Democracy Pictures, Steps International, the BBC, DR, ZDF/Arte, Arte G.E.I.E., NHK, NRK, SVT, VPRO, YLE, the Open University, and ITVS International, 2012); Martin Gilens, *Affluence and Influence* (Princeton University Press, 2012); Christopher Hayes, *Twilight of the Elites* (Crown, 2012); John Judis, 'Rein in the rich: How higher taxes could lift the Economy', *New Republic* (12 December 2012); Nicholas Kristof, 'A failed experiment', *New York Times* (21 November 2012); Alan B. Krueger, 'The rise and consequences of Inequality', Council of Economic Advisers (12 January 2012); Annie Lowrey, 'Income inequality may take toll on economic growth', *New York Times* (16 October 2012); Timothy Noah, *The Great Divergence* (Bloomsbury Press, 2012); Isabel V. Sawhill, 'Are we headed toward a permanently divided society?', CCF Brief 448 (Brookings Institution, 2012); Hedrick Smith, *Who Stole the American Dream?* (Random House, 2012); Joseph E. Stiglitz, *The Price of Inequality* (W.W. Norton, 2012).

2. Lane Kenworthy, 'Has rising inequality reduced middle-class income growth?', in Janet C. Gornick and Markus Jäntti (eds), *Income Inequality: Economic Disparities and the Middle Class in Affluent Countries* (Stanford University Press, 2013).

3. Judt, *Ill Fares the Land*, p. 184.

4. Stiglitz, *The Price of Inequality*, p. 177.

5. Joseph E. Stiglitz, 'America is no longer a land of Opportunity', *Financial Times* (26 June 2012).

6. Christopher Jencks and Lane Kenworthy, *Should We Worry about Inequality?* (Yale University Press and Russell Sage Foundation, forthcoming).

7. Stiglitz, *The Price of Inequality*, p. 177.
8. Sarah Voitchovsky, 'Does the profile of income inequality matter for economic growth?', Working Paper 354 (Luxembourg Income Study, 2003); Lane Kenworthy, *Egalitarian Capitalism* (Russell Sage Foundation, 2004); Dan Andrews, Christopher Jencks and Andrew Leigh, 'Do rising top incomes lift all boats?', *B.E. Journal of Economic Analysis and Policy* 11 (2011); Jencks and Kenworthy, *Should We Worry about Inequality?*
9. Anant A. Thaker and Elizabeth C. Williamson, 'Unequal and unstable: The relationship between inequality and financial crises', *New America Foundation* (2012), p. 1. See also Branko Milanovic, 'Income inequality and speculative investment by the rich and poor in America led to the financial meltdown', *Yale Global Online* (2009); Joseph E. Stiglitz, 'Drunk driving on the US's road to recovery', *Real Clear Politics* (9 January 2009); Michael Kumhof and Romain Ranciere, 'Inequality, leverage, and crises', Working Paper 10-268 (International Monetary Fund, 2010); Raghuram G. Rajan, *Fault Lines* (Princeton University Press, 2010); Reich, *Aftershock*.
10. Anthony B. Atkinson and Salvatore Morelli, 'Inequality and banking crises: A first look', Oxford University (2010); Edward Glaeser, 'Does economic inequality cause crises?', *New York Times: Economix* (14 December 2010); Michael D. Bordo and Christopher M. Meissner, 'Does inequality lead to a financial crisis?', Working Paper 17896 (National Bureau of Economic Research, 2012).
11. Naoki Kondo, Grace Sembajwe, Ichiro Kawachi, Rob M. van Dam, S.V. Subramanian and Zentaro Yamagata, 'Income inequality, mortality, and self-rated health: Meta-analysis of multilevel studies', *BMJ* 339 (2009); Richard Wilkinson and Kate Pickett, *The Spirit Level: Why Greater Equality Makes Societies Stronger* (Bloomsbury Press, 2009).
12. Ken Judge, Jo-Ann Mulligan and Michaela Benzeval, 'Income inequality and population health', *Social Science and Medicine* 46 (1997); Gary Burtless and Christopher Jencks, 'American inequality and its consequences', in Henry Aaron, Pietro S. Nivola and James M. Lindsay (eds), *Agenda for the Nation* (Brookings Institution, 2003); Jason Beckfield, 'Does income inequality harm health? New

cross-national evidence', *Journal of Health and Social Behavior* 45 (2004); Andrew Leigh and Christopher Jencks, 'Inequality and mortality: Long-run evidence from a panel of countries', *Journal of Health Economics* 26 (2007); Andrew Leigh, Christopher Jencks and Timothy M. Smeeding, 'Health and economic inequality', in Wiemer Salverda, Brian Nolan and Timothy M. Smeeding (eds), *The Oxford Handbook of Economic Inequality* (Oxford University Press, 2009).

13. Angus Deaton, 'Health, inequality, and economic development', *Journal of Economic Literature* 41 (2003); John Lynch, George Davey Smith, Sam Harper, Marianne Hillemeier, Nancy Ross, George A. Kaplan and Michael Wolfson, 'Is income inequality a determinant of population health? Part 1. A systematic review', *Milbank Quarterly* 82 (2004); John Mullahy, Stephanie Robert and Barbara Wolfe, 'Health, income, and inequality', in Kathryn M. Neckerman (ed.), *Social Inequality* (Russell Sage Foundation, 2004); Leigh, Jencks and Smeeding, 'Health and economic inequality'.

14. Burtless and Jencks, 'American inequality and its consequences'; Jencks and Kenworthy, *Should We Worry about Inequality?*

15. See also Miles Corak, 'How to slide down the "Great Gatsby Curve": Inequality, life chances, and public policy in the United States', Center for American Progress (2012); Bernstein, 'Inequality, the middle class, and growth'; Sawhill, 'Are we headed toward a permanently divided society?'; Stiglitz, *The Price of Inequality*.

16. OECD, *Starting Strong II: Early Childhood Education and Care*, 2006.

17. James J. Heckman, 'Schools, skills, and synapses', Working Paper 14064 (National Bureau of Economic Research, 2008); Gøsta Esping-Andersen, *The Incomplete Revolution* (Polity, 2008).

18. The r-squared from a simple (one-variable) regression is 0.47 with the Nordic nations included and 0.16 without them. For more detail, see Lane Kenworthy, 'Inequality, mobility, opportunity', *Consider the Evidence* (31 January 2012).

19. Krugman, 'For richer'; Jacobs et al., 'American democracy in an age of rising inequality'; Krugman, *The Conscience of a Liberal*; Paul Krugman and Robin Wells, 'Economy killers: Inequality and GOP ignorance', *Salon* (15 April 2012); Stiglitz, *The Price of Inequality*.

20. Nolan McCarty, Keith T. Poole and Howard Rosenthal, *Polarized America* (MIT Press, 2008), p. 27.
21. Jacobs et al., 'American democracy in an age of rising inequality'.
22. Center for Responsive Politics, www.opensecrets.org/lobby.
23. Bartels, *Unequal Democracy*; Gilens, *Affluence and Influence*.
24. John Hills, Tom Sefton and Kitty Stewart (eds), *Towards a More Equal Society? Poverty, Inequality, and Policy since 1997* (Policy Press, 2009); Jane Waldfogel, *Britain's War on Poverty* (Russell Sage Foundation, 2010); Lane Kenworthy, *Progress for the Poor* (Oxford University Press, 2011); Lane Kenworthy, 'When does economic growth benefit people on low-to-middle incomes – and why?', Resolution Foundation (2011).
25. Lane Kenworthy, *Social Democratic America* (Oxford University Press, forthcoming 2014).
26. Leslie McCall and Lane Kenworthy, 'Americans' social policy preferences in the era of rising inequality', *Perspectives on Politics* 7 (2009); Leslie McCall, *The Undeserving Rich* (Cambridge University Press, 2013).
27. Gøsta Esping-Andersen and John Myles, 'Economic inequality and the welfare state', in Wiemer Salverda, Brian Nolan and Timothy M. Smeeding (eds), *The Oxford Handbook of Economic Inequality* (Oxford University Press, 2009); Kenworthy, *Progress for the Poor*, ch. 7.

CHAPTER 12

Recreating Solidarity via Social Citizenship

Why It Is not Enough to Tax the Rich

Jane Jenson

One of the pernicious legacies of neo-liberalism has been the popularisation of the neo-liberals' normative vision of society as composed of two groups: a large majority of 'good citizens' who are responsible, autonomous and depend only on market and family relations for their well-being; and a minority that does not take responsibility for itself and even lives off government largesse. A corollary of this societal vision has been the notion that taxes should be kept as low as possible so as to reward effort and to leave good citizens with the wherewithal to make their own choices. From the perspective of neo-liberalism, good citizens should pay only the minimum in taxes. With fewer resources, because of reduced revenues, states would obviously have to make cuts in public spending. This ideological commitment to a less active state and to maximising choice implied any social-policy interventions were supposed to be carefully targeted, designed so as to induce everyone to become more responsible. In the meantime, governments systematically reduced their own resources by cutting tax rates.

The mantra of 'no new taxes' dominated political discourse in Europe and North America throughout the neo-liberal years. Political parties hoping to govern, on the left as well as the right, subscribed to this chant.

In the European Union (EU) through the 2000s, the average tax on labour in member states was on a downward trend.[1] These cuts were meant to foster job creation. A second tax-cutting trend also swept the OECD world. The average top personal income tax (PIT) rate among OECD countries was cut significantly between 1980 (65.7 per cent) and 2000 (46.5 per cent) and had fallen even lower by 2010 (41.7 per cent).[2] Thus, what since 2001 have in America been familiarly called the 'Bush tax cuts', which benefited high-income earners in the US, were not unique by any means. Across the EU, both the top PIT rates and the rates on corporate income were also reduced dramatically between 1995 and 2008. In the EU-27 the top PIT rate fell from 47.4 per cent in 1995 to 37.9 per cent in 2008, while the tax rate on corporate income plummeted from 35.3 per cent to 24 per cent.[3]

Not surprisingly, then, the tax-to-GDP ratio dropped, despite healthy economic growth rates. As reported by Eurostat, the 'level of the total tax-to-GDP ratio in 2008 was slightly below the 2000 level'.[4] In other words, even as growth rates climbed after 2004, revenues did not increase as much as they would have in the past, because tax rates were lower. When growth deteriorated after 2008, governments quickly found themselves called on to do more with less.

Having placed a cap on their own income, many left and centre-left parties tried to pull off a juggling feat. They promised to improve social policy (and make other progressive spending decisions), all the while keeping taxes low or reducing them more. The idea was to target social policy to the 'truly needy' on the margins of society, thereby limiting social exclusion, promoting social inclusion and avoiding threats to social cohesion.

A Society of the 'Middle Class' and the Poor

In the neo-liberal portrayal of society as composed of a core and its margins, there was little space for political parties to promote social solidarity across classes. The core was represented as a large and responsible group of citizens who were most appropriately left with their own resources to make their own choices. This idea of the core has become, in the incessantly repeated term of American political discourse in the 2012 elections, 'the middle class'. Or, as Tony Blair once put it, 'we're all middle class' now.

In political discourse before 2008, it was those at the margins who were falling away. This group was represented primarily as the 'poor' or disadvantaged rather than the working class, as in the old days. Indeed, one of the prime descriptors of the poor was their 'worklessness', and therefore the need for policies to promote work and to 'activate' appeared self-evident. Nor in this vision were the poor a homogeneous category; they might be lone parents, youth, immigrants, urban dwellers or even the working poor.

A left and centre-left strategy based on this representation of a society *without* classes but *with* social problems fundamentally altered notions and practices of social citizenship, in three ways. First, it reinforced the neo-liberals' view that paying taxes, and certainly paying *more* taxes, was to be avoided as a matter of principle; everyone needed to be able to choose how to look after her or his own needs. Taxes became a burden to be borne rather than the means to share social risk.

At the same time, the move away from universal provision in the design of many social programmes as well as the declining quality of many public services (which suffered from lack of adequate investment) meant that citizens often found themselves having to pay (and often much more) for services such as education, health, pensions, childcare and so on. These services were private, not social rights. People's investment in their children's future in particular became a serious worry, as the price of university soared in many places and high-quality, affordable childcare was often in short supply. Private schooling also increased in many countries. But, at the same time, these citizens saw their tax dollars used to provide at least minimal and sometimes improved services to the poor and disadvantaged, in the name of social cohesion and even social investment.

Third, the restructuring of capitalism brought a much-documented and massive increase in inequality. Economists tracked rising Gini coefficients, but ordinary citizens lived this social transformation as they struggled even harder to buy quality services for themselves and their children. If monetary and credit policies could be used to induce investments in the housing market – which eventually ended in many countries with the burst bubble after 2008 – the rising cost of private and privatised services meant that families and individuals had even more trouble investing in their own needs.

Austerity Can Be a Political Choice

At the same time, governments were tying their own hands by reducing tax rates. Reductions in tax revenues through the 2000s were generated by political decisions to back off: to lower tax rates on the wealthy and on the costs of labour. When the economy did well mid-decade, the money was left in citizens' pockets. Governments then complained of being too strapped for funds to spend. And, when the crisis hit, they were indeed in trouble. Moreover, even when the picture improved in 2009 and 2010, revenues were still less than they might have been.

By 2010, tax-to-GDP ratios had not returned to the levels of the 1990s. Calculations document that the problem was not only one of lower economic growth. Even after the effects of the business cycle are factored in, the effective revenue rates did not reach the earlier levels.[5] This pattern results from tax cutting. There has been a downward convergence of tax-to-GDP ratios, as the higher-taxing countries moved towards the lower ratios in the EU, these often being found in the newest member states.[6]

This pattern reminds us that public finances are the result of two kinds of choices: how much money to spend but also how much money to collect.

Some New Taxes – At the Top

After 2008 the refrain of 'no new taxes' lost its lustre. This shift occurred in part because of political mobilisation and in part because of the needs created by the post-2008 financial crisis. Political activists and commentators railed against the massive rise of inequality that benefited the very rich much more than anyone else.

Across Europe and North America, in 2011, the Occupy Movement exposed the shift in the Gini with accessible language and images. It protested the fact that the massive increase in wealth at the top had created steeply rising inequality that left the rest of society – the 99 per cent – struggling far behind. In many ways this representation was the mirror opposite of neo-liberalism's vision of the 'middle class' and the poor on the margins. This time the excessively wealthy were the margin, different from everyone else.

An analysis of both wealth inequality and income inequality motivated the Occupy and other anti-austerity movements' demands – which varied widely from place to place, to be sure – for everything from bank regulation and caps on executive earnings to forgiving student loans and limiting offshore production and its accompanying job losses. The absence of clearly articulated demands resulted from the form and strategy of the movement, which refused to make them. But it also came from the absence of any agreed-upon political principles for moving beyond diagnosis to action.

There was, however, some agreement on the need to augment some tax revenues. Very popular was the 'Robin Hood tax' on financial transactions, while London's Occupy movement mobilised dramatically against corporate tax practices. Both these demands received support from political authorities. In Britain the debate often turned to tax 'evasion' (usually the legal use of loopholes) by large corporations, with Amazon, Google and Starbucks targeted. The European Commission and Parliament developed a proposal for a financial transaction tax, justified as one instrument that would allow banks to pay back cash-strapped governments for the support given to the financial sector after 2008.

Many European governments began adjusting their tax claims, usually by updating the cut-offs for tax brackets as well as increasing rates at the top. This was done sometimes with great fanfare and sometimes quite quietly. France lost one of its most famous citizens to the measure for fiscal justice promised by François Hollande in the 2012 presidential election; Gérard Depardieu moved his residence to Belgium and then accepted the offer of Russian citizenship rather than pay the 75 per cent surcharge on the portion of his income above €1 million. Pollsters found that, though ordinary French citizens 'could understand' his decision to move to Belgium's less onerous tax regime, eight out of ten nonetheless believed that it was legitimate for the government to demand more taxes from the very rich.[7]

Since the 2008 crisis there has been a broad trend in the EU to increase top PIT rates, and cuts to corporate income tax rates have virtually halted (although the Eastern European countries tend not to follow the trend). After 2008, eight of the EU-15 countries increased their top PIT rate, including both France (as mentioned) and the UK, the latter deciding on a significant increase to 50 per cent (10 percentage points higher than the previous minimum) in 2010. Germany had just made a major change in early 2008, increasing the top rate to 45 per cent.[8]

It at first appeared that the US might follow suit and raise tax rates on the wealthy. In exit polls after the presidential and congressional elections in November 2012, 60 per cent of American voters said that taxes should go up. Almost 50 per cent set the cutting point for 'making the rich pay' higher taxes at an income of $250,000 for a couple. This definition of 'the rich' would have put the US in line with definitions of high income in the EU.[9] Despite Barack Obama's use of the same cutting point in his campaign (which the polls appeared to validate), when the dust settled after the negotiations to avoid the fiscal cliff on 1 January 2013, income taxes went up only for the very, very wealthy.[10] The tax rate increased for those making more than $400,000 ($450,000 for couples) from 35 per cent to 39.5 per cent. The cuts to income taxes introduced by President Bush stayed in place for everyone else.[11]

Despite the populist appeal of making the rich pay more, this single change is inadequate as the primary strategy for moving ahead for tough times.

Of course, the roll-back of tax cuts is helpful, allowing treasuries to recoup some of the generous benefits they handed out in the heady days of the neo-liberal era. Nonetheless, a political strategy based simply on 'making the rich pay' and continuing to treat tax paying as a kind of taboo is insufficient for several reasons.

There are Simply not Enough 'Rich' to Fill the Gap

The first reason the strategy is insufficient is a pragmatic one. Figure 12.1 indicates the amount of revenue that *would have been* added if Congress had accepted President Obama's proposal for increasing the PIT rate for couples earning above $250,000. While the additional $56.3 billion in revenue would have helped reduce the deficit, it was clearly too limited on its own. Moreover, not even this compromise passed

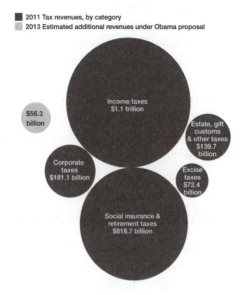

FIGURE 12.1 How taxing the wealthy stacks up.
Source: NPR, 'The value of taxing the wealthy: $56 billion' (Planet Money, 11 July 2012). Available at www.npr.org/blogs/money/2012/07/11/156577573/the-value-of-taxing-the-wealthy-56-billion (accessed 6 May 2013).

Congress as the fiscal cliff deadline loomed. Only the very, very rich saw their income taxes rise. Therefore, revenues will increase even less than in this estimate.

Of course, top PIT rates could and probably should be higher than they are currently in many countries. A return to the rates of the 1980s is no doubt a good idea. But, while increasing the contributions of the wealthiest is certainly a *necessary* component of any way forward in post-2008 progressive politics, it is not enough. It does not raise enough income to make a real change in government finances. Moreover, it does little to halt and reverse the rising inequalities across the world so carefully mapped by the OECD in its studies *Growing Unequal* (2008) and *Divided We Stand: Why Inequality Keeps Rising* (2011).

Moreover, as demonstrated by both the silliness of the discussion of the Depardieu *affaire* in France (provoked by the Socialist president) and the inability of a newly relected Democratic president to prevail over

Congress, this focus degenerates quickly into populism, and progressives often lose. A focus on the unfairness perpetrated on the 99 per cent or the 99.1 per cent does nothing to challenge or reverse the worldview drawn from neo-liberal ideology that taxes are in and of themselves to be minimised.

The reasons for having taxes have been lost in the swing by some lefts towards the premises of neo-liberalism. The language of sharing risk among citizens needs to be brushed off and modernised so that state revenues can be brought back to a level that allows them to address social choices.

The Case for Raising Taxes in Order to Spend Better

The conversation needs to change such that taxes are defined as tools for redistributing income, to be sure. But taxes are the tools we have for expressing collective choices about social citizenship and well-being.

Now that tax increases are happening, it is essential to get the story straight. There are two dangers to avoid. The first is the possibility that the discussion will be allowed to be hijacked by the misery of countries such as Greece and Spain, where the least well off are being forced to pay for the past and egregious errors (and even sometimes corruption) of their leaders. Raising taxes in the context of massive unemployment is neither an effective nor a fair strategy. A fairer tax regime will not – *pace* the Romney Republicans – turn the US into Greece.

The second danger to avoid is one in which the swinging political pendulum redefines taxes simply as a populist tool for punishing the rich. It is too easy to rail against Wall Street and the City for their benefits packages (which are unacceptable!) while leaving aside real issues of social solidarity across all of society.

Both of these dangers can be avoided if government revenues (in other words, taxes) are carefully described as the grounding for social citizenship and the means for making collective choices. There are a number of arguments that progressives can make to explain why taxes benefit everyone, as well as explanations about how the current tax situation can be corrected.

Paying Taxes is a Social Right

Put this way, the statement does sound peculiar. Nonetheless, there are two ways that the years of neo-liberalism undermined the simple idea that everyone should be *able* to contribute to democratic decisions about collective choices and build social citizenship. The first was, of course, restructured employment, in which many people were excluded from participation in work or were paid so poorly for their work that they did not climb above the minimum level for having their income taxed. Of course, as consumers, everyone pays VAT-type taxes, and in many cases even low-wage earners have payroll taxes deducted by their employers. However, moving towards a society in which employment is not only spread more widely but also much better paid – as the calls for 'predistribution' argue – would allow many more citizens to visibly and transparently exercise a real social right of participation.

Sharing Risk is a Principle of Fairness

One of the enduring truths of collective life for centuries has been that there are real advantages not only to helping one's fellows but also to sharing the costs of that aid. Friendly societies and mutuals provided the example of how to prepare for life's inevitable burdens by paying something in advance and using the accumulated capital to look out for those in need when their catastrophe struck – whether in the form of the death of a breadwinner, the cost of a funeral or unemployment. Social-insurance regimes, whether for unemployment or pensions, carry on that tradition. But they are under assault. In their place we now often find tax expenditures or deductions that encourage and reward private savings and the accumulation of privately held wealth.

This strategy of not collecting taxes has consequences.

Pension experts correctly point out the advantages of having retirement-income systems standing on several pillars. But the size and reach of each can be usefully discussed. For example, are the massive tax expenditures – that is, tax revenue foregone by deductions on tax liability against private savings – that support both private savings and the financial firms that organise pension funds and investments in stocks or other financial instruments the best way to provide reliable and fair retirement incomes? Might better outcomes in terms both of greater equality and greater stability be provided by reducing tax expenditures and investing tax revenues in public pension regimes? This is a discussion that could be launched by progressives in the name both of fairness and better outcomes for all. Such a discussion, moreover, helps to exhibit a commitment to older citizens without necessarily committing a greater portion of the budget to them, at the expense of other social groups.

Providing Public Services Redistributes Income and Benefits Everyone

A fairer tax regime is one that provides quality services in exchange for taxes paid. The least solidaristic arrangement and the least likely to promote social citizenship is one in which citizens both pay taxes and are compelled to purchase their own services in the private market. This is what neo-liberal policies did in many countries, particularly for families with children.

Any 'social investment' strategy has to be carefully designed to ensure that the quality services – whether investments in human capital (childcare, schooling, university, etc.) or others – are provided to all citizens who can and wish to use them.[12] Concentrating social investments on the 'disadvantaged' simply perpetuates a vision of society in which there is a deep cleavage between those who are supposedly responsible and those who must be helped to become so. Social investments are, at their best, investments that will benefit the whole of society and, therefore, allow all parents to take advantage of services as a social right.

These three themes, taken up seriously by progressives and linked to other proposals for distributing employment income and services more fairly, would help to move progressive politics away from the pernicious legacies of the neo-liberal era and towards a more promising future.

Notes

1. Eurostat, *Taxation Trends in the European Union* (Luxembourg: Publications Office of the EU, 2012), p. 35. Available at http://

ec.europa.eu/taxation_customs/taxation/gen_info/economic_ analysis/tax_structures/index_en.htm (accessed 6 May 2013).

2. OECD, 'Tax: the average tax burden on earnings in OECD countries continues to rise' (25 April 2012). Available at www.oecd.org/newsroom/ taxtheaveragetaxburdenonearningsinoecdcountriescontinuesto rise.htm (accessed 6 May 2013).

3. Eurostat, *Taxation Trends*, 2012, pp. 33, 36. While the new member states actively reduced tax rates, so too did the Nordic countries. For example, Sweden reduced its top PIT rate between 1995 and 2008 from 61.3 per cent to 56.4 per cent and Finland went from 62.2 per cent to 50.1 per cent. Denmark too reduced its top rate, but less so (from 65.7 per cent to 62.3 per cent), while Norway made little change to its already low rate (from 41.7 per cent to 40 per cent). Throughout these years of Conservative and Labour governments, the UK retained its own rate at only 40 per cent.

4. Eurostat, *Taxation Trends in the European Union: Main Results* (Luxembourg: Publications Office of the EU, 2010), p. 5. Available at http://ec.europa.eu/taxation_customs/resources/documents/taxation/ gen_info/economic_analysis/tax_structures/2010/2010_main_ results_en.pdf (accessed 6 May 2013).

5. Eurostat, *Taxation Trends*, 2012, p. 20.

6. Ibid., pp. 22–3.

7. This was an IFOP (Institut français d'opinion publique) poll for *Le Figaro* conducted in December 2012. 'Les Français "comprennent" Gérard Depardieu' (20 December 2012). Available at www.lefigaro. fr/actualite-france/2012/12/20/01016-20121220ARTFIG00677-les-francais-comprennent-gerard-depardieu.php (accessed 6 May 2013).

8. The value added tax (VAT) has also increased significantly in many member states since the crisis (Eurostat, *Taxation Trends*, 2012, pp. 31–2). After 2008 about half the EU member states raised the VAT rate, with, for example, the UK going from 15 per cent to 20 per cent (Eurostat, *Taxation Trends*, 2012, p. 10).

9. In 2012, for example, the highest tax bracket and rate were above €250,000 and 45 per cent in Germany, above £150,000 and 50 per cent in the UK, and above €181, 000 (SEK 574,300) and 50 per cent

in Sweden. The $250,000 converts to about €188,000, while $400,000 is about €300,000.

10. Payroll taxes had been cut as a stimulus measure in 2011 and 2012. This measure expired and the 2 per cent increase in payroll taxes meant that all the employed would see a decline in take-home pay.

11. There were, however, much less publicised increases to taxes on investment income for those in the top *two* income brackets.

12. Jane Jenson and Denis Saint-Martin, 'New routes to social cohesion? Citizenship and the social investment state', *Canadian Journal of Sociology* 28/1 (2003), pp. 77–99.

CHAPTER 13

The Emerging Intergenerational Conflict

Social Investment and New Forms of Redistribution

Bruno Palier

M any European countries are on the edge of an intergenerational conflict that could hit home forcefully in the coming years. The political residue of fiscal contraction has sparked a situation in which pensioners seem to be against making collective sacrifices to their living standards, while younger people are increasingly frustrated with the opportunities afforded to them by their government and political class. At the heart of the divide lies the fact that public spending on healthcare and pensions, which primarily benefit the elderly, is disproportionately higher than spending on childcare, education and training, which by nature are geared more towards younger generations.

Investing now in children and younger generations would, however, have a triple benefit:

1. It would reach those who need the most social support these days (during the past two decades, poverty has shifted from the elderly to the younger generation).
2. It would lay the foundations to enable the future tax base to finance pension and health expenditure. Social policies for the young should not be classified as 'passive' income support but rather as investment in human capital, as delivery of emancipating and 'capacitating' services (such as childcare, education and training) and as a way to prepare younger generations for new economic realities.
3. It would have the potential to reconcile younger generations with social democratic parties and governments, were they to offer and develop these policies.

The reality is that young people today are not at all seduced by the promises of centre-left parties.

New Intergenerational Inequalities Call for New Forms of Redistribution

Over the past two decades an overwhelming consensus has emerged
around the need to tackle growing inequality. However, most debates
focus merely on income inequalities, and especially inequalities between
those at the top of the income scale and the rest of the population. Yet,
other types of inequalities have increased, and, crucially for social
democracy, they call into question the purpose and structure of current
welfare state settlements and their reforms.

Although the most visible trend described by a recent OECD study
is rising 'inequality […] generally due to the rich improving their
incomes relative both to low- and middle-income people', less discussed
are mounting inequalities between generations and age groups. As
the OECD study also points out: 'the risk of poverty for older people
has fallen, while poverty of young adults and families with children
has risen'.[1] Within the cohort of 'young adults and families with children', those particularly hit are children born in work-poor families
and unskilled young people (especially women, single mothers and
migrants). Moreover, during the crisis, elderly pensioners are faring
much better than young people (see Figure 13.1). Despite these changes
in the distribution of poverty and life-chances, the redistributive structure of our welfare states has not changed. Worse still, expenditure is
increasingly concentrated on the elderly.

We still have old-age-biased welfare states. It is clearly the older generations that benefit most from welfare spending. In almost all OECD
countries, pensions and health care are the two biggest social spending
budgets.

Over recent decades, we have seen an increase in welfare state spending targeted at older generations. While public expenditure on pensions
increased from 6.6 per cent of GDP to 8.3 per cent on average between
1980 and 2007 in the 21 richest OECD countries, public expenditure on
education decreased from 5.6 per cent to 4.8 per cent of GDP during

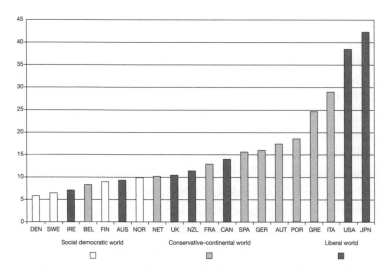

FIGURE 13.1   Elderly/non elderly spending ratio, average 1985 to 2000.
Source: Julia Lynch, *Age in the Welfare State* (Cambridge: Cambridge University Press, 2006), p. 5.

the same period. Meanwhile, spending on vocational training diminished almost everywhere (even in Nordic countries). This, of course, reflects demographic changes in our societies, characterised by the fact that people are living longer (hence benefiting from longer pension periods) and by the fact that more people are retiring (baby boomers have been lucky enough to work at a time of exceptional growth with almost no unemployment, and have thus had full careers entitling them to expensive pensions). In parallel, fertility has gone down, leading to a shrinking active population that is encountering more difficulties in the labour market (the tax base is smaller). Spending may well be driven by demography. Nevertheless, it does not have an answer to the emergence of a new set of corrosive social problems. In most of Europe, the poor are no longer the elderly but rather the young and children.

Should we just let things go, and see expenditure driven by demography rather than by political choice or social justice? Should we, in the spirit of austerity, accept the increased needs of the elderly and collectively do nothing for the younger generations? This is indeed a crucial political dilemma for the European social democratic parties.

The political reality is that those who could contribute more to the welfare state (baby boomers) are increasingly numerous and important voters; and they are also more likely to vote on election day. They feel that they deserve their social benefits (they, indeed, worked and paid for them) and they do not feel selfish since most of them do take care of their children and grandchildren (and sometimes also of their frail parents).

Still, should redistribution really be organised within families, letting rich grandparents dutifully help their grandchildren with generous sums while their poorer elderly counterparts are unable to help theirs? Do these types of intergenerational intra-family transfers not contribute to reproducing social inequalities? Behind this question of social justice and redistribution there is a political question as well. Should social democrats become the parties of baby boomers, only defending those who benefit from the best social democratic invention so far (the postwar Keynesian welfare state) without reaching out to new constituencies who are encountering difficulties in the labour market and are poorly represented and little looked after?

The Sacrificed Groups of Current Welfare Systems

Average unemployment levels have increased since the early 1970s by 5–10 percentage points and have more or less stabilised between 5 and 15 per cent since the 1980s. With the crisis, certain countries are reaching unprecedented levels of unemployment. Moreover, the share of atypical employment in the overall OECD workforce (part-time and fixed-term combined) has grown from an average of around 10 per cent in the early 1970s to 25–35 per cent. More and more individuals are at a particularly high risk of being in atypical employment (short-term contracts, or interim or undesired part-time jobs) or unemployment. This means low levels of pay, low levels of social benefits and low levels of employment protection.

In terms of social protection, there is an increasing dualism between, on the one hand, individuals covered through comprehensive public or statutory social protection (often complemented or supplemented by private or occupational social protection to a level that maintains living standards) and, on the other, those that have to rely on modest (largely means-tested) public provision, primarily intended to alleviate poverty.

Certain groups are over-represented among those outsiders in all OECD countries: women, young labour-market participants, low-skilled workers (especially in the service sector), immigrants and migrant workers. These groups are more likely to be unemployed or atypically employed, and they are more likely to be poor and to suffer from insufficient social rights. The available evidence suggests that their lower status has been consistent over time. And yet governments have increased spending on the elderly and on health, and decreased spending on youth (in education) and on the unskilled (in training).

In order to address these new inequalities, we need to rewrite the social contract between generations and invest massively in childhood and youth services.

Does this mean adding to the welfare state burden, next to already-existing social expenditure? Not so much if those who can contribute do so – not only the very rich but also new pensioners, who continue to benefit from fiscal derogations created for their much poorer predecessors despite the fact that they are not so poor anymore themselves. Furthermore, in a longer perspective, it has to be recognised that spending on children and young people does not constitute 'sunk social costs' ,but rather qualifies as social investment. Here, social justice coincides with economic efficiency.

Indeed, providing all children and young people with much-needed qualifications is also an employment policy at a time when qualifications are required to succeed in knowledge-based economies. Providing such opportunities in a fair and equal way means preparing the future for all, and thus building better and fairer societies in line with social democratic principles.

Under-Qualification is a Pressing Social Risk

In today's economy, qualifications are more important than ever, especially in view of the increasing needs of new sectors of employment (such as 'green jobs', advanced technologies and the digital economy) that lie at the core of the new economy. In this context, the lack of adequate qualifications has become a new social risk. Unemployment risks and rates are much higher for the unskilled than they were a couple of decades ago, and much higher than for those with tertiary education. As the European Commission's *New Skills for New Jobs* report underlines, employment rates vary greatly according to qualification levels.[2] In 2008, the employment rates across Europe as a whole for those with high skills was 83.9 per cent, compared to 70.6 per cent for those with medium skill levels and only 48.1 per cent for those with low skill levels.

Furthermore, the wages of the low-skilled have also fallen relative to those of more skilled individuals. The number of low-skilled individuals has fallen in the labour forces of most advanced economies, which suggests that there has been a fall in the demand for low-skilled labour. In fact, between 2007 and 2010, the number of jobs employing people with high skills has increased in Europe, while the number of low-skilled jobs has decreased.[3]

The fact that the unemployed are predominantly unskilled and that vacant jobs require high skills suggests that we need to emphasise the importance of education, training, skill formation and maintenance and updating of skills as policies that prepare individuals for the current and future economies.

Increasing education and skill levels has a positive effect on employment, both in terms of increasing employment levels and in terms of creating 'good jobs'. If we want not only to reduce unemployment but also to promote employment growth (especially in 'good jobs'), it is important to complement demand-oriented Keynesian measures with supply-side-oriented instruments that go beyond the neo-liberal deregulation of labour markets. Instead of lowering labour costs and incentivising the unemployed to take poorly paid jobs, it is necessary to provide skills training for the unemployed to equip them with the necessary learning capacities, and to safeguard the younger generation against a lack of qualifications.[4]

This is best done through policies that are broad-based, egalitarian and of high quality, and that follow the whole life-course, starting with early childhood education and care.

Social Investment and Equality

While specific policies are needed to support the least skilled in the labour market, social investment strategies cannot exclusively be based on programmes targeted at 'the unskilled' or other disadvantaged groups. They should in the first place be based on the provision of universal high-quality education and training programmes throughout the life-course. Equality and quality must be at the centre of the social investment approach if programmes are to deliver good returns.

Equality appears to be a necessary precondition for promoting growth and employment, especially in good-quality jobs. Both equality of access (to quality childcare, to education, to lifelong training, to quality health and care services) and income equality are at stake. Egalitarian societies perform better.[5] As the Scandinavian countries illustrate, egalitarian societies are more successful in implementing social investment policies and in achieving many of the desired outcomes linked to this strategy.

The experience of the Nordic countries suggests that social investment policies can be used to successfully combine social and economic goals. These countries display high and broad-based education levels, which appear to translate into high levels of social capital and social cohesion, greater learning and innovation capacity at work (making these countries among the most competitive economies in the world), more flexibility on the labour market and good economic growth (including the creation of more and better jobs). These countries also display higher female employment rates and lower poverty rates (including lower transmission of intergenerational poverty), and have been dealing successfully with demographic issues, both in terms of providing care for the elderly and in maintaining fertility levels. The key to this success seems to be the fact that the Nordic countries have not merely pursued a reorientation strategy of their welfare systems towards more activation (i.e. encouraging people into the workplace). They have instead combined strong protection with heavy social investment, with the aim of promoting social equality as well as gender equality.

Thus, it is not just equality of opportunity ('social justice') but also equality of access and equality in benefits and services that matter.

Equality appears to be a precondition for a successful social invest-ment strategy. This urges us to keep in mind the merits of traditional social protection and anti-poverty programmes. It suggests that reduc-tion of income inequality should remain high on the social investment agenda.

Gender equality should also be a central goal of this agenda. Raising female employment rates cannot be enough. Persistent gender inequalities such as the division of unpaid care and household labour, the gender wage gap, labour market segregation and the 'glass ceiling effect' for women must also be addressed. This means that special attention must be paid to the specific design of policies that seek to promote women's employment and to policies for reconciling work and family life.

Public services for dependent and vulnerable persons, as well as early childhood education and care, also seem to be appropriate means to address the issue of increasing women's labour market participa-tion and gender equality. Early childhood education, care and other services create jobs for women, and also enable mothers of young chil-dren to work for pay and their families to balance work and family life. Increasing labour-market participation obviously responds to women's aspirations for economic autonomy, but it goes beyond that. It also helps to reduce child poverty, since poverty is always lower when two parents are employed. It also increases the employment rate, such that reve-nues are higher for states and for insurance-based social programmes. Policies 'for women' have to do with more than simply allowing for a work–family balance; they must also provide gender equality and equality of opportunity. This means, in other words, changing men's trajectories as well as women's, and altering the gender division of labour within the household.

Likewise, more attention needs to be devoted to the structural and political factors that contribute to the kinds of ethnic inequalities that characterise European societies today and that are likely to be of increas-ing importance in the future if not properly addressed. A focus upon upgrading the skills, including the communication skills, of immigrants, appears crucial.

Social Investment and Quality

'Quality' should be another crucial component of social investment strategies. This relates both to the quality of jobs and to the quality of services. Only high-quality childcare can foster good cognitive-skills acquisition among all children and help to reduce social inequalities. Participation in education does not directly translate into high performance: quality matters more than mere participation for skill accumulation, particularly at the low end of the capability distribution.

When it comes to the active labour market, policies directed only towards 'activation' in the sense of pushing people back into the labour market to take up 'any job' have not produced good results. While employment rates have generally increased over the 2000s, the jobs created have very often been of low quality, taking the shape of atypical jobs, short-term contracts, interim work, part-time work and so on. This has resulted in increased in-work poverty.

Thus, active labour-market policy can be considered part of a social investment strategy only if conceived as an instrument of social promotion, and not only as a way to increase employment rates at any cost. Among the various active labour-market measures, only the 'up-skilling' ones seem to fit into the social investment approach. Activation is not enough.

This is all the more important since, if the quality of jobs is forgotten, activation only leads to shifting people from inactivity into in-work poverty. This does not increase the tax base to support future pensions and health-care costs. Furthermore, given the challenges of economic globalisation, one way to remain competitive on the world market is through innovation, and through producing goods and services of high quality.

It is necessary to invest in high-quality services, and thus in the qualifications necessary for and working conditions of jobs in sectors such as transport, construction, health and education, and care services. These areas are too often regarded as not forming part of the economics of quality jobs due to inadequate measures of productivity (based on the number of units processed per hour and on the level of formal education required). The collective utility of these services should be promoted as a criterion for evaluating the 'productivity' of work.

Investing in quality means that substantial investments must be made to improve education, training and up-skilling schemes, as well as to improve working conditions. This, in turn, means that more social spending – or, rather, social *investment* – is needed. The fact that an effective social investment strategy entails increasing social expenditure in the short run cannot be ignored. This may well appear problematic in the aftermath of the 2008 financial crisis and at a time of fiscal austerity. Yet there are good reasons for changing the way such expenditure is considered, and to be serious in presenting these expenditures as *investments* from which economic returns can be derived.

Hence, the future beneficiaries of these investments should be mobilised to support this approach, since they are also the ones who will benefit from these investment returns. In the end, the social investment approach is about the long-term enhancement of the future tax base so that we can avoid severe austerity at a time when the population is ageing.

Investing in the Younger Generations

If social democrats in Europe do not want to become shrinking parties supported mainly by the now retiring beneficiaries of golden-age social democracy, they need to renew their vision of the welfare state. A future-oriented social investment strategy geared towards investment in children and young people through high-quality childcare, education and lifelong training must be adopted and pursued. Investing in the younger generations means reaching out as a society to those who are currently most in need – that is, those who will generate the tax base in years to come and who may become the pillars of a renewed social democratic political force.

Notes

1. OECD, *Growing Unequal? Income Distribution and Poverty in OECD Countries* (2008), Executive summary. Available at www.

oecd.org/els/soc/growingunequalincomedistributionandpoverty inoecdcountries.htm (accessed 1 May 2013).

2. Commission of the European Communities, *New Skills for New Jobs: Anticipating and Matching Labour Market and Skills Needs* (2008). Available at http://eur-lex.europa.eu/LexUriServ/LexUriServ.do? uri=COM:2008:0868:FIN:EN:PDF (accessed 1 May 2013).

3. Ibid.

4. Nathalie Morel, Bruno Palier and Joakim Palme, *Towards a Social Investment Welfare State? Ideas, Policies and Challenges* (Bristol: Policy Press, 2011).

5. Richard G. Wilkinson and Kate Pickett, *The Spirit Level: Why More Equal Societies Almost Always Do Better* (London: Allen Lane, 2009).

CHAPTER 14

Affordable Social Investment and the Euro Crisis

European Integration and the Future of Welfare

Anton Hemerijck

The shape of the welfare state has people worried in the aftermath of the deepest economic crisis since the Great Depression. For member states of the European Union (EU), where collective coverage of modern social risks is comprehensive and welfare spending accounts for 16–30 per cent of GDP, the long-term social and economic repercussions of the 2008–12 financial crisis mark a serious 'stress test' for twenty-first-century welfare provision. The global economic crisis has already fundamentally redrawn the boundaries between states and markets. Will its aftermath, like the Great Depression and 'great inflation' predecessors, mark a new opportunity to reconfigure and relegitimise social policy? Or are European welfare states in danger of becoming a 'crisis casualty' in the cascade of violent economic, social and political aftershocks unleashed by the first crisis of twenty-first-century global capitalism?

Since the 1980s, various trends have fundamentally altered the policy environment of European welfare states. Because of greater capital mobility and accelerated European economic integration, fiscal pressures have increased. In addition, population ageing and declining fertility rates, together with a trend towards early retirement of baby boomers, have come to overburden pension systems. Rapid technological change has meanwhile reduced the demand for low- and medium-skilled work in advanced economies. The shift towards a post-industrial labour market has opened up job opportunities for women, but deindustrialisation has come with declining levels of steady lifetime jobs and rising job precariousness, especially for females and young people. Changing family structures and gender roles – with longer education spells, later child-birth and lone parenthood – have additionally created new tensions between work and family life and raised new demands for the provision of social care, especially for young children and the elderly. The 'new social risk' profile of social exclusion both within and outside labour markets has triggered growing income polarisation between high-skilled and job-rich 'dual-earner' families, and low-skilled and work-poor male-breadwinner and single-parent households.

Although the drivers behind long-term socio-economic change are common across Europe, the pressures they create for existing social-policy repertoires, together with the policy responses they trigger, vary from country to country. While some welfare systems have been quite successful in *updating* their policy repertoires in light of the social transformations preceding the global financial crisis, others have fared less well for various economic, political and institutional reasons.[1] Add to this the differential impact of the global financial crisis and it is easy to see that European welfare states have entered a new era of flux that will see major reform and adaptation to unfolding long-term social changes, and short- to medium-term economic aftershocks.

High and rising (youth) unemployment, strained pensions and fiscal consolidation packages enforced by recent EU agreements today put enormous pressure on nationally elected politicians in the majority of EU member states, where citizens continue to hold high expectations of social protection from economic uncertainty. The outcomes of the 2012 elections in France, Greece and the Netherlands, local elections in the UK and regional elections in Germany all testify to mounting popular backlashes against the fiscal austerity regime promoted by the European Commission, the European Central Bank (ECB) and the Merkel–Sarkozy tandem from 2010 to 2012.

In this essay, I argue that there is ample room for a more realistic (slower) pace of fiscal adjustment, coupled with participation and productivity-enhancing social (investment) reforms and informed by readily available evidence about the efficiency–equity frontier. It is not that I am overly optimistic; I just wish to challenge, on both economic and political grounds, the false 'necessity' of the prevailing *pensée unique* of fiscal austerity.

Revisiting the Idea that Social Policy Enhances Productivity

Social reform dynamics over the past decades are difficult to pigeon-hole in terms of a crude 'black-and-white' dichotomy of more or less retrenchment. Given the available evidence, we are well advised to resist easy generalisations about the complex dynamics of changing welfare states. An underspecified polemic of 'Americanisation' of European social model(s) is particularly unhelpful. According to former International Monetary Fund chief economist Raghuram Rajan, the lack of adequate welfare provision has played a particularly important role in the US economy's growing private indebtedness since the 1980s. Increasing job insecurity and the general stagnation of wages of the American middle class since the late 1970s were compensated by easy credit and subprime mortgages, allowing spending patterns of the squeezed middle to be kept up by reductions in household savings and mounting private indebtedness. In other words, in a free-wheeling 'disembedded' market environment, access to easy credit and subprime mortgage loans to low-income households seemingly replaced the welfare state as the basis of the American social contract. Consequently, weak social safety nets, growing inequality and increasingly unequal access to education and privatised health care have, since the 1980s, deepened the 'fault lines' of the overleveraged US economy, and tempted consecutive American governments and the Federal Reserve to pursue extremely risky expansionary fiscal and monetary policies.[2]

The overall scope of social reform across the EU member states has been far more heterogeneous, disparate and uneven. Social-policy reforms have indeed become more 'employment-centred'. This included a drive towards greater labour-market flexibility and a strong emphasis on 'making work pay' in social insurance provision. The employment turn largely appeared in two guises: one inspired by social retrenchment and labour-market deregulation; and a second based on proactive 'productivist' social policy, bent on increasing labour supply and productivity through 'capacitating' family, training and employment services. The available evidence suggests that the latter 'high road' strategy of employment-centred social reform has been able to produce more productive, competitive and sustainable job growth, while the 'low road' of social retrenchment and labour market deregulation has produced a greater number of less productive, low-paid and low-quality jobs.[3] In this respect, the competitive strengths of Scandinavian economies, before and after the 2008 credit crunch, can be recognised as a product of active and capacitating social reform. By contrast, welfare-related competitiveness gaps in the southern eurozone periphery, notably Greece and Italy, seem inherently related to their antiquated, passive, pensioner-biased social contracts and two-tiered labour markets, inhibiting both high-quality employment opportunities and adequate social protection and services support for highly educated women, young people and single-parent households.

Social-policy programmes can create important returns. Adequate social protection in terms of income support during periods of short-term unemployment can reduce the search costs for new jobs, fostering more efficient employment matches. Universal social protection potentially enhances, rather than distorts, labour market flexibility. Similarly, a comprehensive system of collective bargaining permits macro-economically responsive wage-setting. Even employment protection, together with legally sanctioned worker participation through works councils, can contribute to competiveness by engaging workers in production and training processes that can be beneficial to productivity. Finally, social protection expenditures are powerful stabilisers of economic activity because they help to sustain effective demand in times of recession.

This kind of Keynesianism through the back door continued to prove highly functional in response to the immediate credit crunch after the Lehman Brothers bankruptcy in the autumn of 2008. Security against the adverse effects of illness, disability, unemployment, old age, divorce and child-bearing is of value to citizens who are protected by social policy but also to society and the economy at large, to whom the cost burden of poverty and social instability would fall if there were no social protection provision.

It is important to underscore that future 'productive social policy' has to factor in far more adverse demographic conditions compared to the era of social-insurance expansion after World War II. Labour market reforms promoting higher employment levels, together with pension reforms aimed at increasing the (effective) retirement age to counter early retirement, have been important strategies for addressing the looming demographic challenge. Therefore, the welfare state's present economic sustainability hinges on the number of and productivity of future taxpayers.[4] From this reading, social policy should contribute to mobilising the productive potential of citizens in order to mitigate the risks of care obligations or obsolete skills, causing atypical employment, long-term unemployment, working poverty, family instability and lack of opportunities for labour market participation. Labour market participation and retirement decisions are more than ever contingent on the available supply of health and care services in the market and the family. A fall in fertility implies fewer daughters and (less often) sons to take care of increasing numbers of frail elderly.

One of the fundamental reasons why the 'active' welfare state today must provide enabling and capacitating social services is related to the erosion of the effectiveness of the social-insurance principle, upon which the postwar male-breadwinner welfare state was based.[5] When the risk of industrial unemployment was largely cyclical, it made sense to administer collective social-insurance funds for maintaining steady consumption during spells of demand-deficient unemployment. However, as the risk of unemployment became structural, caused by radical shifts in labour demand and supply, unemployment insurance could no longer function as a reserve income buffer between similar jobs. In order to better connect social policy with a more dynamic economy and society, citizens therefore have to be supported by ex-ante capacitating services tailored to particular social needs over the life cycle.[6]

Although comparative welfare-regime analysis at the macro level supports the plausibility of 'productive social policy' claims, traditional cost–benefit economic policy analyses of social programmes only measure immediate budgetary costs and never their long-term economic gains. Policy analyses rarely gauge the longer-term impact of early childhood education and parental leave arrangements, which help to reconcile work and family life with the effects of raising employment levels (especially of married women), and active labour market policy interventions on employment participation levels and earnings.

In addition, the long-term productivity gains from investing in quality education and vocational training are not taken seriously enough in traditional economic cost–benefit policy analyses. As argued by Nelson and Stephens, long-term human capital investment 'crowds in' growth in high-end and high-quality service-sector employment and shifts low-end services from price competition to quality competition, thereby increasing the value-added (individual and societal) returns of these jobs.[7] By the same token, the costs of a universal day-care policy can easily be reimbursed by working parents via higher tax payments and social contributions throughout their working lives. Since day care minimises parents' employment interruptions, cumulative lifetime earnings increase, implying higher future tax revenues.[8] In other words, capacitating welfare provision can advance the efficiency–equity frontier, provided that access to labour markets is available and generally promoted.

The social investment approach rests essentially on policies to raise the human capital *stock* (early childhood education and care, vocational training, education and lifelong learning) and *flow* policies, serving to make the most efficient use of human capital (through policies supporting single-parent employment, active labour market policies that facilitate access for vulnerable groups and social-protection supports that promote security) across the life-course. By emphasising *flow*, the social investment perspective is wider than traditional human capital policies.

Managing Social Policy Coherence

Policy choices are never made in institutional isolation. Institutional characteristics relate to how social provisions target risk groups, how they are financed and anchored in tax systems, and how they are run by public and/or private actors. Some policy legacies are better able to incorporate social investment innovations than others. It is impossible to judge the quality of early childhood education and care in isolation from the institutional opportunities for mothers to participate in the labour market and have access to training, supported by policies of gender equality and parental leave arrangements. In terms of administrative capacities, to the extent that welfare states are becoming more service-oriented, this requires much improved public administration and professionalisation, also with respect to improved tax collection and fighting of corruption. On the other hand, tax systems that penalise dual-earner couples offset opportunities created by raising the employment participation of young children's parents. By the same token, social protection arrangements that continue to guarantee jobs for life and/or high social benefits to labour market insiders disincentivise lifelong learning and productive employment mobility, with the likely adverse effect of excessive youth unemployment. For contemporary social policy to be successful, the devil is in the details of coherence in substantive policies and institutional co-ordination across social services and transfers, in close connection to labour-market governance.

Social investment is no panacea for all social ills. There are also inherent tensions and potential conflicts in pursuing social protection and investment under tight fiscal constraints. However, to the extent that social investment deficits are partly explained by the current disequilibria in the EU, it is clear that we need more social investment, not less.

Governance Deficits of the Economic and Monetary Union

Can European welfare states survive the latest stage of the eurozone's sovereign debt crisis and, if so, in what shape will they reappear from the resolution that is chosen? The deepening of the euro crisis reveals how deeply interconnected Europe has become in recent decades – economically, legally, politically. And, as the successive twists of the crisis also reveal, the complexity of a highly economically integrated Europe raises the stakes for devising effective governance arrangements within and across national boundaries. It likewise increases the importance of developing a better understanding of the evolving capacities of European institutions, member states and private actors to respond to these conditions of greater interdependence and uncertainty. This also intensifies the urgency of sharing such understanding with the European public in order to secure the legitimacy of eventual solutions.

Politically, further economic and political integration can only be successfully achieved with citizens' support, which is conditional on popular trust in democratic governments able to handle the social consequences of the crisis. Since the onslaught of the global financial crisis, closer integration implies that welfare-policy proficiency (or deficiency) in one country strengthens the prosperity (or stagnation) of the EU economy as a whole and vice versa. With public social spending averaging between 16 and 30 per cent of GDP, European welfare states are powerful macroeconomic buffers. On the other hand, macroeconomic policy leeway has become more constrained since the European sovereign debt crisis of 2010.

Currently, we are witnessing a particularly strong backlash against austerity recipes, in Greece and France but also in Germany, the UK and the Netherlands. The election of François Hollande, based on his advocacy of 'giving growth a chance', is challenging Angela Merkel's policy preference for fiscal austerity. Between rising anti-austerity national protests and the EU's inquisitive demand for overnight fiscal consolidation, a 'political vacuum' has emerged at the heart of the integration project. The more the European Commission steps up austerity, the more European voters, from Greece to France, the Netherlands and Finland, seek refuge with extreme anti-EU left- and right-wing populist parties. This trend is not new, however. Before the near economic meltdown of 2008, middle-class fears of falling behind, especially for their offspring, invoked a nostalgic narrative of 'golden age' welfare paradise lost, pitted very much against the alleged globalising ambitions of the EU.

An *economic policy regime* failure lies at the heart of the eurozone's political conundrum. The original theory behind the Economic and Monetary Union (EMU) was based on the faulty assumption that the ECB's strong mandate on price stability and member state governments' equally strong commitment to fiscal consolidation, enforced by the Stability and Growth Pact, would raise competitive pressures among member state economies. Enhanced competitiveness in financial and product markets would subsequently translate into greater tax and cross-border labour-market competition. This, in turn, would force democratic governments to launch incisive reforms in their welfare states and labour markets, if need be by blaming the EU for their inevitability. The architects of the EMU, in short, conceived that the new macroeconomic policy regime would naturally trigger 'structural' reforms, ultimately resulting in Pareto-optimal economic growth hikes all across the EU.

The eurozone sovereign debt crisis has exposed the weaknesses of this economic policy theory. No happy equilibrium has been forthcoming. Instead, we are confronted with destabilising high current-account deficits in Greece, Ireland, Italy, Portugal and Spain; housing bubbles in Ireland, the Netherlands and Spain; and current-account surpluses in Germany and the Scandinavian countries. Additionally, the low interest rates that came along with the introduction of the EMU slowed down the proactive welfare-reform momentum in the countries that needed it most, with passive and insider-biased welfare systems and labour markets. Paradoxically, it was the countries with current-account surpluses and that were more concerned with competitiveness, such as Germany and the Nordic countries, that intensified the social reform momentum after the 1990s.

Today, the real economic consequences of pre-emptive austerity seem increasingly self-defeating, given the negative growth numbers in many eurozone economies. Moreover, ratios of gross public debt to GDP are rising, not falling, in distressed economies. As a consequence, real economy divergences between the competitive north (which is paying close to zero interest rates on moderate levels of public debt and government deficits at manageable rates of unemployment) and the uncompetitive south (which is facing exceedingly high spreads on high debt and deficits, two-digit levels of unemployment and politically unmanageable rates of youth unemployment) continue to increase. Belated 'structural reforms' offer no relief in asymmetric adjustment processes.

Collectively, EU institutions preside over enough action resources to restrain contagion. In addition, the EU writ large as a regional economy is fiscally in better shape than the US and Japan. Practically all leading European economists believe that a fiscal union is essential for the survival of the EMU. In the absence of fiscal solidarity, eurozone economies with unsustainably high interest rates have no room for manoeuvre. The good news is that a banking union is no longer a taboo.

Politicising EU Social Investment

The global financial crisis originated in the behavioural excesses in deregulated financial markets, not in excess welfare spending. The fundamental insight that (re-)emerged from the crisis is that economic markets are not self-regulating, self-stabilising or self-legitimising.[9] While this important lesson is certainly not new, a whole generation of domestic and EU policy-makers and academic economists seem to have forgotten the basic truth that the benefits of global economic interdependence rely heavily on robust social and political – both domestic and supranational – institutions. The EU's original sin of pushing for rapid market and currency integration to let the social-political-institutional underpinnings of European economic integration catch up later is in dire need of correction. In their cognitive bias of further liberalising the internal market through monetary integration, EU economic policy-makers, from the European Commission to the ECB, declined to really appreciate the Lisbon Treaty's macroeconomic importance in terms of 'productivity-enhancing', 'participation-raising', 'employability-friendly', 'family-capacitating' social investments for the greater good of a more prosperous, equitable and caring Europe.

Both the survival of the eurozone and the imperative to recalibrate welfare provision in the knowledge-based economy conjure up a democratic predicament of national and European dimensions. The EU can no longer advance as a mere project of market integration and fiscal austerity. A joined-up social and economic policy strategy is required. In his important 2010 report on the future of European economic integration, Mario Monti urged for an 'appropriate reconciliation' between the single market and social-policy priorities in the wake of the crisis.[10] It is my contention that 'appropriate reconciliation' between economic and social prerogatives is not advisable merely for political reasons of popular disenchantment with European integration. A Pareto-superior social investment policy mix, as I have argued in this chapter, comes with a comparative advantage for Europe and an orderly resolution of the sovereign debt crisis, and is a *sine qua non* for the survival of the welfare state and vice versa.

The social and economic policy challenge is to make social investments and fiscal consolidation mutually supportive and sustainable, through improved macroeconomic governance. To this end, a more realistic (slower) pace of fiscal adjustment should be coupled with productivity-enhancing social (investment) reforms, in a form of what my colleagues Frank Vandenbroucke and Bruno Palier and I called an 'EU social investment pact'.[11] The EU is in need of a political deal wherein *all* governments pursue medium-term budgetary discipline *and* long-term social investment, supported therein by an effective macroeconomic euro crisis resolution mechanism to help the euro-zone regain aggregate competiveness. An EU social investment pact implies significant burden sharing. In terms of budgetary policy, north-ern European governments should avoid austerity overkill, as part and parcel of a mutual effort. The competitive north could tolerate higher levels of inflation so as to make price and wage adjustments in the Mediterranean south realistic, provided that Greece, Italy and Spain use leniency to continue with structural social (investment) reforms.

A social investment strategy is not cheap, especially not in the short run. Simultaneously responding to rising needs in health care (and pensions) and implementing a successful transition to fully fledged social investment strategies will require additional resources. Moreover, there is no denying that a social investment strategy gener-ates tensions and trade-offs between various social-policy preferences in the short term. As public resources committed to welfare provision continue to be directed at 'old' social risk categories, including unem-ployment insurance and (particularly) old-age pensions, increased fiscal pressure because of population ageing could easily crowd out the policy space to counter social investment policy innovation. The demographic advantage of older workers and pensioners makes them well poised to successfully oppose profound reform in pensions and health care. Demographic ageing over the past decade has not stood in the way of fundamental reform, including the freezing of pension entitlements, the raising of the statutory retirement age, the phasing out of early exit benefits, the partial privatisation of pension provisions and the strengthening of the minimum income protection function in public pensions. Old-age policies are more successful the better they are integrated into life-course policy supports in health, family and labour-market programmes that allow societies to adapt to demo-graphic ageing as a whole.

Together with the intrinsic value of social protection and care, the social investment perspective may offer a substantive redefinition of the EU's political purpose, a purpose that must be defined if we are to achieve the long-term sustainability of the eurozone (and thus the EU). European integration can only be maintained if citizens support it and trust governments to handle the social consequences of the crisis fairly. Moreover, the social investment edifice is at least rhetorically in line with the Europe 2020 policy strategy, which is based explicitly on the commitment to 'inclusive growth', aimed at 'fostering a high employment economy delivering economic, social and territorial cohesion'.[12] Taxation is crucial. The crisis has tightened budget constraints, and this makes it difficult for governments to trade short-term revenue losses for long-term competitiveness gains through selective tax-rate reductions. Given these twin financial and political constraints, greater tax co-ordination across countries and even tax harmonisation, including a tax on financial transactions, should be placed on the economic policy agenda in the aftermath of the global financial crisis.

To give Europe 2020 more bite, structural funds could be granted to fiscally constrained member states under the proviso that subsidies should be spent on social investment policy priorities. Without a stronger economic *and* social Europe, the EU is likely to remain trapped in self-defeating policy indecision, which conjures up the image of a 'double-dip' recession across the eurozone economy far worse than Japan's 'lost decade' of the 1990s.[13]

At this critical juncture, it is important not to discount the massive achievements of over half a century of European regional integration and welfare state development. The unprecedented deepening and widening of regional integration from six to 27 member states, creating a community of some 500 million people, was accompanied by the establishment and expansion of comprehensive welfare systems, boosting prosperity and social progress while promoting democracy and securing peace to an extent barely conceivable at the start of reconstruction after World War II. A 'social investment pact', bolstered social investment project bonds and more generous human capital promoting access to structural funds (discounted in national budget accounts) could be an important step towards a Pareto-superior 'caring Europe', based on better domestic solidarity and supranational European cohesion.

Notes

1. Anton Hemerijck, *Changing Welfare States* (Oxford: Oxford University Press, 2013).
2. Raghuram G. Rajan, *Fault Lines: How Hidden Fractures Still Threaten the World Economy* (Princeton: Princeton University Press, 2011).
3. Anton Hemerijck and Frank Vandenbroucke, 'Social investment and the Euro crisis: the necessity of a unifying social policy concept', *Intereconomics* 47/4 (2012), pp. 200–6.
4. Thomas Lindh and Joakim Palme, *Sustainable Policies in an Ageing Europe: A Human Capital Response* (Stockholm: Institute for Future Studies, 2006).
5. Charles Sabel, AnnaLee Saxenian, Reijo Miettinen, Peer H. Kristensen and Jarkko Hautamäki, *Individualized Service Provision in the New Welfare State: Lessons from Special Education in Finland* (Helsinki: SITRA, 2010).
6. Gøsta Esping-Andersen with Duncan Gallie, Anton Hemerijck and John Myles (eds), *Why We Need a New Welfare State* (Oxford: Oxford University Press, 2001); Gøsta Esping-Andersen and John Myles, 'Inequality and the welfare state', in W. Salverda, B. Nolan and T.M. Smeeding (eds), *The Oxford Handbook of Economic Inequality* (Oxford: Oxford University Press, 2011).
7. Moira Nelson and John D. Stephens, 'Do social investment policies produce more and better jobs?', in N. Morel, B. Palier and J. Palme (eds), *Towards a Social Investment Welfare State? Ideas, Policies and Challenges* (Bristol: Policy Press, 2011), pp. 205–34.
8. Gøsta Esping-Andersen and Sebastian Sarasa, 'The generational conflict reconsidered', *Journal of European Social Policy* 12/1 (2002), pp. 5–21.
9. Dani Rodrik, *The Globalization Paradox: Why Global Markets, States, and Democracy Can't Coexist* (Oxford: Oxford University Press, 2012).
10. Mario Monti, *A New Strategy for the Single Market at the Service of Europe's Economy and Society: Report to the President of the European Commission José Manuel Barroso* (2010). Available at

http://ec.europa.eu/bepa/pdf/monti_report_final_10_05_2010_
en.pdf (accessed 1 May 2013).

11. Frank Vandenbroucke, Anton Hemerijck and Bruno Palier, 'The EU
needs a social investment pact' (OSE Paper Series, Opinion Paper 5,
2011).

12. Europe 2020 strategy, *Executive Summary* (English version) (2010).
Available   at   http://ec.europa.eu/eu2020/pdf/COMPLET%20EN
%20BARROSO%20%20%20007%20%20Europe%202020%20%20
EN%20version.pdf (accessed 1 May 2013).

13. Richard C. Koo, *The Holy Grail of Macroeconomics: Lessons from
Japan's Great Recession* (Hoboken: John Wiley & Sons, 2008).

CHAPTER 15

Beyond GDP

A Post-Crisis Agenda for Measuring Government Performance

A.B. Atkinson

It is often asserted that progressive parties are 'lost' and 'rudderless' in the wake of the 2008 financial crisis and its aftershocks. Statements such as this seem to me exaggerated. It may be that political parties are disorientated, but my assessment is that individual citizens, at least in Europe, have a reasonably good idea of where they would like to be heading. They want to live in a society where there are secure jobs, where their children are well educated, where they are able to take advantage of new opportunities and technologies, where we are taking steps to offset climate change and where we are genuinely 'all in it together'. This is the agenda on which post-crisis policy should be based.

My assertion is based in part on the fact that, in 2010, the European Union (EU) was able – with relatively little dissent – to adopt the Europe 2020 strategy:

> The Union has set five ambitious objectives – on employment, innovation, education, social inclusion and climate/energy. Each member state will adopt its own national targets in each of these areas. Concrete actions at EU and national levels will underpin the strategy.[1]

Explicitly, the EU targets for the decade are:

- *employment*: 75 per cent of 20–64-year-olds to be employed;
- *innovation*: 3 per cent of Europe's GDP to be invested in research and development and innovation;
- *climate change and energy*: greenhouse gas emissions to be 20 per cent lower than in 1990; 20 per cent of energy to come from renewable sources; a 20 per cent increase in energy efficiency;

- *education*: reduce school drop-out rates to below 10 per cent and at least 40 per cent of 30–34-year-olds to have completed third-level education;
- *poverty and social exclusion*: at least 20 million fewer people in or at risk of poverty and social exclusion.

These objectives were agreed by an EU dominated by right-wing governments, and it would be easy for the centre-left to reject Europe 2020 or to dismiss it as empty rhetoric. However, I believe that it provides a valuable point of departure, and rhetoric itself is important. The detail of the objectives can be challenged, but they constitute a minimal set of aspirations with which many people can identify.

The centre-left should therefore seize the opportunity of the Europe 2020 strategy to insist on measures that can make these objectives realisable. We need to provide a narrative as to how the ambition can be translated into a reality. The great success of the Beveridge Report in the UK in 1942 lay not in the details of reform but in the narrative as to how the problems of society could be addressed. Today, we lack such a story line. In this short chapter, I consider three elements that can contribute to and that will be important for post-crisis policy-making: the way in which government performance is assessed, distributional cleavages, and the balance between distribution and redistribution.

Assessing Government Performance

Statistics are often seen as an anorak subject, but they are of key political importance. The political success and survival of governments depend on the way in which their performance is measured. It is therefore essential that these measures reflect our ultimate objectives. A centre-left government needs to establish the criteria by which it wishes to be judged. In this respect, the work of the Stiglitz-Sen-Fitoussi Commission pointed the way forward, but there has been a disappointingly slow response.[2] The current crisis is still discussed solely in terms of GDP (not even expressed per head). Yet there are simple changes that would lead to better measures, measures that would – crucially – be more meaningful to individual citizens.

First, the Stiglitz Commission recommended that, when measuring material well-being, we should look at income and consumption rather than production, and that these factors should be seen from the perspective of the household. I believe that we should be concentrating on what is happening to household disposable incomes per person, expressed in terms of what they will buy. GDP may go up or down for reasons that have no implications for the living standards of households. Indeed, it was one of the successes of the initial G-20 response to the crisis that household incomes were maintained in the face of a sharp fall in GDP (having previously risen less than GDP in the boom). It is household living standards that influence well-being – and how people vote.

Second, we need to incorporate inequality into the headline indicator in order to understand how the fruits of growth, or the burdens of recession, are being shared. Even in good times, people may feel they are being left out: 'we all hear about the amazing growth in GDP, but none of us ordinary people feels the benefit' (*Financial Times*, April 2012, writing about Hong Kong).[3] The simplest way in which distributional considerations can be introduced is to show what is happening to median, rather than mean, incomes. If growth is accruing only to the top 1 per cent, this would be revealed by the stagnation of median incomes. The median income has been used (along with the top and bottom decile incomes) by the European Commission in its analysis of the changes in the distribution in the first years of the crisis.[4] Or we could use mean income adjusted for inequality in the way proposed by Amartya Sen, where the performance of a society is judged by its growth in mean income multiplied by 1 minus the Gini coefficient.[5] (The Gini coefficient is one of the most commonly employed measures of inequality.) Thus, a country that allows its Gini coefficient to rise from 0.25 to 0.3 will see its growth performance docked by 6.75 per cent.

Third, we should look at more than one number. Just as drivers can look at more than the speedometer, so too citizens are quite capable of studying a dashboard with several indicators. The Europe 2020 targets, with their five dials covering key areas of performance, provide a good starting point.

Statistics may be boring, but they have proved in the past to be highly effective levers for change. At the end of the nineteenth century, the findings of Charles Booth and Seebohm Rowntree about poverty gave momentum to the calls for the creation of the welfare state. More recently, Jacques Delors used statistics on poverty in Europe to plead for a social dimension (now incorporated in Europe 2020). The placards of the Occupy Movement showing the income share of the top 1 per cent were a highly visible political statement. The centre-left needs to establish a clear benchmark by which it – and its opponents – should be judged.

Distributional Cleavages and Their Implications for Living Standards

The 'inequality' just discussed relates to the traditional 'vertical' inequality between rich and poor. This is highly important, but there are two other cleavages that are likely to be critical in policy-making after the crisis.

The first concerns equity between generations. Intergenerational distribution and redistribution are at the heart of many of the pressing policy problems, such as climate change, ageing and pension policy, the national debt and student funding. The burden of the current austerity measures is being disproportionately borne by younger generations. The intergenerational dimension needs to be made explicit, and doing so may help unlock some of the log-jams in policy-making. In the debate about climate change following the Stern Review, too little attention has been paid to the question as to *who* should pay for it. Put starkly, should mitigation actions be funded by cutting student support or by cutting pensions? This does not necessarily mean that there will be intergenerational conflict. By posing the intergenerational equity question explicitly, it may be possible to reach an intergenerational pact covering a wider set of issues. The *Report of the High Level Group on the Future of Social Policy in an Enlarged European Union* proposed such a pact, arguing that the debate about the reform of social policy was too much based on fear (of ageing populations, migration, etc.) and that such a pact would provide a positive approach to future challenges.[6] At a national level, such a pact would mean an explicit link between the decisions made about increases and reductions in government spending. Grandparents, for example, may accept pension cuts for the better-off elderly if they are accompanied by increased child benefits and a more sustainable future for their grandchildren. It would mean that the removal of tax privileges for older generations (such as abolishing the exemption of older workers from National Insurance contributions) could be seen as having a counterpart in benefits to younger generations.

The second concerns the global distribution. Critics of globalisation point to growing inequality across the world, but we must remember that the world has been highly unequal for centuries. One of the most important contributions of the Blair–Brown governments was, in my judgement, to bring about a shift in public attitudes towards global justice. In the spending cuts in the mid-1970s, one of the first casualties was overseas aid; in contrast, in 2010, the coalition agreement stated that the government would honour the UK's commitment to spending 0.7 per cent of gross national income on overseas aid from 2013, and to enshrining this commitment in law. But the issue goes much further. We have to recognise that the next decades will see a major shift in the world distribution of income. It always seemed to me totally unrealistic that the EU Lisbon Agenda called for Europe to be 'the most dynamic economy in the world'. Europe may aspire to keep pace with other rich countries, but the rest of the world will – we should hope – increasingly catch up. As a result, many of the 'rents' that Europe has enjoyed on account of its earlier start will be shared globally.

Both of these concerns have significant implications for the potential growth of living standards in rich countries. We cannot, in my view, expect Europe to grow as fast as the world economy, nor can we expect household spendable incomes per head to grow at the same rate as GDP per head. Indeed, living standards in Europe may not grow much at all. This may sound as though I have given up on growth, as though I am espousing a stationary state, but this is far from the case. Growth in GDP per head is essential. We need rapid technological development to meet the challenges of climate change and the depletion of natural resources. We need the resources generated by growth of GDP to provide for investment in education and training, and to accommodate an ageing population. For all these reasons, sustainable growth in GDP is essential.

What I am saying is that we have to consider the proper allocation of the fruits of growth. We have to recognise that household spendable incomes will not grow at the same rate, and indeed – in the face of the challenges just described – we may have to set ourselves the more modest objective of maintaining the current levels of spendable income. Future generations will of course benefit from new technologies, with products and processes that we cannot conceive, but they will not necessarily be better off in terms of spendable incomes.

Distribution and Redistribution

Redistribution through social transfers and progressive taxation must remain a key element in a centre-left programme. At the same time, there is increasing realisation that this cannot be the sole policy platform. Pragmatically, this is because of the current fiscal crisis and the perceived limits to such redistribution. Criticism of 'tax and spend' policies from the right has gained traction because fiscal redistribution is seen as increasingly ineffective.

How can the pre-redistribution market outcomes be modified? The standard economic textbook explanation of rising market income inequality is based on an increased demand for skill (typically equated with education) as a result of globalisation and skill-biased technological change. The policy prescription that follows is that of investment in skill. In my view, this approach needs to be developed in at least two directions. First, we need to go beyond a simple supply-and-demand model of the labour market, and move to a more subtle understanding of the working of markets and of the motives of economic agents. Where remuneration is more about bargaining over the division of rents than about productive contribution, there is scope for intervention that brings about improvements in both efficiency and equity. In such bargaining the institutions of the labour market play a crucial role, and it can be argued that increased earnings inequality owes as much to the individualisation of pay as it does to the skill story. In my judgement, the centre-left needs to give careful consideration to the restoration of collective bargaining and to ensuring parity between the social partners.

The second reason for questioning whether investment in skill is sufficient is that, while earnings are important, we also need to look at capital incomes and the capital market. It can indeed be argued that technological change is now damaging the prospects not only of unskilled workers but also of skilled workers – to the profit of capital. We need to return to the classical question of the division of national income between wages and profits. Some 50 years ago, James Meade described the impact of automation as making labour redundant and the ownership of property more profitable.[7] He went on to discuss how the distribution of property could be made more equitable, and this is as much a challenge to the centre-left today. This means actively considering taxes on wealth, such as a properly progressive tax on wealth transfers received, and looking to restore the role of the state as a beneficial owner of property (via sovereign wealth funds).

Intervention in the capital market should not be viewed solely in terms of market regulation. I accept that deregulation of capital markets was one of the reasons why we moved from an era of (very) few financial crises from 1945 to 1970 to one in which they have been as frequent as before 1939. But the difficulties in reinstating effective regulation of the capital market have demonstrated that it is not easy to put the clock back. The same applies to another form of intervention that was used with (modest) success in the past: incomes policies. Today's situation, in which individual governments in the eurozone are limited in their macroeconomic policies by loss of control over both monetary and fiscal policies, is reminiscent of times in the past when governments were similarly constrained, and made use of incomes policy as a third instrument. Arguably, such a policy has been, tacitly, employed by Germany in the past decade. But the enforcement of such a policy cannot be achieved by legislation alone; it depends on public acceptance.

This brings me to my final point: the role of public discourse and of moral suasion. In the previous section, I argued that we need to address the division of the fruits of future growth. This should be the subject of public debate, with the aim of achieving a broad consensus about the sustainable level of consumption, the level of public investment and the provision for global convergence. This debate is significant not only for the design of policy but also for its impact on the decisions of individuals.

Where individuals are motivated not solely by individual economic advantage but by a wider set of concerns, there is scope for achieving a fairer market outcome. Put bluntly, if politicians tell people that they should pay taxes as part of their civic duty, and if their neighbours frown on those who do not, then there is likely to be less tax avoidance. Market regulation can only be truly effective in a context where people 'buy in' to the underlying rationale. An effective incomes policy would require government 'by consent'. This brings me back to the urgent need for a narrative as to how centre-left goals can be achieved.

A Post-Crisis Policy Agenda

This contribution represents a pragmatic argument by an economist. The key elements may be summarised as follows: the European centre-left should seize the opportunity offered by the Europe 2020 strategy and seek to make its goals a reality by providing a centre-left narrative as to how they can be achieved; the centre-left should seek to establish the criteria by which its actions should be judged, focusing on household living standards rather than GDP and making inequality an integral concern to make sure that progress is for the many and not just the few; policy log-jams can be 'unlocked' by explicit consideration of equity between generations via an intergenerational pact; the position of Europe has to be seen in terms of global convergence and the costs of ageing and climate-change mitigation, which means that there can only be modest increases in household spendable incomes; the state needs to intervene to change the distribution of market incomes, but neither investment in skills nor regulation is enough; the centre-left needs to pay attention to labour market institutions, including the role of social partners, and to the capital market; and an important role has to be played by public discourse and moral suasion.

Notes

1. Europe 2020 strategy, *Highlights of Europe 2020* (2010). Available at http://ec.europa.eu/europe2020/index_en.htm (accessed 1 May 2013).

2. Stiglitz Commission, *Report on the Measurement of Economic Performance et Social Progress* (2009). Available at www.stiglitz-senfitoussi.fr (accessed 1 May 2013).

3. Enid Tsui and Henny Sender, 'Hong Kong: a majority to accommodate', *Financial Times* (23 April 2012). Available at www.ft.com/cms/s/0/90f19c96-8942-11e1-bed0-00144feab49a.html#axzz2MfGuZaUS (accessed 1 May 2013).

4. European Commission, *Employment and Social Developments in Europe 2011* (2011), p. 25. Available at http://ec.europa.eu/social/main.jsp?catId=738&langId=en&pubId=6176 (accessed 1 May 2013).

5. Amartya K. Sen, 'Real national income', *Review of Economic Studies* 43 (1976), pp. 19–39.

6. European Commission, *Report of the High Level Group on the Future of Social Policy in an Enlarged European Union* (2004), p. 18. Available at http://www.pedz.uni-mannheim.de/daten/edz-fd/gds/hlg_social_elarg_en.pdf (accessed 1 May 2013).

7. James E. Meade, *Efficiency, Equality and the Ownership of Property* (London: Allen and Unwin, 1964).

CHAPTER 16

Corporations, Elites and Inequalities of Power
Building Broad-Based Societal Coalitions

Colin Crouch

Inequality has returned as a problem in the political, social and economic agenda. This provides a major opportunity for social democracy to challenge neo-liberalism at a highly vulnerable point. To frame and tackle the issue directly, however, social democrats must give priority to an aspect that they have often forgotten in the past: inequality is a problem of power at least as much as it is one of access to goods and services. They must also break out of the defensive stance to which many have retreated following the decline of their traditional social bases, and assert themselves as uniquely equipped to confront the key challenges of today's world.

Before we become too celebratory at this new opportunity, its sober backdrop must be kept prominently in mind. The reason for the return of a concern over inequality is the fact that it is increasing almost everywhere in the advanced world, in the US dramatically so. This both demonstrates how far social progress has moved backwards in recent years and serves as a warning about the accumulations of wealth and power that stand ready to combat any new egalitarian challenge.

Economic globalisation stands behind the rise in inequality. It both builds up large concentrations of power in multinational corporations and releases millions of workers in the developing world (who have to accept very low wages and poor working conditions) into competition with workers in the existing advanced economies. While large multinationals may engage in competition with each other, it is not the pure market competition envisaged by economic theory but one in which leading firms can control the terms. Further, the global locational choices available to them enable them to drive very hard bargains with governments concerning labour conditions, taxation and other public-policy issues. In turn, governments fear the giants and allow themselves to be very vulnerable to lobbying and other exercises of corporate influence.

An important aspect of this is the threat that, unless labour standards are weakened, business will be lost to countries in the developing world whose governments and populations are more amenable. This political lobbying intensifies the inequalities being generated in the economy through the changed balance between scarce capital and abundant labour. The spiral then gathers further speed. One result of the lobbying and political penetration is more wealth and more privileges for the giant corporations, and the individuals and families who own them. Part of this wealth can be used to purchase more political influence (by such means as owning media outlets or funding parties and think-tanks), which produces even more favourable policies and thus even more concentration of wealth in their hands.

These processes were behind the growth of the deregulated global financial system that collapsed in 2008, a growth that was closely associated with the rise in inequality. One might have expected that the collapse of that system might therefore have produced a reversal of the trend. In fact, the opposite has happened. The main political response to the crisis was acceptance of a need to save the banking system from itself, as we had all become so dependent on it. This has had two consequences. First, as governments have come to the rescue of their banks, they have diverted resources to them from their welfare states. The earnings of bankers have therefore been protected at the expense of the poorer populations, for whom welfare states are important. Second, although there have been some gestures at re-regulating finance, governments had become so dependent on the earnings of the deregulated system that they are desperate to have it up and running again, propping up its essential unsustainability for as long as they can. This is giving bankers even more influence over policy. And so the spiral continues.

Recognising Inequalities of Power

The rise in inequality has now reached the point where the OECD[1] and at least some economists at the International Monetary Fund[2] have concluded that it might be holding back economic growth through the restraints it imposes on consumption by the less well off. This is an important moment. The main standard argument used by the defenders of inequality is that it is needed for economic progress, on the grounds that entrepreneurs need incentives to produce the economic innovation on which growth depends. But, if inequality reaches a point where it is itself damaging growth, that argument is undermined. This gives social democrats an opportunity to unapologetically bring the issue back to the political agenda.

It is then essential to recognise that the problem of inequality is not simply one of the distribution of income, wealth and access to goods, but one of power. For too long social democrats concentrated solely on the distributional aspects of inequality, enabling right-wing critics to complain that they were motivated by 'envy'. More seriously, it eventually led to the claim – by both conservatives and Third Way social democrats – that inequality did not matter provided everyone had access to a reasonable standard of living. But this does not apply to power, which is always exercised over someone and therefore at their expense. We see this whenever global corporations threaten relocation in China if workers' rights are not reduced, or use their monopoly position to set up highly unequal contracts with customers. The old compromise solution of easing distributional problems through economic growth, enabling everyone to have more, does not work where inequalities of power are concerned.

Avoiding Defensiveness

But inequality and the power of global corporate wealth must be contested by favouring innovation rather than lapsing into defensiveness. The first danger of defensiveness would be to turn against globalisation, despite the problems it is causing. Protectionism leads only to the protected economy producing poor-quality goods and services, as domestic producers face no external competition. Eventually the day of reckoning comes: the country returns to free trade and its uncompetitive producers are swept aside. In the long run, globalisation will enable the vast working population of the world to become consumers as well as producers, buying goods and services from the existing advanced world as well as selling them to it. This process has already started for the enormous Asian middle class, as many European, Japanese and North American producers are finding. We simply need, while this process is developing, active economic and social policies that will protect us, not from competition itself but from the insecurity and deterioration in personal and collective living conditions that it brings.

The idea of a social investment welfare state, discussed elsewhere in this book by Palier (Chapter 13) and Hemerijck (Chapter 14), is central to the project of an assertive, innovation-friendly social democracy. It involves using collective resources to prepare a confident, skilled work-force, supported by a strong infrastructure, that can enable a country or a region to compete at the 'high end' of the global economy, avoiding the challenge from low-cost producers competing on the basis of low wages and taxes, and poor infrastructure and working conditions.

In general, innovation is not normally seen as a hallmark of social democracy, though generations of social democratic politicians have tried to associate themselves with the idea of 'modernisation'. Today, social democracy's claim to be a source of innovative energy lies in its capacity to challenge neo-liberal hegemony. Hegemony implies the exclusion of alternatives, and that exclusion limits the amount of innovation that a system can entertain. This is now happening with neo-liberalism, as its anti-collectivist dogma and refusal to take market externalities seriously prevent it from developing novel approaches and from anticipating challenges to which its stock responses have no answers. A defining characteristic of liberalism is its ability not just to tolerate diversity and criticism but to use them creatively to innovate. In its increasing inability to do this, neo-liberalism is becoming deeply illiberal.

As I have argued elsewhere, social democracy, not neo-liberalism, represents the highest form of liberalism.[3] Because it exists alongside a capitalist economy and private economic power, social democracy always has to seek compromises with that power. Whether social democrats have historically intended this or not, it leads to a society of constant diversity and tension, without historical victors or lasting hegemony. No interest dominates entirely, and therefore alternatives and innovation are favoured.

If social democracy has found its strongest and most enduring expression in the Nordic countries, it is not just because social democratic parties have enjoyed their longest periods of government there, but because they have done this while maintaining capitalist economies that have always had to compete in the open international market, these countries being too small to become protectionist. Nordic social democracy has had to cope with permanent challenge, and has therefore had to embrace constant innovation. It is not surprising that today this part of the world contains the strongest examples of the social investment welfare state, and combines the world's lowest levels of inequality with some of the highest rates of economic innovation.

Compiling a New Agenda

The potential for actions that simultaneously challenge power while favouring innovation can be seen in several areas of policy. For one example we can return to the core social democratic area of labour-market and social policy embedded in the social investment welfare state. The key question is: how are people to be persuaded to accept the risk and uncertainty of a rapidly changing working life and not just to demand protection from it? The neo-liberal answer is to offer glittering prizes for a few and to coerce the rest with workfare and cuts in welfare spending that force them to seek protection through money earnings (and, with the help of the financial sector, private debt). Through the social investment welfare state, social democracy develops its own supply-side alternative. Social policy becomes not part of a welfare state 'burden', but an innovative solution to the problem of improving labour-market participation and quality while also reducing insecurity in workers' lives.

But issues of power also need to be confronted here. Working people are being called on to accept risk and change, and this requires an ability to trust. Why should workers trust employers, who are constantly seeking ways to dispense with them and maximise profits at their expense? Why should they trust governments, the lives of whose personnel are so remote from their own? Only trade unions can provide an effective and genuinely autonomous representation of employees' interests, provided they are also structured in a way that enables them to go beyond defensiveness and become committed to the need for change. Countries such as France and the UK, where politicians on both the right and the left have largely given up believing in the possibility of such a form of trade unionism, are losing a potentially valuable resource.

Another key policy area for assertive social democracy is the necessary challenge to the power of the corporate rich, and also to the power of markets when these ignore important externalities. The traditional regulation of industry operated by placing constraints on economic activity, and requiring permissions that increasingly became mindless bureaucracy and have little to do with really checking power. Under neo-liberalism this has been replaced by an approach that tries, in oligopolistic sectors, to create the outcomes that would have resulted from more perfect competition. This has brought some real improvement to regulation, but it necessarily has difficulty dealing with externalities, and it is highly vulnerable to lobbying and regulatory capture.

Virtually all regulators spend far more time socialising with the firms they are supposed to be regulating than with the customers for whose interests they are supposed to be working – unless the customers are also corporations. An approach to regulation is needed that is based on the identification of clearly defined externalities, a transparent process of negotiating between the need to address these and the need to let markets and enterprise work, and a tough approach to concentrations of corporate power. The campaigning groups that have usually been behind most such measures also have to accept that they cannot fade away after their initial victory and leave it all to the state. Bureaucratism and regulatory capture always lie in wait. Campaigners need constant vigilance.

Many parts of the regulation agenda require international action, a fundamental source of corporate power being the ability to play national jurisdictions off against each other. For Europeans this means strengthening the role of the European Union (EU), both to co-ordinate among member states and to be a powerful actor in relations with other major geopolitical centres, most of which are dominated by single large nation states among whom individual European countries cannot carry much clout. In recent years the EU and the European Court of Justice have pursued an increasingly neo-liberal agenda, and many social democrats, from Sweden to Greece, are tempted to turn their backs on it and return to protecting their national achievements. But there is no way that they could achieve a regulation of global financial capital through that route, and, while it remains unregulated, capital will retain its bargaining strength against states, workers and consumer interests alike. Europe is the only region of the world where many countries combine reasonable levels of equality, good welfare states and dynamic economies. These achievements can no longer be protected solely through defensive national measures. Either the EU is turned away from its current neo-liberal path to become their advocate or the social democratic cause is lost.

The logic of social policy development and its relationship to marketi-sation seems to work differently in the US. The political and economic elites in many European countries envy the ability of that country to combine advanced economic success with high and rising levels of inequality, dominance of politics by corporate lobbies, and a neglect of negative externalities and environmental problems. They do not under-stand why they cannot have such a happy combination, and increasingly try to seek it. But the US benefits from major positive network exter-nalities that cannot be imitated. Although the market economy is itself a general phenomenon and no respecter of nation states, in practice the institutions of one hegemonic nation state, the US, dominate the form taken by many global economic institutions: the role of the US dollar and the country's unique ability to resolve its internal economic tensions by printing more money; its global military dominance and associated opportunities for state aid to industry that are not seen as state aid because they are concerned with military-based sectors; and the US base of much rule-setting for the international economic system achieved through the perspectives of US-dominated economic theory and global accountancy rules determined by US accountancy firms and ratings agencies.

These characteristics confer advantages on the US that cannot be imitated by countries in less powerful positions. The US was also a particularly important example of where workers on stagnant wages were able to fund consumption through extensive mortgage and credit-card debt, which was in turn funded by the secondary markets that collapsed in 2008. While that crisis rocked the US, it cannot undermine it in the way that a similar crisis can rock, say, Spain because, as the US administration pointed out when the federal government was downgraded by the ratings agencies, the US can solve its problems by printing more dollars, the global leading currency.

In this context, and given that the power of corporate lobbies more or less guarantees that the US will remain a force hostile to labour rights and an advanced welfare state, social democratic values will only be able to be protected and advanced if an alternative source of global network externalities can be developed. Europe is the only potential candidate, hence the need for a strong euro, fiscal federalism and the transcendence of national autonomy. At the same time, European elites are still contemplating how their societies can be made to correspond more closely to the US 'new inequality' model. A struggle for the direction of EU social policy is fundamental to the future of social democracy.

Building Broad-Based Societal Coalitions

An agenda of this kind, which assumes a capitalist economy, requires co-operation between public policy and private business. Is the latter (and especially its financial sector) in a frame of mind to accept compromise of this kind, when powerful business interests have demonstrated their power to play states off against each other? This is now a serious challenge for democracy.

In the twentieth century, powerful elites were able to maintain elements of their position and accept democracy by making alliances with broad elements of the middle classes against a perceived threat to all property owners from a socialist working class. That threat has now passed, while economic elites have become increasingly global, not caring particularly about embedding themselves in relations with broader classes. We are living at a dangerous moment. One outcome could be a residualisation of democracy so that it avoids all challenges to elite power. Arguably, this has been the main response to date; but new middle-class discontent with elite behaviour threatens it. An alternative, highly dangerous, response is for democracy to be used to place the blame on foreigners – either poor foreign immigrants and minorities seen as a symbol of globalisation or ethnically defined foreign finance capitalists. There are also strong signs of this in several countries.

The third possibility is to harness the growing climate of criticism of the irresponsible exercise of economic power by seeking broad coalitions of a range of negatively affected interests, but doing so alongside the innovation-friendly agenda considered here. Business leaders then have the option of collaborating with a broad alliance that is critical of them, but also offers them a high-quality labour force and rich infrastructure.

The time is ripe for this. The wave of disgust at the behaviour of the banking elite that swept through the populations of Europe and North America after the financial crisis has proved to be more than ephemeral. Campaigns related to it have gone on to target tax avoidance by global concerns that locate themselves for fiscal purposes in countries with the lowest tax levels, and firms that exploit contracts to provide privatised public services. The slogan of the Occupy Wall Street movement – 'We are the 99 per cent' – summed up a new sensitivity to the gap that separates a tiny politico-economic elite from the rest of the population. (In fact, the elite of the powerful super-rich is considerably smaller than 1 per cent.) There is a widespread feeling, extending beyond campaigning radicals to include large numbers of middle-income people, that a small elite is gaining in both power and wealth at the expense of everyone else. We see this particularly clearly in the negative externalities that accompany many exercises of corporate power, particularly environmental damage but also in such diverse things as the damage done to urban amenities when all shopping centres are dominated by the same few global brands, or the anxieties caused to employees at all levels who fear losing their jobs through corporate restructuring.

Social democrats need to be confident in asserting their new paradigm. It is not the case that neo-liberal ideology has conquered everywhere, and that the left's only choice is to give in to it (broadly the approach of the Third Way) or resist it stubbornly in a few declining redoubts. This is to mistake an intellectual dominance for a popular one. Very few people outside the ranks of the wealthy believe that market forces should rule unchecked, or that the rich should keep becoming richer and more powerful. The extension of markets into areas previously seen to have some moral or communal importance is fiercely resented, not only by a few activists. Social democrats need to see themselves at the centre of a wide circle of unease at the current development of modern capitalism – not by seeking to absorb all expressions of that unease within social democratic organisations, but by making a virtue of the fluidity of a diversity of alliances.

From communists to social democrats, the left has tended to believe in the centrality of its parties as the only acceptable expression of political dissent. The situation on the conservative (though not the extreme) right has been different. Its parties have just been part of a broad swath of interests that find their expression in religion, local communities, businesses and elsewhere. The inability of parties to monopolise this breadth has been seen as a strength, not a weakness. It is high time that social democrats saw things the same way. There is no need to choose between action through parties, through citizens' actions, through green campaigns and through participation in non-political organisations that increasingly resent market forces and corporate interests intruding into their world. All these need to thrive and to accept their co-existence, with occasional collaboration.

There are real dangers today that the combination of a major economic crisis and a disembedded global capitalist elite will undermine democracy or give it a nasty xenophobic turn. Assertive, innovation-friendly social democracy provides the only path that can avoid this. A new social compromise based on it is entirely viable, but whether it is feasible will depend on how well social democracy is able to develop its side of the offer, and on how business interests rate the choice between it and its darker alternatives.

Notes

1. OECD, *Divided We Stand: Why Inequality Keeps Rising* (2011). Available at www.oecd.org/els/soc/dividedwestandwhyinequality keepsrising.htm (accessed 1 May 2013).

2. Andrew G. Berg and Jonathan D. Ostry, 'Inequality and unsustainable growth: two sides of the same coin?' (Staff Discussion Note SDN/11/08, IMF, 2011).

3. Colin Crouch, 'Markets, power and politics: is there a liberalism beyond social democracy?', in *Priorities for a New Political Economy: Memos to the Left* (London: Policy Network, 2011); Colin Crouch, *Making Capitalism Fit for Society* (Cambridge: Polity Press, 2013).

CHAPTER 17

The Next Social Contract
Progressive Politics after an Era of Plenty

Alfred Gusenbauer and Ania Skrzypek

The political discourse in the aftermath of the crisis is dominated by two sentiments. The first revolves around the assumption that we have come to the end of an era. The postwar social and economic order of the western world has collapsed and the framework for a new social contract has not yet been erected. In this moment of suspension, it is widely felt that no new promise of progress and broad-based prosperity is affordable – neither for politicians to make nor for societies to believe in.

This connects with the second element: there is a belief that we have reached a historical moment of ideological decline. Indeed, the schools of political thought that have shaped the second half of the twentieth century face a profound test. The practices and processes of politics have become detached from the societies they serve; it seems that political ideas and political will can make very little difference when they are pitched against current levels of public cynicism and distrust.

In these circumstances, the centre-left faces a particularly stiff challenge. Even though the electoral tide seems to be more sympathetic in absolute terms, social democrats continue to drift on the changing waves of public opinion without the anchor of a solid position. The movement lacks a modern, convincing story to highlight what sort of a society it strives for. The times call for a new narrative stretching far beyond contemporary political conceptions of social democracy.

The Next Social Contract

The recent resentment towards institutionalised politics is borne of the inability of politics to deal with the challenges of the modern world. The shortcomings of liberal democracy have been exposed by the rapid processes of globalisation and further exacerbated by the global financial and economic crisis. Politics, instead of being a driver for change, has been slow to react to social, economic and cultural transformations. Though this is true for all traditional ideologies, it presents an even greater moment of truth for social democracy, as the centre-left redefined its historic mission from overthrowing capitalism to changing and regulating it. Thus, when hit by the financial crisis, social democrats found themselves defenceless.

This partly explains why there was no automatic shift towards social democracy, even though the crisis had clearly been induced by neo-liberalism. It succeeded in corroding societies in so far that an ideology (social democracy) based on communitarian values of equality and solidarity lost its power to appeal to people.

This relates to another issue, which is the fate of the welfare state. In its traditional form, its weakness in the face of new social risks was evident before the crisis came, despite numerous reform attempts. The inadequacy of the welfare state vis-à-vis the needs of contemporary society was one side of the coin, while the cost and affordability of proposed reforms was the other. In this sense it not only failed to address growing inequalities resulting from both the 'old' and 'new' social risks, but also deepened inequalities in certain areas and created new societal divisions.

There was criticism levelled at the fact that, despite the welfare state's burdensome costs for certain groups such as the middle classes, neither they nor the most impoverished truly benefit from its provisions. All these issues were significant in discrediting the sustainability of the welfare state, making it vulnerable to attack by conservatives, who duly set upon dismantling elements of social security and public services under the auspices of austerity. Such cuts have given rise to popular protest in many European countries, but the centre-left should be wary that this anger should be read as public opposition to further cuts, not public support for social democracy.

Nevertheless, the mood created by these popular mobilisations has produced a fertile climate for social democratic renewal. It brings the focus back onto the social contract, which has traditionally been at the core of the progressive mission. Its specificity has always been grounded in providing a modern translation of core progressive values within a social deal, which would ensure equilibrium of powers between the worlds of capital and labour. In that sense it has always focused on connecting and framing relations between politics and society. At the same time, it aimed to establish the primacy of democratic politics over economic forces to deliver a better, more prosperous life for all. This does not mean that the modern definition of progressivism should be defined by the social contract alone – but that it should become the key competence of social democracy.

Putting a new social contract centre stage while reconnecting it with a feasible promise of progress is likely to be a decisive factor in determining to what degree a profound renewal and consequently a re-emergence of social democracy is possible. But the construction of a new social contract also reveals a fundamental dilemma which divides the social democratic movement. Should the focus be primarily on safeguarding and strengthening existing safety nets or should it rather be on investment in skills and productive potential? Both options gain support within social democracy, where there also seems to be a growing belief that there is no longer sufficient resources to do both. This exemplifies a confined reasoning, which the age of TINA (there is no alternative) succeeded in pressing upon the centre-left, and speaks to the core inability of social democracy in Europe to decisively position themselves vis-à-vis both new social mobilisations and those who decide to entirely sink in their political alienation and withdrawal. A new societal contract therefore requires a change in attitude.

First of all, it requires reviving societal thinking beyond the terms of *financialised* capitalism. The erosion of communities and the increasing individualisation of society are the core elements that need to be addressed. Therefore, a new discourse that rebalances the rights and responsibilities of individuals towards each other within society is crucial.

Second, it demands dealing with the soiled reputation of the welfare state. It necessitates a new conceptualisation that is based on a modern understanding of equality, solidarity and social justice. It requires a commitment and contribution from all to the best of their capacities, while at the same time retaining the mechanism for achieving prosperity for all. Herewith, social democracy must seek to become associated with a strategy for sustainable social progress. Disentangling social policies from simplistic associations with charitable missions is crucial for allowing social democrats to be seen as a political force that can govern and not just manage and repair situations after crises occur.

This also means that social democrats cannot remain confined within redistribution policies alone. The new social contract should, in fact, address more effectively the question of equality, reclaiming primacy in education, work and care sectors. Redistribution as a secondary form of distribution is insufficient for solving many societal problems in the long term, while at the same time there is a growing polarisation between the real value of labour and the profits of its application. A new social contract would rephrase the economic debate on progressive terms and address questions about levels of productivity in the growing care sector, and about high-quality employment and fair work conditions, as well as reconnecting the real economy with the financial sphere and ensuring fair profit sharing among employees of successful enterprises.

Putting forward a vision for a new social contract involves progressive politicians taking the lead and framing the debate. In these circumstances it might be easy to engage in pessimism about the future of the welfare settlement, but formulating a new vision can make social democracy distinctive again on the political stage. This is an indispensable prerequisite for winning elections and returning to power. It will sharpen the political debate overall, even though with the current climate of anti-politics it needs to be clear that divisions no longer cut cleanly across the left–right axis within the political sphere. Formulating a new vision would also allow social democrats to respond to a key question about representation and therefore define which compromises, and hence coalitions, remain within the scope of progressivism.

Rephrasing the Debate about Contemporary Capitalism

Fashioning a new social contract is possible if social democrats settle on their vision and relationship with contemporary capitalism. This dispute has always been, and remains, an essential element of any deliberations on the mission and future of social democracy. In this context, however, neither the traditional anti-capitalist rhetoric nor the later conciliatory one can nowadays provide much help. They both critically fail to grasp the nature of the system. As much as politics and all the ideologies within the political sphere should be seen as continuously evolving under the influence of different factors, ideas and interests, so should capitalism. The current stage is what social democracy has to grasp. No less important, social democrats need to try to find common denominators in their evaluations of the challenges across the European continent.

The approach to this debate needs to be revisited – stripped of prejudices on one hand and catchy but empty descriptions on the other. Merely labelling instead of analysing capitalism may prove harmful, as it can thus become a political story that may easily be rejected as a result of anti-political resentment. Comprehending contemporary capitalism requires an understanding of its systemic character. And this is where the movement appears divided again, drifting in between critics of neoliberalism on one hand, and anti-market fundamentalism on the other. The narrative that progressives should be constructing requires that they establish a certain socio-political understanding that can be translated into a popular approach. Only then can progressives succeed in addressing capitalism's evolutionary character with feasible, long-term policy proposals. This is where the potential lies in arguing in favour of labour and social policies that require a certain amount of time before individuals and societies can enjoy their real benefits.

Furthermore, capitalism has always been at its core a system that produces unjust and unsustainable results. Hence there is a necessity for corrections through adequate policies, which should be conceptualised along the lines of a new social contract. Financialisation lifted capitalism to another level, which made it even more vulnerable to different failures and consequently crises given that the link between the real economy and the financial sector has been weakened. It means that, on one hand, there is no translation between economy-based values and financial profits, which allows secondary financial markets to operate faster, with greater risks and potentially larger profits. On the other hand, any disruption on the financial side seems contagious, infecting primary levels and instigating difficulties within the real economy. This explains why the recent financial crisis so quickly transformed into an economic and a social one as well.

The problem with the present capitalist system is that, while there are no limits to making a profit, there is also no clarity concerning existing competition objectives. Profit has become an aim, detached from notions of productivity, wealth or progress. It is a market rule that a company needs to make a profit in order to survive; however, as much as non-profitable enterprises are unsustainable, neither in the long run are corporations, whose profits have no function within societies. Excessive gains that are not translated beyond the financial sphere are the reasons behind financial bubbles, resulting as they do from the misallocation of economic means. This causes further distortion and economic imbalances. The solution is multi-layered; however, two main guidelines should remain: a redefined social contract and a reconnection between the world of finance and the real economy. There are multiple ways of making this a reality, including accelerating the quality of the world of labour through fairer sharing of profits with workers, improved working conditions and better social security.

Another difficulty is related to the international character of capitalism. Despite the pledge of international solidarity, social democracy and its parties have remained confined within national state circumstances regarding economic and social policies. The difference between the types of social arrangements across countries has vastly limited the possibilities for enhanced co-operation in labour or social dimensions of European integration or within international institutions. Hence, still, the capitalist economic order rules itself with *hard* laws on all levels while the social and labour policies remain *soft*.

This above-described mismatch means that national and European Union policies related to the welfare state are not in a position to contain and correct the negative effects of international financial capitalism. This is also why there is a need to reformulate the social contract accordingly and push the boundaries of political imagination beyond the nation-state approach towards society. In that sense, the social contract should also provide a significant guideline for a progressive discourse on Europe and the approach towards much-needed reform of international co-operation frameworks of global institutions.

In circumstances that have been created by globalisation and determined by contemporary international capitalism, transnational co-operation is indispensable. This argument shall be highlighted, especially in the difficult times that Europe is facing, with different internal processes fuelling a rise in nationalistic approaches. Since the crisis hit and various austerity measures were put in place, the feeling across the continent has been one of injustice. For some this is because they have been required to contribute more in order to rescue others, for others it is because they have been compelled to accept stricter cuts and face severe consequences. This fuelled a rise in nationalist and populist approaches on the one hand, and on the other it has undermined the EU's credibility, providing reasoning for the imposition of more inter-governmentalist methods in policy-making.

In this situation, social democrats have been advocating alternative ways out of the crisis, mostly focusing on two pillars. The first has been a demand for tougher regulations on the financial world. The second has been a demand for strategies to generate growth that would again translate into an improvement of living and working conditions. Both ambitions are correct; however, they do not seem to exhaust all possible solutions.

It is evident that no process exists without occasionally facing a crisis. No matter what regulations are put in place, they will not ensure that calamities are avoided in the future. However, if they are based on solid analyses of what may cause problems, they may ensure that calamities deal a lesser blow and pass more quickly. They must follow the logic of a newly determined social question, anchored on an understanding of capitalism and hence on its potential developments. Progressive policies are compelled to ensure that the effects of crises on 'ordinary people' are limited, which is synonymous with them not having effects on the spheres of public goods and public services, for example.

Re-Energising Democratic Politics

The framing of a new social contract is closely linked with efforts to alleviate the growing democratic crisis in western political systems. Resentment towards the world of politics is one of its features; and it is particularly damaging as it erodes the belief that individuals can change society through collective action. The popular understanding of contemporary capitalism is that it is overpowering and that there is very little that politics can do to tame its negative impacts. The paradox remains that, in this era of citizenry in which we enjoy the largest number of codified civic rights and the broadest access to information in history, the 'TINA' (there is no alternative) demagogy can be so widely spread. This naturally induces anti-political approaches and causes further resentment towards the world of politics.

The *professionalisation* of politics has repositioned political life away from being a mission to serve society towards a sphere in which the various interests and conflicts are dealt with by professional career politicians. Though it is not a new phenomenon, its extent has become vast in recent years. Decisions are too often based on 'expertise' provided by groups of 'specialists' and on opinion polls. Both limit the eventual range of available choices, as the deliberative process is distanced from the people, transforming democracy from a participatory to a monitoring one. The declining support and membership within traditional parties, combined with a general withdrawal from practices of inner-party education, make groups of 'party faces' shrink further in size. This also provokes a popular feeling best captured in the weary expression of 'same old, same old' politics.

Another characteristic of contemporary politics is its *mediatisation*. While deliberative societal dialogue is in decline, weakening the traditional links between society and politics, the vacuum is being filled with different media. Herewith the so-called 'fourth power' arrives to set the terms for politics through instruments such as 24-hour televised information cycles and internet portals. The criteria that politicians and their ideas need to meet are today primarily related to the appeal of their looks and short messages rather than what their ideological commitment means in a long-term perspective. Consequently, the scope of politics becomes further narrowed and the range of choices even further limited.

This understanding poses a great challenge. Until now, social democrats have been rallied behind a commitment to restore the primacy of politics. This has especially been emphasised in relation to the economy, while rejecting the dominance and dictates of market rule. The question, nevertheless, relates to what sort of politics should retain primacy. Progressives should formulate a response through the conceptualisation of a new social contract, ensuring in that way that politics is first and foremost about framing a societal process in which alternatives are commonly deliberated and democratically decided upon.

Engaging citizens is crucial for empowering the political process, while democratic legitimacy is needed for politics to gain the capacity to act on behalf of society and defend its interests. It is a bond through which the public sphere and all that it entails, including public policies and public goods, is being determined. It is therefore a relationship with mutual responsibility and a common objective to restore democratic rule while balancing the power represented by international capitalistic markets. Social democrats can succeed in this mission, once again placing themselves in between the worlds of labour and capital. However, in order to do so they must find new ways of recreating their movement and reaching beyond the sterile circumstances of contemporary institutionalised politics.

In this way, a newly defined social contract may prove useful in two ways. The first is the reconstruction of the centre-left in organisational terms. Social democracy has undergone a great transition since its beginnings, shifting from a broad movement into a mass political party. It became an element of the twentieth-century partisan system, benefiting in many ways from becoming a constituting element of intra-partisan democracy and consequently suffering together with others from processes such as the recent decline of partisanship. A remedy lies in realising that a new stage of democracy will require a new sort of political organisation that will be able to aggregate and mobilise public opinion. Social democracy should therefore aim to evolve, reformulating its construction towards a form that fits the social relations and lifestyles of individuals in contemporary times. Its support may no longer depend on numbers of members or activists at the parties' internal meetings, but rather on the ability to instigate a larger societal discourse and shape it according to progressive values and principles. This engagement, which is a more open formula, should then appear motivating for others, becoming a base for the mobilisation of electoral support.

Second, defining a new social contract and constructing a narrative based upon it is an ideological denominator that can help social democrats to reach out and build coalitions with potential allies. Today, social democracy finds itself trapped in this regard. On the one hand, a number of its traditional partners face the prospect of becoming socially obsolete. Social democracy, which is still struggling with its own renewal debates, nevertheless feels compelled to stick to them while also being accused of treachery if it moves to reach out to the others. On the other hand, in the context of the multiplier divisions within contemporary societies and the fragmentation of political systems, it is unlikely that centre-left parties will win landslide victories in the majority of proportional electoral systems in Europe. Hence, the need to build coalitions to govern is a fact. Progressives may be more successful in closing coalition agreements once they orientate eventual agreements as consolidations of different forces in a mission to realise policies resulting from the newly determined social contract.

Progressive politics after the era of plenty will be a prelude to the times in which social democracy will either succeed in defining a new narrative or face a further, and perhaps this time final, decline. There are a number of reasons to believe that the first, positive, scenario is feasible. The post-crisis political landscape, economic deficiencies and social climate constitute a welcoming habitat for new ideas. They will extract a political legacy in societal terms and, while safeguarding it, orientate all efforts towards progress, prosperity and participation for all. Social democracy, which is still battling with its own profound crisis, is aware that there will not be any true revival by default, and that it needs to reformulate its mission for the twenty-first century.

Reformulating and championing a new social contract that would become an analytical and ideological lens for modern times would constitute a profound step forward in defining a new socio-economic paradigm. Its methodology should be anchored in a fundamental debate on the current stage of international financial capitalism on the one hand and the necessary re-energising of democratic politics on the other. In both cases, the approach must be open and sober, without sentiments or habitual assumptions. The final query remains how far social democracy is able to think beyond the boundaries of contemporary political conceptions to mobilise the will and courage to complete its own historical transformation.

Bibliography

Allen, A. (ed.) (2011), *Democracy in What State?* (New York: Columbia University Press).

Bazillier, R. (2011), 'The economic meaning of progressive values', in E. Stetter, K. Duffek and A. Skrzypek (eds), *Progressive Values for the 21st Century* (Brussels: FEPS).

Beck, U. (2012), *Twenty Observations on a World in Turmoil* (Cambridge: Polity).

Benabou, R. (2000), 'Unequal societies: Income distribution and the social contract', *The American Economic Review* 90/1 (March), pp. 96–129.

Berman, Sh. (2006), *The Primacy of Politics. Social Democracy and the Making of Europe's Twentieth Century* (Cambridge: Cambridge University Press).

Byrne, L. (2012), 'The squeezed middle and the new inequality', in O. Cramme and P. Diamond (eds), *After the Third Way: The Future of Social Democracy* (London: I.B.Tauris/Policy Network).

Caney, S. (2010), 'Global distributive justice and the state', in G.W. Brown and D. Held (eds), *The Cosmopolitanism – Reader* (Cambridge: Polity).

Clark, Ch. and Clark, S. (2011), *Global Crisis and The Search for a New Social Contract* (Bloomington, IN: iUniverse).

Cramme, O. (2011), *Social Europe's New Battleground*, Policy Network Social Democracy Observatory. Available at www.foresightproject.net/mailout/pno/mobile.asp?h=347 (accessed 21 March 2011).

Crouch, C. (2004), *Post-Democracy* (Cambridge: Polity).

Crouch, C. (2011), *The Strange Non-death of Neo-liberalism* (Cambridge: Polity).

Diamond, P. (2012), 'National and global governance in crisis: Towards a cosmopolitan social democracy', in E. Stetter, K. Duffek and A. Skrzypek (eds), *Building New Communities: Notes from the Transatlantic Dialogue of Dialogues*, Next Left Book Series, vol. 5 (Brussels: FEPS/GLP HLS).

Dworkin, R. (1975), 'The original position', in N. Daniels (ed.), *Reading Rawls* (Oxford: Blackwell).

Erckel, S. (2008), 'Classical social contract theory', in E. Stetter, K. Duffek and A. Skrzypek (eds), *A New Progressive Vision. A New Social Contract for a Better Society*, Next Left Book Series, vol. 5 (Brussels: FEPS/GLP HLS).

Esping-Andersen, G. (2002, 2009), 'Towards a good society', in G. Esping-Andersen, D. Gallie, A. Hemerijk and J. Myles (eds), *Why We Need a New Welfare State* (Oxford: Oxford University Press).

Flinders, M. (2012), *Defending Politics. Why Democracy Matters in the Twenty-first Century* (Oxford: Oxford University Press).

Freeman, S. (2007), *Justice and Social Contract* (Oxford: Oxford University Press).

Gauthier, D. (1986), 'Morals by agreement', in P. Vallentyne (ed.), *Contractarianism and Rational Choice* (Cambridge: Cambridge University Press).

Giddens, A. (1984), *The Constitution of Society: Outline of the Theory of Structuration* (Cambridge: Polity).

Giddens, A. (1990), *The Consequences of Modernity* (Cambridge: Polity).

Ginsborg, P. (2008), *Democracy: Crisis and Renewal* (London: Profile Books).

Greve, B. (ed.) (2012), *The Times They Are Changing? Crisis and the Welfare State* (Oxford: Wiley-Blackwell).

Gualmini, E. and Rhodes, M. (2011), 'Welfare states in trouble. Policy reform in a period of crisis', in E. Jones, P. M. Heywood, M. Rhodes and U. Sedelmeier (eds), *Developments in European Politics* (Basingstoke: Palgrave Macmillan).

Gusenbauer, A. (2011), 'Defining the path forward', in E. Stetter, K. Duffek and A. Skrzypek (eds), *Progressive Values for the 21st Century* (Brussels: FEPS).

Gusenbauer, A. (2013, forthcoming), 'For a new social deal: Believing in the hopes that social democracy aspires to be entrusted with', in E. Stetter, K. Duffek and A. Skrzypek (eds), *For a New Social Deal*, Next Left Book Series, vol. 6 (Brussels: FEPS).

Habermas, J. (2010), 'A political constitution for the pluralist world society?', in G.W. Brown and D. Held (eds), *The Cosmopolitanism – Reader* (Cambridge: Polity).

Hanke, B. (2011), 'Varieties of European capitalism and their transformation', in E. Jones, P. M. Heywood, M. Rhodes and U. Sedelmeier (eds), *Developments in European Politics* (Basingstoke: Palgrave Macmillan).

Hannan, K. and Kelly, J. (2011), *Parties, Elections and Policy Reforms in Western Europe: Voting for Social Pacts* (London: Routledge).

Hemerijk, A. (2006), 'Social change and welfare reform', in A. Giddens, P. Diamond and R. Liddle (eds), *Global Europe, Social Europe* (Cambridge: Polity).

Jun, U., Niedermayer, O. and Wiesendahl, E. (eds) (2009), 'Zukunft der Mitgliedpartei', in A. Gusenbauer, *Lessons for the 'Next Left': Reaching Beyond our Own Limitations*, Queries, vol. 3 (Brussels: FEPS).

Kant, I. (1797), *The Metaphysical Elements of Justice: Part 1 of The Metaphysics of Morals*, 1st Edn. Translated by J. Ladd (1965) (Indianapolis: Bobbs-Merrill).

Kenny, M. (2012), 'Identity, community and the politics of recognition', in O. Cramme and P. Diamond (eds), *After the Third Way: The Future of Social Democracy* (London: I.B.Tauris/Policy Network).

Kymlicka, W. (2003), 'The social contract tradition', in P. Singer (ed.), *A Companion of Ethics* (Oxford: Blackwell).

Lansley, S. (2012), *The Cost of Inequality: Why Equality is Essential for Recovery* (London: Gibson Square).

Lessnoff, M. (1986), *Social Contract* (London: Macmillan).

Lind, M. (2007), *A Citizen-Based Social Contract*, New America Foundation. Available at www.newamerica.net/files/NSC%20Citizen%20Principles%20 Paper.pdf (accessed 10 July 2013).

Muldoon, R. (2009), *Diversity and the Social Contract*, Unpublished PhD Dissertation, University of Pennsylvania.

Rawls, J. (1971), *A Theory of Justice* (Cambridge, MA: Belknap Press of Harvard University Press).

Reiman, J. (1990), *Justice and Modern Moral Philosophy* (New Haven, CT: Yale University Press).

Rousseau, J.J. (1762), *The Social Contract*. Available at www.ebooks.adelaide. edu.au/r/rousseau/jean_jacques/r864s/ (accessed 10 July 2013).

Skrzypek, A. (2011), 'The core values for the next social deal', in E. Stetter, K. Duffek and A. Skrzypek (eds), *Progressive Values for the 21st Century* (Brussels: FEPS).

Skrzypek, A. (2012), 'Core values of social democracy: A comparative analysis of the PES member parties' ideological statements', FEPS Next Left. Available at www.feps-europe.eu/uploads/documents/2012-02-12-short-article-on-progressive-values.pdf.

Skrzypek, A. (2013), 'The next social contract: A new vision for European Society', in E. Stetter, K. Duffek and A. Skrzypek (eds), *For a New Social Deal*, Next Left Book Series, vol. 6 (Brussels: FEPS).

Skyrms, B. (1996), *Evolution of the Social Contract* (Cambridge: Cambridge University Press).

Southwood, N. (2010), *Contractualism and the Foundations of Morality* (New York: Oxford University Press).

Stetter, E., Duffek, K. and Skrzypek, A. (eds) (2011), *Progressive Values for the 21st Century* (Brussels: FEPS).

Stiglitz, J. E. (2012), *The Price of Inequality: How Today's Divided Society Endangers our Future* (New York: W.W. Norton and Company).

Vandenbroucke, F., Hemerijck, A. and Palier, B. (2011), *The EU Needs a Social Investment Pact*, Observatoire sociale européen, No. 5, May. Available at www.ose.be/files/OpinionPaper5_Vandenbroucke-Hemerijk-Palier_2011. pdf (accessed 10 July 2013).

Véron, J., Pennec, S. and Légaré, J. (eds) (2010), *Ages, Generations and the Social Contract: The Demographic Challenge facing the Welfare State* (Dordrecht: Springer).

Vries, C. de (2011), 'New challenges for social democracy – lessons from the Netherlands', in E. Stetter, K. Duffek and A. Skrzypek (eds), *Next Left – Towards a New Strategy* (Brussels: FEPS).

Index